NAMIBIA

DUE DATE	BRODART	10/95	16.95

NAMIBIA
The Independent Traveler's Guide

Scott and Lucinda Bradshaw

HIPPOCRENE BOOKS
New York

Copyright © 1994 Scott and Lucinda Bradshaw

Maps by Jason Han.
Original drawings by Linda Parkinson.

For information, address
HIPPOCRENE BOOKS, INC.
171 Madison Avenue
New York, NY 10016

Library of Congress Cataloging-in-Publication Data
Bradshaw, Scott
    Namibia: the independent traveler's guide/ Scott and Lucinda
Bradshaw.
        p.   cm.
    Includes bibliographical references and index.
    ISBN 0-7818-0254-7 $16.95
    1. Namibia—Guidebooks. I.Bradshaw, Lucinda. II. Title.
DT1517.B7   1994
916.88104'4—dc20   94-13986
                                                  CIP

Printed in the United States of America.

Contents

Maps

Thanks

We wish to thank all the Namibians we encountered who guided us to new and unexpected places and who were a wonderful source of information and insights essential for this book.

We wish to especially thank Kent and Denise Elsbree whose support was essential for gathering material; the Passanos, who made us part of their family; the people of Uis; the Estorff reference library's helpful staff; the many outstanding people with the Department of Nature Conservation whose knowledge and willingness to help was invaluable; Grant Burton and Marie Holstenson; Sharon Montgomery; Franco and Janet Bossi; Fred Thyer; Déne and Hendrick Herselman; Bill and Kathy Gasaway; Tim and Caitlin; Jason Han; Linda Parkinson; Bubette, Chuck and Elvis, whose everyday lives kept us entertained, and our friends and family who supported us in getting here.

General Impressions

Namibia is one of Africa's newest countries, having achieved nationhood on March 21, 1990, effectively ending colonialism on the continent. It is arguably the freest country in Africa today. While Africans know a bit about this unusual place, most of the Western world has scarcely heard of it. Unlike many African countries, Namibia now has an infrastructure that is first rate and lends itself to tourism. The roads, both tar and gravel, are excellent and well maintained and the facilities are generally well above average for Africa and on a par with many Western countries. There also is the opportunity for the tourist to get off the beaten track—well off in fact—and see the wild and untamed beauty that exists in abundance here with or without the luxuries of modern accommodations.

Tourism has grown rapidly here since independence and non-stop flights are now available from several Western European countries into the capital city of Windhoek.

You will find a wide range of accommodations, ranging from tents and sleeping bags, to luxury hotels. You can arrange an all-inclusive tour to even the most remote parts of the country or for a real adventure, go it on your own in a rented 4-wheel drive.

Namibia is one of Africa's (and the world's) least densely populated countries, which offers the visitor plenty of room to roam around the deserts or the game parks without having to deal with crowds. In fact you won't find near the number of people here as in the popular East African game parks. Namibia is known for its wild game viewing, most notably at the renowned Etosha National Park, but game is spread over the entire country. Namibia will likely soon be well known for its ruggedly magnificent desert wildernesses where life has adapted to the unique and forbidding environment, its remote coastal areas where weathered shipwrecks dot the shoreline, rich fishing grounds that provide superb angling, and its friendly, hospitable and incredibly diverse people who are probably its greatest asset. The air is crystal clear, allowing views of a hundred miles or more over many parts of the country.

From the largest population of wild cheetah in the world to the highest sand dunes anywhere on Earth, it has much to offer.

It also provides a fascinating opportunity to see a new country going through growing pains as a stable democracy develops in place of the apartheid system that was so long in force. There is freedom to speak, print and go where one pleases and the ubiquitous soldiers and road blocks seen in many countries are not seen here. People will openly give you their opinions and criticism of government is not limited to the opposition—the government is often critical of itself.

We hope that this guide will acquaint you with the options that are available here and give you an idea what the country has to offer while pointing you in the right direction to go off and explore new terrain.

Please tread lightly on this fragile land, respect its uniqueness and its natural heritage, yet leave it with many memories.

Some information provided in this guide becomes dated due to price changes, inflation, facilities closing or opening. Every effort has been made to make all information as current as possible; if you find something new that you think would be an interesting addition to this guide, please write us.

— Scott and Lucinda Bradshaw

CHAPTER 1

The Country and People

Geography

Namibia is situated in southwest Africa, bordered on the south by South Africa, on the north by Angola and Zambia, on the east by Botswana and on the west by the south Atlantic Ocean. Its land area is 824,268 sq. km. (approximately 317,000 sq. miles, or twice the size of California), and its population is about 1.6 million, giving it a population density of roughly 2 per sq. km.—one of the lowest in the world. It has a growth rate of approximately 3.5 percent—one of the highest in the world.

Namibia can be divided into 4 sections geographically:

1) **The Namib Desert** stretches the entire length of the coast and inland from 65-160 km. This area is probably the world's oldest desert and covers 15 percent of the land area of Namibia. The mean annual rainfall is less than 100mm (4 inches) and there is very little vegetation except in the riverbeds that cross it. Parts of the Namib have long lines of huge sand dunes, typified by the Sossusvlei area.

2) **The Great Escarpment** is the semi-arid mountainous plateau with an average altitude of 1,100 meters, though mountain masses within this region reach 2,500 meters. This region covers most of the central part of Namibia including the capital, Windhoek. Much of the plateau is covered by grassland.

3) **The lower lying northeastern and southeastern areas** are mostly the Kalahari's extension into Namibia. This is not

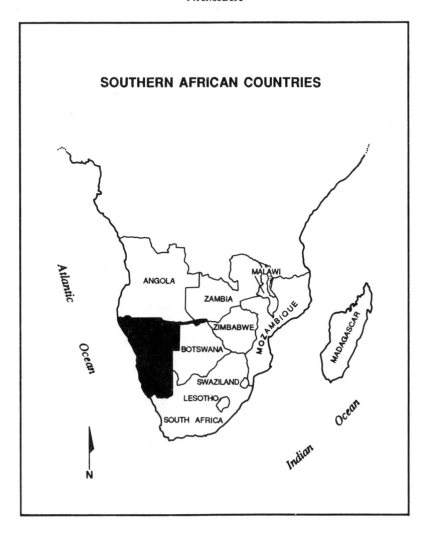

SOUTHERN AFRICAN COUNTRIES

as dry a desert as the Namib and in the northeast is in fact quite lush.

4) **The northern plains** are predominately tree savannah and woodland where the rainfall is greater and border rivers flow year round. This area includes the Caprivi strip.

Economy

Namibia has an economy based on export of unrefined goods and the import of most consumer goods. The major contributor to the GDP is mining followed by government, wholesale and retail trade and agriculture (including fishing). Namibia actively encourages foreign investment since independence as sanctions have ended and it is searching for new export markets for its raw materials.

The largest businesses are CDM (Consolidated Diamond Mines), Rössing Uranium and Tsumeb Corporation (lead and other base metals).

CDM operates diamond mines on Namibia's southern coast, stripping the sand off the ground near the beach to reach the bedrock's rich diamond deposits. They provide a substantial part of the tax base that contributes to the income of government.

Rössing operates the largest open pit uranium mine in the world east of Swakopmund in the Namib desert. They are one of the largest exporters of raw materials in Namibia, but have hit hard times recently due to a depressed uranium market. It seems that with the end of the cold war, the demand for uranium for nuclear weapons has dropped and the world's good fortune is Namibia's bad luck.

Tsumeb Corporation Limited mines lead, copper, zinc, silver, cadmium and arsenic trioxide in the town of Tsumeb in northern Namibia.

Namibia's economy traditionally has been and largely still is in the hands of whites. Blacks from indigenous tribes and to a lesser extent mixed race or 'colored'people work in the lower paying jobs, many of them farm labor on white farms or in the mining industry. Manual labor wages are typically very low-ranging from R150-R1000 per month.

Jobs that were not available to people of color under apartheid are now opening up but many people find they don't have the experience or qualifications for the jobs. Many government jobs were retained by the whites who remained in the country after independence, while the new government created many posts currently held mostly by non-whites. You'll find that most whites enjoy a living standard comparable to western Europe, while most blacks, especially in the countryside are living in the third world.

History

The oldest inhabitants of Namibia are the San people. They are commonly referred to as "Bushmen" but this has a derogatory connotation and is being replaced by San in reference to the linguistic group of their speech (Khoi-San), characterized by clicking sounds made with the tongue. There is a Herero word *Ovakuruvehi* meaning "the ancient or original ones" which is little used but may appropriately describe these people as they have no name in their language for themselves. Their ancient rock art found throughout Namibia dates back at least 28,000 years.

The Damara are also long time residents, perhaps descendants of ancient immigrants from the north.

The black population consists mainly of three groups of tribes— the Owambo, Kavango and Caprivi—along with the Herero and Tswana. Early Herero cattle herders moved into the Kaokoland-Kunene area sometime in the 18th century. They then left the area to go further south where they clashed with the Namas leaving behind a sub-group today known as the Himba.

Groups of mixed descent, mainly the so-called Hottentots and Basters moved from the Cape region to what is now Namibia in the 18th and 19th centuries. Missionaries started arriving and though they helped prevent some inter-tribal clashes, especially between Nama and Herero, they sought annexation by German or British colonial powers. Particularly strong were the Rhenish missionaries who, along with other churches, established Afrikaans as the *lingua franca*. White traders moved in and became a prominent economic force. When German military colonialism started to exert itself in the late 1800s and early 1900s the Namas and Hereros revolted and were put down, with the Hereros decimated and eventually forced into labor at mines and other developing industries. German control continued until World War I, when the Union of South Africa, a British ally, attacked the Germans as part of the war effort.

In 1915 German South West Africa was surrendered to South African forces. In 1920, the League of Nations entrusted the country to South Africa as a Class C mandate territory. In 1946 the U.N., which replaced the League of Nations, denied South Africa's request to annex South West Africa, and South Africa refused to place it under U.N. control. Eventually the South West Africa People's Organization (SWAPO) demanded independence and fought a war against South African troops, mostly in northern Namibia and southern Angola. This led to prolonged negotiations by the international community, complicated by the fact that there were at the time Cuban troops in Angola supporting the pro-SWAPO government there. A settlement plan, Resolution 435, was accepted by South Africa, SWAPO, and most internal parties. Resolution 435 required a peaceful transition to independence after free elections under U.N. control.

During the transitional period, Administrator-General Advisor Louis Pienaar administrated the country, while the implementation of the resolution was overseen by Martti Ahtisaari, Special Representative of the Secretary-General of the U.N. and the United Nations Transitional Assistance Group (UNTAG) . UNTAG consisted of military, police and civilian teams from 109 different countries to ensure a fair and safe transition period.

The overall peace plan included the partial withdrawal of the Cuban troops from Angola, the withdrawal of South African troops from Namibia, the demobilization of Namibian military units, the return of refugees, release of political prisoners, the repeal of discriminatory laws, the end of apartheid and registration of voters followed by free and fair elections.

In November, 1989, 97 percent of the registered voters voted for the Constituent Assembly. On February 9, 1990, the

Assembly adopted the Constitution of Namibia and on March 21,1990, Namibia finally gained independence witnessed by the entire international community in a huge country-wide celebration.

The current SWAPO-led government headed by president Sam Nujoma is faced with a severe drought, the problems of dismantling the vestiges of apartheid and the disparities of income between different groups. Building an economy with foreign ownership of many industries and developing farmland susceptible to drought are serious challenges as well. Reconciliation between former warring parties is a major policy of the government though it will have to come from the people expressing their desire to move on and develop a new nation.

Namibia's current district boundaries run along divisions created by the Odendaal commission during the apartheid era. They were implemented in 1967 dividing the central part of the country into farms which were given to the whites and creating communal areas mostly on the perimeter for black "lands" such as Damaraland and Hereroland. Existing groups which conflicted with the sometimes artificial divisions were moved. The current SWAPO government is drawing up new boundaries for regions within Namibia so for a while there will be two sets of districts shown on maps. We include both districts so the traveler can adapt to signs and boundaries in either case. (See Appendix map section for new and old regional maps.)

People

Namibia has a mix of people from diverse ethnic backgrounds. This is reflected by the language, dress, physical characteristics and customs. The ethnic groups making up Namibia are described below.

Owambo—The much talked about "Owambo nation" centered in the north of the country doesn't really exist. There are actually seven tribes in the north that are quite distinct and are usually grouped into one Ovambo nation. They live in the north central part of Namibia in Owamboland and are the main population group comprising about 50 percent of the country's people. The SWAPO- led independence movement was centered in Owamboland and the struggle for independence was most intense here. They speak many different related Bantu languages and herd cattle and goats and grow subsistence crops in the north. Many have jobs in mining and industry and they are the major force in Namibian government.

Damara—The Damara originally lived a scattered servile existence though their origins are still a mystery. The Damara people speak a "clicking" language almost identical to the Nama language that is part of the Khoi-San group of languages. Around 1870 missionaries helped them gain land near Okombahe which was later extended into what is now Damaraland. They traditionally herd goats and cattle though many do small scale mining for semi-precious gems. Today 55 percent live in cities or towns and make up 7.5 percent of Namibia's population.

Kavango—The Kavangos consist of five tribes, with Kwangali and Mbukushu being the dominant languages. Centered in Kavangoland in the north near the Caprivi strip, they primarily grow crops and fish as well as herd cattle and goats. Much of Namibia's fine wood work comes from this area. The people comprise about 10 percent of the population and live almost entirely in rural areas.

Colored—These are a people of mixed black and white origin. Their "native" tongue is Afrikaans although many speak English. Most live in cities or towns and they make up 4 percent of the population.

White—Namibia's white population is mostly of German (18 percent) or South African (80 percent) descent. They are Namibia's most well-off group, used to a style of living with European standards. They are the dominant economic force in the country though only 6 percent of the population.

Himba—The Himba live in Namibia's far northwest region of Kaokoland. Most dress in their traditional garments, with body paint and animal skin clothing. Comprising less than 1 percent of the population, they are perhaps least affected by modern society.

Herero—These formerly pastoral nomads share a common tongue and heritage with the Himba. The Herero fought with the German troops during colonial times and are very proud of the part they played in Namibia's history. The women are particularly noticeable for their huge, colorful, Victorian style dresses, (which take 10 meters or more of material to make) and their triangular hats made from the same material. These come from the times when missionaries thought it would be better to have the half-naked women in clothing. They comprise 7.5 percent of the populace and live all over the country, though primarily in the central and northwest areas with about 40 percent in cities or towns.

Nama—The Nama are descendants of the Khoi-Khoi or Hottentot people and are centered in the south central area of Namibia. They speak a Khoi-San "clicking" language and a large percentage work on white farms in the area, though 40 percent live in cities or towns. A few make weavings and rugs from hides and sell them on the roadside. Namas comprise 5 percent of Namibia's people.

Baster—In the Rehoboth area live the Basters. They are descendants of Nama and white settlers, who moved into the Rehoboth area in the late 1800s. They call themselves Basters, as their heritage is from "bastard" offspring of white and Nama. Primarily Afrikaans speaking, 62 percent live in cities or towns, namely Rehoboth and Windhoek and make up 2.5 percent of the population.

San (Bushmen)—San were the earliest inhabitants of Namibia, living mostly in the northeast. They have lost their traditional nomadic hunter-gatherer way of life as the encroachment of modern societies has forced them to change. Some were used as trackers by the South African Army where they encountered a strange world indeed. Many find living in today's world a perplexing situation, and alcoholism and poor health are rampant. They make up 2.5 percent of the population of Namibia.

Caprivian—The Caprivi people consist of many tribes that due to their geographic isolation often feel like part of another country. Their tribes enjoy a large degree of political autonomy, with tribal courts existing and tribal chiefs having a say over land use in the area. There are two main tribes, the Bafwe and Basubia and a common language, Silozi, is spoken by most Caprivians in addition to their own tribal tongue. Few speak Afrikaans, though English is widely used. Some 84 percent live in rural areas and they comprise 3.5 percent of the population.

Tswanas—Namibia's smallest population group (.5 percent), they are separated geographically from their relatives in neighboring Botswana. They are primarily centered around the Gobabis area.

Government

The Namibian government is a multi-party democracy. The Namibian Constitution guarantees fundamental rights and freedoms and divides powers between the Executive, Legislative and an independent Judiciary. The president, Dr. Sam Nujoma, heads the Executive assisted by the Cabinet of ministers. The President is elected by direct popular vote for a term of 5 years and can be re-elected once. During Namibia's first election, however, the President was elected by the Assembly.

An interesting feature of the Namibian Constitution is the Ombudsman. The Ombudsman reports to the executive and the judiciary on irregularities or violations of fundamental rights by an organ of state or private institution. The Ombudsman is independent and subject only to the Constitution and the law.

Namibia is a member of the United Nations, the Commonwealth, the Organization for African Unity, the Southern African Development Co-ordination Conference and the Non-Aligned Movement.

Climate

Coastal

The coastal climate is characterized by markedly moderate temperatures in comparison with inland. Due to the influence of the cold Benguela current that runs offshore of the Namibian coastline, the temperature extremes are minimal. Fog is a common occurrence when the air over the ocean is cooled by the colder currents then condenses and rolls inland. In summer the coast is much cooler than inland and in winter the nights can be warmer on the coast when often it freezes in the higher regions of the central plateau. Days can be quite cool in Swakopmund any time of the year and a sweater or light coat will be needed. Swakopmund's pleasant cool weather is also the reason why people flock from Windhoek's summer heat to the coast, making it Namibia's premier resort. A rare, reverse trend occurs when a hot east wind blows towards the coast, baking it in temperatures approaching 40°C (104°F).

Northern

The northern region of Namibia, with the exception of the Namib desert coast and parts of Kaokoland, receive the most rainfall of the entire country. This becomes more apparent the farther east you go, with Katima Mulilo being the wettest part of the country, although with the current drought the area has taken on a drier than normal look. This is the main agricultural area of Namibia as it is the only area with sufficient rainfall for non-irrigated crops.

Southern

In general, the farther west and south you go in Namibia, the drier it gets. The southern parts of the country contain the Namib and parts of the Kalahari desert and are known for their hotter temperatures, which can be in the 40°C (104°F) range or higher in summer, though winter temperatures can get quite cold.

Central

The central part of the country is dominated by the high plateau that varies from 1,000-2,000 meters above sea level (3,300-6,600 feet). The weather can still get quite hot here in the summer and very cold (below freezing) in the winter. Camping here in the winter can be a cold proposition, so be prepared! The daytime winter temperatures are usually perfect: 15-25°C (60-75°F), which is why many people choose to come to Namibia during May-September.

TEMPERATURE CHART

PLACE	JAN. AVERAGES			JULY AVERAGES			RAINFALL
	High	Low	Rain	High	Low	Rain*	Annual
Windhoek	30°C	17°C	77mm	20°C	6°C	1mm	366mm
Swakopmund	20°C	15°C	1mm	18°C	9°C	0mm	16mm
Lüderitz	22°C	14°C	1mm	18°C	10°C	2mm	17mm
Grootfontein	30°C	18°C	159mm	24°C	4°C	0mm	591mm
Katima Mulilo	31°C	19°C	177mm	25°C	5°C	0mm	706mm
Keetmanshoop	35°C	19°C	25mm	21°C	6°C	1mm	168mm
Runda	31°C	19°C	144mm	26°C	6°C	0mm	605mm
Mariental	35°C	21°C	36mm	23°C	5°C	1mm	196mm

CHAPTER 2

Getting There

Getting to Namibia

From Europe

From Europe there are non-stop flights on Air Namibia from London and Frankfurt to the capital city of Windhoek that take about 10-11 hours. Lufthansa also flies from Frankfurt to Windhoek non-stop. UTA/Air France has flights from Paris direct to Windhoek with a short stopover in Luanda, Angola. South African Airways (SAA) has flights from London to Windhoek via Johannesburg that take a little longer due to a layover in Johannesburg. Other African airlines fly from London or Paris to southern Africa where you can catch a short flight to Windhoek. Try Zambian Airways or Air Zimbabwe or some of the discount "bucket shops" in London.

From the U.S.A. and North America

Probably the quickest (but not the cheapest) way to get to Namibia from the U.S. is to take the South African Airways flight from New York to Johannesburg that only stops to refuel in the Cape Verde Islands, and then grabbing another SAA flight or Air Namibia flight to Windhoek. If you're not in a hurry or are on a budget try any one of the "bucket shops" in a large U.S. city such as New York or San Francisco. These companies are consolidators—that is they buy large quantities of seats from many international airline companies at a discount and can often arrange the cheapest way to get from point A to point B. Try New York or San Francisco to Paris, then UTA/Air France to Windhoek, or New York or San Francisco to London then Air Namibia to Windhoek. It's worth trying these companies because you essentially have a reserved seat like any other but with the usual restrictions against changing or canceling your ticket.

From South Africa

Both SAA and Air Namibia have flights from Johannesburg and Cape Town to Windhoek. Over land the system of highways connecting the R.S.A. to Namibia is good with 24 hour border posts at Noordoewer and Ariamsvlei as well as other smaller border crossings which you should contact beforehand for hours of entry. There is also a train that crosses near Nakop (Ariamsvlei) from De Aar and Upington in the R.S.A and goes to Windhoek. Buses regularly ply the route between South Africa and Namibia—check the "Getting Around" chapter for schedules.

From Botswana

You can cross into Namibia from Botswana at Buitepos (Namibia) after a long drive through the Kalahari, but be very well prepared before you go this route as there aren't an abundance of services on the Botswana side and the road is much rougher, possibly requiring a 4-wheel drive vehicle. You can also enter from Botswana into Namibia at a couple of places in the Caprivi region, namely Ngoma (2 WD) and Shakawe (4WD). There are also flights into Namibia with Air Botswana or Air Namibia.

From Zambia

In addition to regular air service from Lusaka, there is a border crossing at Katima Mulilo where you must take a ferry across the Zambezi. There is also a bus from Lusaka to Grootfontein once a week—see "Getting Around" chapter.

From Angola

Assuming you've made it through war-torn Angola and

come to the main southern border post of Oshikango, you'll find Namibia a welcome relief.

What to Bring

Passports and Visas

A valid passport is required to enter Namibia. Visas are also needed except for nationals of the following countries: Angola, Austria, Belgium, Botswana, Canada, Denmark, Finland, Germany, Luxembourg, France, Italy, Ireland, Japan, Liechtenstein, Mozambique, the Netherlands, Norway, the former USSR, Singapore, South Africa, Sweden, Switzerland, Tanzania, the United Kingdom, the United States, Zambia and Zimbabwe.

Visas can be obtained from the Ministry of Home Affairs, Private Bag 13200, Windhoek or at Namibian embassies around the world.

International Driver's License

It's a good idea to get one of these before you come if you are planning to rent or drive a vehicle, as they are required for all overseas visitors to drive in Namibia. You can get one at your local Automobile Association.

NOTE: Driving in Namibia is on the left side of the road.

Vaccinations

No proof of vaccination is required to enter Namibia although you should take necessary precautions against diseases. See the health section for details.

Clothing

If you are coming to Namibia during the winter months (May-September) the chances of your encountering rain are much slimmer and rain gear may not be needed. Check under the climate section of this book to see what weather might be and dress accordingly. Light polyester-cotton clothing is usually best as it is cooler and easy to wash. A jacket or at least a sweater is necessary during the winter months as the temperature falls below freezing in many parts of the country. If you are camping, warm clothing is essential in winter and light but durable clothing in the summer. A hat is recommended for any time of the year as the sun is fairly strong at this latitude, especially in the summer (October-April), when it gets downright hot and sunburn and exposure can be a problem.

Photography and Game Viewing

Binoculars—are essential for game viewing and bird watching. Often the game are distant and to really get a decent look at lions hidden in far-off grass or a funny bright green bird you want to identify, you should have a good, preferably lightweight pair.

Film—is available in most towns. You can use a lower speed film for most daytime shots of scenery and still objects; ASA-ISO 100-200 is fine. For lower light shots and action (running animals, etc.) you will want ASA-ISO 400. Something in between, like ASA-ISO 200, offers flexibility for your shots.

There are several one-hour film developers in Namibia and while the price may seem high (R40 for a roll of 36), they usually give you a free roll of whatever you had developed so the price you pay is for the film and—the developing costs. Check on this before you leave your film.

Cameras, binoculars and other sensitive equipment should be protected from Namibia's often dusty roads in a dustproof case or plastic bag.

Other Essentials

Sunscreen—is readily available at pharmacies in the larger towns for protection against Namibia's constant and often intense sun.

Malaria pills—are available as well, but if you are going to an endemic area you usually must start taking the pills some time before entering the area. Consider this ahead of time. Insect repellent can come in very handy especially during summer months and in endemic malaria areas. See the health section in this book about malaria protection.

Camping, Backpacking and Hiking

For any camping or backpacking trip, there are many essential items. Please look under the backpacking and hiking section in the "Getting Around" chapter.

Arriving by Air

If you are arriving by air, chances are that you will land at the International Airport 40 km. outside the capital city of Windhoek. Formalities are kept to a minimum here; if your papers are in order you should be through in less than 30 minutes, depending on how many disembarking passengers there are. You can get up to one month on your visa but it can be extended at the Ministry of Home Affairs. You are supposed to show an onward ticket, but they don't always ask.

You are allowed to bring in hunting rifles (but not handguns), which must be declared, 2 liters of wine, 1 liter of spirits, and 400 cigarettes. Pornography and drugs are illegal—don't try bringing them in.

The airport has a post office, foreign exchange bank and an information counter. A bus is available for each arriving flight and will take you into town for R20. Taxis will also take you into town for R40-50.

Car Rentals—can be arranged at three car rental agencies at the International Airport, namely Avis, Budget and Imperial.

Arriving by Land

If arriving by land, you'll need a passport, visa (if necessary) and proof of ownership of the vehicle—have all your registration papers in order. Third party insurance is not necessary in Namibia, the cost being included in the price of petrol (gas).

CHAPTER 3

Getting Around

Money Matters

The currencies currently in use in Namibia are the Namibian dollar and the South African Rand. Since independence Namibia has continued to use the South African Rand as its currency. In July of 1992 Namibia announced that it would be issuing its own currency, the Namibian dollar. It hit the streets in mid 1993 but was not widely available at that time. The Namibian dollar will be tied to the Rand for an indefinite time period, depending on the fortunes of the Rand on the international market. The Rand may eventually be phased out as legal tender in Namibia, so check your currency when you exchange money.

The Rand comes in notes of 5, 10, 20, and 50; 100 and 200 Rand notes are planned for introduction in 1993. The Rand is divided into 100 cents with coins of 1, 2, 5, 10, 20, and 50 cents and 1 and 2 Rand in circulation. See below for the approximate rate of exchange. Prices in this book are quoted in Rands which are currently equivalent to Namibian dollars.

Changing Money

There is no black market here as in some African countries, so you'll probably be changing money at a bank or hotel, though banks will usually give a better rate. The commissions charged vary slightly from bank to bank, averaging 1 percent for traveler's checks or cash with a certain minimum charge, usually from R3-10.

EXCHANGE RATE

US$= R or $N3.05
DM = R or $N1.92
£ = R or $N4.63
FF = R or $N .57

Use the above rates to compute approximate prices given in this guide into your currency. Remember, however, that prices will change yearly as will exchange rates.

Credit Cards

Credit cards are accepted at most major hotels, restaurants, rental agencies and safari companies. Many shops in larger towns and even some smaller ones will take plastic but it is always better to check first!

About Prices in This Book

Prices quoted in this book will definitely change due to inflation, owners raising prices due to renovations, or any of a number of reasons. Don't expect that the prices quoted here will be the same in 1995 or beyond. Exchange rates fluctuate as well so the relative pricing may go up or down. As the new Namibian dollar is introduced the prices may differ substantially from those quoted here depending on whether it is tied to the Rand or not. Use prices quoted here as a guide only. To account for current inflation, add 10-15 percent per year to any price listed in this book to get an estimate of the prices.

Tax

There is an 11 percent sales tax (GST) on all consumer goods, including lodging. Check to see if this is included in the price. Lodging quoted in this book includes GST while restaurant prices do not.

Tipping

There is usually no service charge in restaurants and tipping is not always expected though usually appreciated. Around 10 percent is normal for most nicer restaurants. Porters can be tipped a Rand or two. Safari guides are tipped according to service.

Telephones and Mail

Mail and Post Offices

Mail is generally reliable and safe in Namibia, though never send cash and insure anything of value. Air mail letters to the U.S.A. and Europe sent from larger towns usually take one to two weeks to reach their destinations while packages sent by surface mail, though much less expensive, can take up to a few months, but sometimes arrive within a few weeks. Many smaller towns have only weekly or less frequent postal service. Postage rates are very reasonable in comparison with other countries although air mail packages can be expensive. Currently, a letter within Namibia costs 20 cents, to South Africa 25 cents, while overseas letters cost 60-85 cents for up to 10 grams.

Telephones

The telephone system in Namibia is good, especially in the larger cities. For more information check the front of the phone book— it has plenty of information about making calls to anywhere in the world. If you plan on traveling around Namibia and making frequent calls either to points in Namibia or overseas, it is very handy to get a copy of the telephone book from the post office and carry it with you. Public telephones are found almost exclusively at post offices throughout the country.

International Calls

You can call direct (with a lot of one Rand coins!) or collect to most countries in the world from the public telephones. At post offices in larger cities you can place direct calls at the long distance section and pay after the call is complete, eliminating the need for a pocketful of change. The international calling office in Windhoek is open M-F 8:30-1 and 1:30-4:15, and Sat. 8-noon. Some credit cards are accepted.

NAMIBIA

To place a collect international call, insert any coin that will fit in the public phone, dial 0690 and wait for the international operator to answer. Sometimes it takes a minute or two of ringing, so be patient. The operator will ring you back and ask you for the details of your call. Your coin should be refunded.

To place a direct call have plenty of one Rand coins handy and a friend to help feed in the coins; then dial the international access code 09, the country code and city codes (if applicable), which you can find in the phone book, then the number.

For some distant places, you must dial 0690 for operator assistance.

The current cost of an overseas call is approximately R9 per minute. If you want someone overseas to call you they must dial the international access code from their country (if applicable) then Namibia's code 264, then the town code (omitting the 0—see below under calls within Namibia), then the number.

Local Calls and Calls within Namibia and South Africa

Local calls currently require 20 cents to start. If you're dialing locally, no prefix is necessary except for farm lines outside the town. For calls to other Namibian towns you must first dial the prefix code (which starts with 0) then, depending on where you're calling, you will:
1) Dial the number (for larger towns with automatic exchanges).
2) Dial no further and wait for the exchange to answer, then give the operator the number you wish to reach (for towns with operator exchanges).
3) Dial no further and wait for the exchange to answer, then give the operator the exchange you want and the number (for small places and farms).

For some small out-of-the-way places in Namibia that have no code you must dial 0020 and give the operator the exchange and number.

Some exchanges are being automated and the old phone numbers have been changed—check on this if you believe you have the correct number. Charges for calls within Namibia vary according to distance and the time called. Cheaper rates are available during certain evening and weekend hours.

Calls to South Africa are dialed like calls within Namibia with a prefix code and number. Conference calls for business people as well as person to person calls are available for an extra charge.

Telephone Codes For Major Namibian Towns

Windhoek 061
Swakopmund 0641
Walvis Bay 0642
Lüderitz 06331
Otjiwarongo 0651
Okahandja 06221
Keetmanshoop 0631
Mariental 0661
Rehoboth 06271
Gobabis 0681
Karibib 062252
Outjo 06542
Tsumeb 0671
Oshakati 06751
Ondangwa 06756
Katima Mulilo 067352

Faxing

If you are faxing to and from Namibia it is done in the normal way from an automatic exchange. To or from an operator exchange, you must dial the number, (or ask the operator for the number) and tell the operator you wish to fax. When the fax beep is heard, start your fax. Some overseas lines are a little rough and it may take a few tries to complete your fax, so be sure your fax machine tells you that the

NAMIBIA

transmission has gone through. Public faxes are available at many hotels and larger stores.

Electricity

All electricity is 220/240 volts 50 cycles. Outlets are the 3-pin, 15 amp plugs. There are 110 volt plug-ins in many hotels for electric razors. Adaptors are not readily available.

Language

Before independence the official languages were Afrikaans, English and German. Upon independence, the new government decided to make English the only official language. Most people in Namibia speak their native tongue and Afrikaans, the lingua franca, and you will find in the outlying regions many people speak little or no English (except in the Caprivi, where English is widely used). In some areas, such as Swakopmund and Lüderitz, German is widely spoken. Government and official business is supposed to be done in English, but this not always possible and people do use Afrikaans.

School is taught in the student's native tongue for the first few years. Before independence, older students were taught in Afrikaans but now English is being introduced as the instructional medium and will eventually replace it. This is difficult for the students who come into high school with no English background and their grades often reflect this. The high school teachers are often no better off as their English is sometimes rudimentary and certainly not at the level it should be for teaching a class. These are some of the challenges that the newly independent, multi-lingual people of Namibia are dealing with.

The native languages you will hear frequently are of two main groups: Bantu and Khoi-San. Owambo and Herero belong to the Bantu language group. Damara and Nama are the most frequently used languages of the Khoi-San group and are similar to the language used by the San (Bushmen), containing a variety of clicking sounds.

Following are some common words and phrases in the four main languages you are likely to come across:

Afrikaans—is derived from 17th century Dutch with Malay, Bantu and English thrown in. It has evolved greatly over three centuries and is one of the official languages (along with English) of South Africa. It originated with the early Dutch settlers there and is simpler than its mother language, lacking conjugations and other more complex grammar. For an excellent guide to learning Afrikaans try *Teach Yourself Afrikaans* by H. Van Schalkwyk. Hippocrene Books also publishes an *Afrikaans/English English/Afrikaans Dictionary*.

Afrikaans Words and Phrases

Hoe gaan dit?	How's it going
Goeie more	Good morning
Goeie middag	Good afternoon
asseblief	please
dankie	thank you
lekker	nice, great
bakkie	pickup truck
braai	barbecue
mieliemeel	corn meal
veld	countryside
pad	road
kos	food
waar is die.... ?	where is the.... ?
ek	I
ek is	I am
jy	you
jy is	you are
ons	we
ons is	we are

Damara Words and Phrases (#=click with tongue)

matisa	how's it going?
#leinchees	good day
#lein se haray	goodbye (when you are leaving)

#lein se #on re	goodbye (when someone else is leaving)
moro	good morning
ayó	thank you

Owambo Words and Phrases (Kwanyama dialect)

ongahe lipi	how's it going?
iyaloo	thank you
kalapo nawa	goodbye
nawa	good
oshiwa	beautiful

Herero Words and Phrases

perivi	how's it going?
okuhepa	thank you
karanawa	goodbye
nawa	good, fine

Holidays

Public Holidays in Namibia

January 1	New Year's Day
March 21	Independence Day
Early April	Good Friday
Early April	Easter Monday
May 1	Workers Day
May 4	Cassinga Day
May 25	Africa Day
Late May	Ascension Day
August 26	Heroes Day
December 10	Human Rights Day
December 25	Christmas Day
December 26	Family Day

School Holidays

It should be noted that during the school holidays, accommodations are in high demand and you are advised to make reservations during these times well in advance. School terms in Namibia are changing from the quarter system to the trimester system during the 1993 school year and traditional school holidays will change as well. You should also be aware of South Africa's school holidays as many tourists come from South Africa.

School Holiday Periods for 1993-4 include the entire month of May. Schools close again from August 25 to September 20 or August 20 until September 13. The Christmas holiday season is from December 8 or 9 until January 18, 1994.

South African school holidays are roughly the first two weeks of April, the end of June until the middle or end of July and in late September/early October for two weeks. Christmas holidays are approximately the same as Namibia's.

Social & Cultural Matters

Greetings

When shaking hands or giving or receiving gifts, some peoples of southern Africa use both hands, often using one to "support" the other. This is a sign of respect and although less frequently encountered in the cities, you will see many people in rural areas doing this. Both men and women will hold hands for quite a bit longer than the traditional western handshake and often talk while still holding on to the hand of the person they are with.

Television

Currently, Namibia has only one television station, Namibian Broadcasting Corporation (NBC), which uses Channel 1. Its programs are mostly in English and are locally produced or imported from a host of countries. Cable TV companies from South Africa have stations broadcasting here as well.

Radio

Radio stations are in English, Afrikaans, German and most native languages. Turning the dial is an interesting way to experience the linguistic diversity of Namibia.

Arts, Crafts & Curios

Typical Namibian crafts include painted or sculpted ostrich eggs, animal skins of all sorts, carved Makalani palm nuts, wood carvings of game animals, weavings, rock carvings and basketry.

Sports & Activities

Fishing—Namibia's coast is well known for its rich fishing grounds. The coastline from Sandwich Harbor up to Terrace Bay is very popular with mobs of people descending on some beaches to surf fish for cabeljou, caljoun and steenbras. Lüderitz is popular for crayfishing and the northern rivers are good spots for tigerfish and bream.

NOTE: Check locally or with the Ministry of Fisheries and Marine Resources for all current fishing regulations.

Swimming—Many towns have municipal swimming pools and diving boards. Swimming in the ocean, though a bit cool, is safe in a few spots but check locally before diving into the surf as currents are strong.

Windsurfing and Boating—There are some fine spots offshore or on several of the dams around the country to enjoy water sports.

Hiking and Backpacking—Namibia has many "official" trails in the National Park system and elsewhere in addition to many hiking trips that you can create yourself with a little adventurousness and planning. See the backpacking and hiking section.

Hunting—Hunting is popular activity in Namibia and the source of much needed foreign revenue. For trophy hunting, you must hunt with a professionally registered hunter. There are several guest farms that specialize in hunting as well as companies which do hunting safaris.

Bicycling—While you don't see hordes of people bicycling in Namibia, it is easy to get around on Namibia's good road system. Care should be exercised as many of the tar roads are narrow. Namibia has many suitable locations for mountain biking though there are few organized trips. Make your own!

Tennis—Many towns have courts in various states of repair though balls and equipment are available only in the larger towns.

Golf—There are many golf courses around the country, but only a handful such as Rössing country club near Swakopmund and the Windhoek course are fully grass. There are several challenging desert courses with lots of sand!

Soccer—Soccer is a popular sport and matches between the major clubs as well as international matches are held around the country.

Rugby—Rugby is a popular spectator sport.

Guest Farms

An institution in Namibia, guest farms are a unique way to visit the country. Situated on farms of very large size (usually 1,000-10,000 hectares\1 hectare = 2.5acres), they offer the traveler something a little different than hotels or rest camps. Mostly upmarket in price (ranging from R 100-300 per person per night, though some go for more) and small in size (usually 5-10 bedrooms) they offer personalized attention that you won't find in a hotel. Most have game on the property and offer game drives while some specialize in hunting. They are usually run by a family and visitors get to know their hosts on a first name basis.

Scattered all over the country except in the far north, guest farms are located in the desert areas as well as bushveld. It's best to stay more than a day to experience the area and to get to know your hosts and a little bit about Namibia.

NOTE: Guest farms are listed regionally at the end of each chapter.

Food and Drink in Namibia

Drink

Wine is not produced commercially in Namibia, but the imported South African wines compete with the best from France and California. They are widely available and the centuries old history of wine making in South Africa makes the quality exceptional. The prices are low compared to their foreign counterparts and some truly memorable vintages are sold in *drankwinkels* (bottle stores) all over the country. Almost all restaurants have a decent wine list, making wine lovers feel at home in Namibia.

Beer and local lagers that go down easily on a hot day include Windhoek, Tafel and Hansa. Guinness is also brewed locally. Namibia Breweries has come out with a Maibock beer, a dark semi-sweet brew with excellent flavor. German brewmasters have set up good brewing facilities in Namibia and the quality is consistent.

Juices are imported from South Africa, and are widely available, all natural and delicious. Ceres and Liquifruit brands make a wide variety including mango, granadilla (passion fruit), pear, litchi (delicious), strawberry-banana, youngberry (like boysenberry), apple and mixtures of many of the aforementioned. They come in small boxes of 200ml or 250ml, 1 liter boxes and 12 ounce cans.

Coffee sometimes may be a coffee-chicory mixture which has an unappealing taste. Check to be sure you're getting real coffee rather than this less expensive substitute. It's sold under various brand names so check the label.

Tea is a common drink any time of day. Try the delicious health tea called Rooibos.

Food

Game meat is widely available in Namibia, and is often raised on farms for this purpose.

Kudu steaks are available from most *slaghuis*/butcheries. The meat is very lean and should be spiced up and tenderized for the *braai*.

Oryx-Gemsbok steaks are widely available. A bit more tasty than kudu and very lean as well.

Eland tastes the most like beef, however it is very scarce.

Ostrich filets are sold mostly in restaurants. This is a delicious meat if prepared properly. It has a wonderful gamey wild bird flavor, yet not too strong. The red meat is very low in cholesterol. You can get it at large meat processing plants such as Hartlief's in Windhoek. The ostrich at the Mokuti lodge in Etosha is smoked as an appetizer and as a main course in a rich gravy.

Crocodile, when served as a cocktail or filet steak, is chewy and delicious, a bit like chicken. Crocodile that is served for food is raised on a croc farm in Otjiwarongo.

Springbok, much like kudu in flavor, is available in some restaurants and butcheries.

Guinea fowl is very tough if not prepared carefully, but has an excellent wild game bird flavor if tenderized and cooked right.

Warthog is a delicious alternative to farm raised pork.

Seafood is usually very fresh if eaten at the coastal towns of Henties Bay, Swakopmund, Walvis Bay or Lüderitz. It is also served in many other towns, though in the outlying areas it is harder to get.

Cabeljou is a delicious white meat fish with few bones—very flaky and firm—try the cabeljou at De Duine hotel in Henties Bay.

Crayfish, like the North American spiny lobster, is a delectable treat fished off the coast mainly near Lüderitz. It's expensive and the meat is a little tougher than its American counterpart.

Caljoun and **Steenbras** are two other locally caught white fleshed fish.

Prawns, not the huge ones, but those served here are usually much smaller; when you're paying as much as most restaurants charge, ask first.

Mussels are black shelled and very tasty.

Oysters we've been served have been fresh and clean tasting—absolutely delicious with cocktail sauce and lemon juice. They're farmed near Swakopmund.

Beef in Namibia is excellent and exported to the European Community. If you are a beef lover and a thick steak on the *braai* is your thing, you will not be disappointed. Beef is relatively cheap—we bought two nice T-bones for less than R7.

Boerewors are famous little sausages seen on *braais* throughout Southern Africa, and you'll find them at most every market or *slaghuis*. These tasty little treats are usually made with beef and spices, with cloves being the telltale flavor. They are often eaten as appetizers before the main meat course, right off the *braai*!

Dröewors or "dry sausage" is basically dried boerewors. It keeps quite a while and is good for the trail as it needs no refrigeration.

Biltong—something must be said about biltong. It is practically an institution in Southern Africa. The rough equivalent of American "jerky," it is made from practically any meat, usually marinated in someone's special recipe and cut into long strips and air dried with fans for several days. Hunters will make biltong from game but butchers make it commercially from beef. It keeps very well but will dry out if left uncovered. We've seen biltong made from oryx, kudu, ostrich, springbok as well as beef and mixed meats, both wild and domestic. It's a wonderful treat for those who like jerky—this African version is addicting! Another excellent food for the trail.

Lamb & Mutton are readily available as there are plenty of sheep in Namibia. Some of the chops we've had in restaurants have been particularly scrawny, though, with just a dab of meat on the bone.

Goats are a measure of wealth and are traded for goods, but not always eaten. Would you put a wad of dollar bills on the *braai*? Goat can be had however as many people raise them for meat these days and the taste is a little like lamb.

Pork is widely available—domesticated as well as wild warthog.

Fresh produce—is mostly imported from South Africa. The closer you are to a major city or town the wider the availability and selection, which is quite good in the large towns.

Groceries are mostly imported from South Africa. You will find a wide selection of western style groceries in the main cities and towns with a smaller selection the farther out you go.

Roads and Traveling

Namibia maintains a good system of paved and dirt roads. In most parts of the country the main roads are in good shape and you can travel without being jarred to pieces by washboard, potholed roads found throughout some parts of Africa. The main danger is wildlife on the roadway, especially at night. Traveling at night or even at dawn or dusk presents dangers; coming over a rise or around a corner in the dark and seeing a large bull kudu standing unwavering in the middle of the road is a bit chilling. Many animals are nocturnal, so you will only see them when your headlights hit them, and often that is too late. If you do happen to hit an animal and are able to drive on, remove it from the road if possible. Try to avoid driving at night except possibly along the coast where wildlife is more scarce. Game populations are generally more dense the farther north you go. If you do travel at night, drive at a minimum speed and keep your eyes open for anything wandering into the road. Even in the day wildlife cross the roads in search of food and care must be taken particularly at dusk and dawn when animals are very active.

As Namibia has been currently experiencing a long drought, some of the livestock herders have taken to grazing their goats, cattle and sheep on the thin strip of grass between the road and the nearest fence. This is often the only place left where there is anything to eat. These sometimes large, slow herds might be crossing the road over the next rise. Watch for people on the road, especially in the north of the country where population density is higher. Roads are frequently used corridors for foot transportation.

On some of Namibia's seldom traveled rural roads, it's best to take plenty of water and some food with you. Being stranded on a road in the hot desert summer (and even in the winter) where 2 or 3 vehicles pass per day is not an exciting prospect!

It is also recommended that you take one or two spare tires, especially if you are traveling off the main tourist roads or on a 4-wheel drive excursion. A hand or foot pump and a tire repair kit for tubes or tubeless tires could also save you from being stranded.

There are petrol stops spaced throughout Namibia, so it is usually easy to plan a trip between towns, but there are some areas where you must carry extra fuel to make it to the next petrol stop, especially in the northwest and parts of the northeast.

If you are traveling on dirt roads, it is often difficult to pass vehicles, especially large trucks, if the wind is blowing the dust towards you. You must be patient and wait until you can see a long, clear stretch of road. The vehicle in front often can't see you because of its own dust. Some of the gravel roads are graded so that the middle of the road is higher than the shoulder, which is often sandy. If you drift onto the shoulder it is easy to lose control and send your vehicle rocketing into whatever lies beyond.

You must drive carefully on dirt roads; locals and tourists have been injured and even killed by overturning their vehicles. If you are involved in an accident, report it to the nearest police station.

The speed limit on the highways is 120 km./hr but you should consider driving slower, especially on the gravel roads.

An international driver's license is required to operate a vehicle in Namibia. You can get one from your local Automobile Association. If you are a member of a foreign Automobile Association, your coverage is generally good in Namibia and you can call a list of AAN approved towers or garages for help if you get stuck on the road. Stop by the AAN office in Windhoek near the Kalahari Sands Hotel for assistance with any motoring concerns.

Offroad and 4-Wheel Drive Roads

Driving on tracks with 4-wheel drive vehicles presents its own set of challenges. Make sure before setting off on a trip that you have enough water, food and spare tires for an emergency. When driving in sand it's sometimes best to lower your tire pressure about 20 percent or so to increase traction—although you will need to be prepared to reinflate them when driving on tarred or rocky roads. Avoid "oily" looking sand in places like Sandwich Harbor as you will get stuck there. When driving through grassy areas, check your radiator for grass seeds that will clog your grill and eventually overheat your vehicle.

Border Crossings

Botswana

When crossing into Botswana, you'll need your passport, visa (if required, check with the Botswana Mission in Windhoek, Tel. 221941 or 41961), and if you're bringing a vehicle, proof of ownership from the Namibian police (available at the Windhoek police station at Independence and Bahnhof Sts.), or forms supplied by the rental agency. You'll need to pay 5 pula (7.5R) for third party insurance at the border. You will be issued coverage for a year. You no longer have to report to the police station in the next town after crossing. There are official borders at Buitepos in the east and in the Caprivi at Ngoma and Mohembo. Four-wheel drive vehicles are recommended after Buitepos and Mohembo, though during the dry season 2-wheel drive may suffice (inquire locally or at the AAN). Make sure you have the proper vehicle for the roads in Botswana. (See the "Getting There" section.)

South Africa

You'll need a passport and visa (if required, check with the S.A. Interest Office in Windhoek, Tel. 227771), as well as proof of yellow fever inoculation if coming from an endemic area. A return ticket is necessary if you can't convince the immigration officer that you have the means to pay for one. Third party insurance is also necessary for vehicles. There are two main border crossings at Ariamsvlei and Noordoewer and several other smaller border posts.

Zambia

You'll need a passport and a visa (if necessary, check with Zambian High Commission in Windhoek, Tel. 37610), as well as a police clearance, that is, proof of ownership. Third party insurance is more expensive for Zambia, so check first.

Just outside Katima Mulilo, there is a ferry border crossing into Zambia with roads going north towards Mongu and a road going east towards Victoria Falls and eventually Lusaka.

Zimbabwe

You'll need the same documents as for Zambia. You will be issued third party insurance at the border for a nominal fee if you don't have proof of your own coverage. Check with Zimbabwe High Commission in Windhoek for changes, Tel. 228134. Take either the border crossing at Ngoma and then travel 85 km. through Botswana to the Zimbabwe border or the road through southern Zambia towards Victoria Falls.

Angola

Should you really want to go through Angola, which has just been through a long civil war, you might be able do so at the main border post at Oshikango. Check with the Angolan embassy and locally first.

Hitchhiking

Hitchhiking in Namibia is fairly good—the problem is not that people won't stop—it's just that the volume of traffic is so minuscule on some roads that you could wait quite a while for a ride. On main tarred highways, traffic volume is good, though don't expect anything remotely resembling a constant flow of traffic. In some of the more remote regions on less traveled roads, it pays to get rides only from town to town or to be prepared to have enough water and food to wait it out. Don't get caught in the summer desert heat between towns on a minor road as this can be dangerous.

Dressing neatly will help you get a ride. People hitch in Namibia by extending their arm and wagging their hand up and down, sometimes with a frantic motion. This adds more urgency to the matter than a motionless thumb. Some people will ask for money in exchange for a lift.

Conversely, if you are driving you'll notice people hitching all over the country as most do not have and cannot afford regular transportation. At exits to most towns there are usually people flagging down traffic. Even in the hinterlands, you come across people hitching, sometimes hours from the nearest town without food or water and you can't help but wonder how long they've been there or where they came from. We once stopped for a man wildly waving his hand in the Namib desert and found out he didn't want a ride, just some water, which he gulped down thirstily. Although you occasionally read about incidents involving hitchhikers, most people just want a ride. We've picked up literally hundreds of people and never had a problem. If you have some room, it really helps, especially where there is no other system of transportation to get from town to town.

NOTE: **No hitchhiking is allowed in Etosha National Park.**

You can call in on NBC radio to advertise free of charge a ride needed or offered. In Windhoek, call 2912002 between 12:30-1:00 for English speakers, 2912003 between 12:00-1:00 for German speakers and 2912007 between 2:30-4:00 for Afrikaans speakers.

Buses

Mainliner Bus Service

The Intercape Mainliner offers luxury bus service at a reasonable price (by western standards anyway) between some of the larger towns and cities in Namibia and South

Africa. They go as far as Cape Town, Johannesburg and East London in South Africa, following the main highways and stopping at many towns in between. In Namibia they go as far north as Tsumeb and as far west as Walvis Bay and Swakopmund. Check with them as far as taking bicycles, surfboards and other large items as these may not be allowed depending on space available. Smoking and alcohol consumption are taboo. You are allowed two bags, but if space is available you can bring more for a surcharge. They serve drinks and snacks but meals are left up to you—either bring your own or get something at one of the stops. Telephone in Windhoek, (061) 227847, or fax, (061) 228285. You must make reservations 24 hours prior to departure. Intercape Mainliner has a 24 hour information line in Cape Town, (021) 9344400.

Mainliner Schedules and Fares

On the following routes you may get on or off the bus at most major towns between the starting point and final destination. Fares are based upon mileage traveled.

Windhoek-Cape Town—3 times weekly. Sample fares: Windhoek-Keetmanshoop, R85; Windhoek-Cape Town, R210

Windhoek-Upington (S.A.):—4 times weekly. Sample fares: Windhoek- Upington, R150

Windhoek-Walvis Bay—4 times weekly. Sample fares: Windhoek-Walvis Bay, R70

Windhoek-Tsumeb—4 times weekly. Sample fares: Windhoek-Tsumeb, R75.

For complete schedules, call Mainliner office. From Cape Town, buses are available to George, Port Elizabeth, East London, Velddrif and Upington. From Upington, buses are available to Cape Town and Johannesburg. Windhoek-Upington bus continues on to Johannesburg.

TransNamib Buses

Telephone (061) 2982032 for reservations or 2982217 for information. A para-statal transportation company, Trans-Namib operates buses, trains, airlines, trucking and other transportation related businesses in Namibia. They run buses that take a limited number of passengers and cargo between major cities in Namibia. These buses are not well advertised and you should phone TransNamib or the local station master; in Windhoek, 2982217, during office hours.

Schedule of Transnamib Buses

Grootfontein-Rundu: 2 times weekly, T & Th

Rundu-Katima Mulilo: Service starting soon once a week; call for details.

Outjo-Khorixas: once a week, Th

Outjo-Walvis Bay: once a week, M; return Th via Khorixas

Outjo-Opuwo: once a week, Th; return same day

Gobabis-Leonardville: once a week, Tu

Gobabis-Aranos: once a week, W

Gobabis-Botswana Border (Buitepos): once a week, F

Mariental-Walvis Bay (through Namib Park): once a week, M

Mariental-Aranos: twice weekly: M & Th

Mariental-Gochas: once a week, W

Keetmanshoop-Bethanien: twice a week, M & Th

Keetmanshoop-Helmeringhausen: once a week, Th

The charge for travel on TransNamib is roughly 6 cents per kilometer and travel is definitely third class. It is an inexpensive way to move about the country and a good chance to mix with Namibians.

Namib Contract Haulage

Namib Contract Haulage: 68 Bismarck St. Windhoek, Tel. 229871 or 225333. This new company offers inexpensive transportation from Windhoek to Swakopmund, Keetmanshoop, Rundu, Khorixas and Okakarara. They pickup from various points in the city; call for rates and times.

Bus to Zambia

There is a United Bus Company of Zambia (UBZ) bus to Lusaka, Zambia, that leaves every Saturday afternoon at 5PM from the Grootfontein train station. It stops at Rundu, Bagani (Popa Falls), Katima Mulilo, Livingstóne in Zambia, and other points in between. It overnights at Rundu and Livingstone, arriving in Lusaka around 2PM on Monday. Tickets are sold at the Grootfontein station from 2 to 4:45PM the day of the trip. The return trip from Lusaka leaves at 5AM every Wednesday, overnighting at Katima Mulilo and arriving Grootfontein at 9:30PM on Thursday. It will drop off or pickup people at any point along the way—thus the lengthy voyage. Fares run roughly R10¢ per km.; Grootfontein to Katima is R82, and to Lusaka R150. The bus is not a luxury bus, but we've seen worse along African roads.

Trains

Telephone (061) 2982032 for reservations or information. Namibia has an efficient, if slow, train system. Schedules usually change yearly. Current fares are approximately .20¢ per km. 1st class; .15¢ per km. 2nd class; and .08¢ per km. 3rd class. Kids under 12 are half fare and kids under 7 are free. There is a dining car only on the Windhoek to De Aar train. The trains stop at most major towns along the way.

Train Schedule

Windhoek-Tsumeb-Windhoek: 2 times weekly
Otjiwarongo-Grootfontein-Otjiwarongo: 2 times weekly
Windhoek-De Aar, S.A.-Windhoek: 3 times weekly
Windhoek-Gobabis-Windhoek: 2 times weekly
Windhoek-Walvis Bay-Windhoek: 3 times weekly
BUS: Outjo-Otjiwarongo-Outjo: 3 times weekly
BUS: Keetmanshoop-Lüderitz-Keetmanshoop: 2 times weekly

Vehicle Rentals

Car, 4-Wheel Drive and Caravan (RV) Rental

Renting cars and bakkies (pick-ups) is not cheap in Namibia. You must be 25 years of age and have a valid driver's license and passport to rent a vehicle.

Sample rates for renting a vehicle are R85-300 per day plus—R1-3 per kilometer for vehicles ranging from a compact to luxury or van. You usually have an option of renting the same vehicle for between R220-500 per day with 250 free kilometers. If you rent for 6 days or longer, rates are approximately R175-425 per day with 250 free kilometers. Insurance (if you aren't covered with a credit card) runs from R22-32 per day.

Kessler Car Hire, probably the largest 4-wheel drive car rental in Namibia, has a large stock of vehicles but is more expensive than Namib4X4. You can take the vehicle to Zimbabwe for an extra R100 charge for documents allowing you to cross the border and you can go to Botswana as well. They have eliminated the VW Synchro4X4 vans due to problems with the vehicles.

Namib 4X4 is less expensive than Kessler, but some of their vehicles are a little older. Check restrictions involved when renting, such as deductible on insurance (called "Excess" in Namibia), non-coverable items such as windshields and tires, deposits equal to 10 percent of the vehicle value, and kilometer charges versus unlimited kilometers, etc. Both companies also rent camping equipment.

For RV rental—try Woodway service at the corner of Gobabis and Klein Windhoek Rds. in Windhoek, Tel. 229917/8

Car Rental Companies
Windhoek
Adventure 4X4 Hire: P.O. Box 9544, Tel. 226188

Avis Rent-a-Car: P.O. Box 2057, Jeans St., Tel. 33166, Fax 223072

Bonanza Car Hire, Woodway Motors: Tal St., Tel. 33196 or 35678, Fax 228264

Budget Rent-a-Car: P.O. Box 1754, 72 Tal St., Tel. 228720, Airport (0626) 225, Fax 38748

Imperial Rent-a-Car: P.O. Box 1387, Stübel St., Tel. 227103 (after hours Tel. 52222), Fax 222721

Kessler Car Hire: P.O. Box 20274, Tal St., Tel. 227605, Fax 224551

Namib4X4: P.O.Box 9544, Tel. 220604, Fax 220605

Pegasus Car & Camper Hire: P.O. Box 21104, Tel. 0800-1600 397 2020 1700-2100 223423

Swa Safaris: 43 Independence Ave., Tel. 37567

Tempest Car Hire: 49 John Meinert St., Tel. 38745

Trip Car Hire: Levinson Arcade, Tel. 36880

Woodway Service: P.O. Box 11084, Corner of Gobabis & Klein, Windhoek Rd., Tel. 229917/8, Fax 220335

Zimmerman Car Hire: 5 Wright St., Box 2672, Tel. 37146

Swakopmund

Avis: 38 Kaiser Wilhelm St., P.O. Box 1216, Tel. 2527

Bonanza Car Hire, Dolphin Motors: 38 Kaiser Wilhelm St., Tel. 4503, Fax 5273

Imperial Car Hire: P.O. Box 748, Tel. 61587

Namib4X4: P.O. Box 4048, Tel. 61791, Fax 62184

Swakopmund Caravan Hire: P.O. Box 3497, Tel. 61297

Trip Swakopmund: 11 Post St., Box 882, Tel. 4031

Walvis Bay

Avis: P.O. Box 758, 121 10th St., Tel. 5935

Bonanza Car Hire: BP Garage, 18th Road, Tel. 5936/5, Fax 6506

Imperial Car Hire: P.O. Box 1591, Tel. 4624

Nechville Car Hire: Toyota Bldg., 9th St., Box 336, Tel. 4414

Keetmanshoop

Avis: P.O. Box, 164 Fenchel St., Tel. 2337

Lüderitz

Avis: P.O. Box 11, Bahnhof St., Tel. 2054

Tsumeb

Avis: P.O. Box 284, Safari Center, Tel. 2520

Ondangwa

Punyu Car Hire: Tel. 58

Katima Mulilo

Avis: P.O. Box 98, Tel. 203

Taxis

Taxis mainly operate in the Windhoek area and you can catch one across from the Kalahari Sands Hotel above the airport bus terminal. They charge about R1.50-2.0 for the first kilometer and the same for each additional kilometer. For pickup at other locations, call one of the following companies:

Namibia Radio Taxis:—Tel. 211116 or 225222

Windhoek Radio Taxis:—Tel. 37070

Funk Taxis:—Tel. 226119 or 34166

There are also vans that take people from the main population centers northward to Owamboland and other areas. They often put in as many people as they can cram into the van and then load the roof high with luggage. This would be an interesting way to meet some of the local populace, though not necessarily a safe or comfortable one. The vans leave from the bus terminal next to Wernhil Park shopping center in Windhoek as well as from the singles quarters in Katutura. Ask locally for other locations.

Bus to Windhoek Airport

There is a regular bus from Windhoek to the international airport 40 km. away that costs R15. It leaves a couple of hours before every flight from the small terminal across from the Kalahari Sands Hotel. Check the schedule there for exact times.

Airline Service within Namibia

The national carrier, Air Namibia, has regular flights from Windhoek to Swakopmund, Walvis Bay, Lüderitz, Oranjemund, Keetmanshoop, Tsumeb, Etosha, Ondangwa, Rundu and Katima Mulilo. Flights are usually on large twin engine propeller aircraft. Many internal flights and a few international flights, mostly to South Africa, leave from Eros Airport, a smaller strip on the south side of town near the Safari Hotel. It's a short cab ride from the city center, saving you the longer 30 minute trip to the international airport.

Airplane Charters

If you want to charter an aircraft for business or pleasure, try Namibia Commercial Aviation, which has single, twin engine or jet aircraft available. Tel. (061) 223562 or after hours 51897, 31369 or 227043, Fax (061) 34583.

In Swakopmund-Walvis Bay area, try Air Charters at Tel. (0641) 5782, (0642) 5871 or after hours (0641) 61398, (0642) 6644 or 3752; Fax (0641) 62719 or (0642) 4217. Also in Walvis Bay, try Safair at 144B 8th St., Tel. (0642) 5806

Health

Namibia has high quality health care with the sixth best doctor/patient ratio in Africa. The ratio of 166 people per hospital bed is the third best in Africa. Through a system of regional hospitals, clinics and bush and mobile clinics, the government aims to put health care within reach of most of the inhabitants. There are private hospitals as well in Windhoek and Otjiwarongo. Medical care is not expensive compared with western standards. For example, an x-ray at the Windhoek State Hospital cost only R30.

Water

Water is very safe in all the main cities and towns. Most guest farms have their own boreholes and the water is good, but in rural areas, you might want to inquire about the source of the water. It is always a good idea to keep a bottle of purified water with you whenever you travel, especially off the beaten track.

Malaria

This is one of the most common diseases in Namibia, affecting mostly people in the northern part of the country. Precautions should be taken when going into the north, especially during the rainy season.

Malaria is a disease of tropical and sub-tropical areas worldwide, although it has been eradicated in some areas of the world. Malaria is transmitted to humans by the female Anopheles mosquito. The Anopheles mosquito can be recognized by its posture when biting, its body in a straight line and more perpendicular to the skin, as opposed to being bent or humped. They are most often active at night. After a bite, it usually takes 12 days or so for the fever to appear.

A malaria attack may begin with chills and shivering accompanied by an often high fever with headache, then copious sweating and a lowering of body temperature. If you experience these symptoms during your stay or after your return from an infected area, have your blood checked for malaria. If caught early, medication can be taken to control it. People usually experience relapses at varying intervals after the initial infection, with symptoms less severe than the original attack. People living in an infected area will often develop an immunity if repeatedly bitten, with attacks of lessening severity that eventually diminish.

Most travelers who wish to avoid malaria take a prophylactic such as chloroquine, beginning two weeks before entering an infected area, weekly during a stay and weekly for six weeks after leaving the area. There are currently strains of malaria which are resistant to chloroquine and other prophylactics, so check with the World Health Organization (WHO) or the Center for Disease Control (CDC) in Atlanta, Georgia. Various strengths and prescriptions for chloroquine may have instructions different from the above. Drugs such as Fansidar are taken if you get malaria. These will relieve or eliminate symptoms rapidly although some have side effects.

A good way to prevent malaria in addition to taking prophylactic drugs is to use a repellent, wear long pants and sleeves, and sleep under mosquito netting.

AIDS

AIDS is increasingly common in Namibia. It hasn't hit the country as it has central Africa but it is only a matter of time if preventative education does not reach the people and social customs continue to get in the way of practicing safe sex. The government is actively educating the public through radio, TV and newspaper ads, but these don't reach all people; AIDS is a growing problem, especially among the young, spread most often by unprotected sexual contact.

Blood products in Namibia are generally regarded as safe. Only highly screened unpaid volunteers give blood. All blood and blood products are screened for various transmissible diseases, including AIDS and hepatitis.

Bilharzia

Also known as Schistosomiasis, bilharzia is a very common disease worldwide, occurring in most of Africa. The disease is caused by the parasitic Trematode worm which is transmitted by freshwater snails. The worm develops in the snail and emerges as a free-swimming organism that can penetrate skin. An open sore is not necessary. This causes an often intense itching. The organism somehow makes its way to the liver where it further develops for about six weeks. It then emerges from the liver and swims to the bladder or intestine, where it lays eggs, which are passed in urine or feces. It then travels to another snail to repeat the cycle. This process doesn't sound very appealing, so it's best to avoid bodies of water where bilharzia is suspected. It is usually found in still or stagnant water. Check locally.

Symptoms include fever, headache, aching muscles, sweating, chills, blood in the urine and feces and diarrhea. If caught early, treatment is effective but should be carried out in a hospital.

Sleeping Sickness (Trypanosomiasis)

Caused by the bite of an infected tsetse fly, sleeping sickness is endemic in the Caprivi, but is controlled by annual spraying. After a bite, a large bump appears, though this is not a sign of infection unless it turns into a large, relatively painless boil and is accompanied by fever 1-3 weeks later. Lymph gland enlargement is common as are headaches and joint pain which may last months if not treated. The name comes from the later stages of the disease in which fatigue and the tendency to fall asleep are common. If treated during the early stages full recovery is possible.

Other Diseases

Tuberculosis, typhoid, meningitis, cholera, hepatitis and trachoma are diseases usually associated with poor socio-economic conditions and occur in overcrowded areas where food and water may be contaminated.

Backpacking, Hiking & Camping

Namibia has some excellent backpacking trails, among them the Fish River Canyon and the Naukluft Range trails. For the more adventurous, cross country hiking and climbing in areas like the Brandberg can be rewarding. There is nothing like being in the desert and coming across an unexpected waterhole, splashing its cool waters upon your tired feet and seeing wild oryx, zebra, springbok and other game not from your vehicle, but from a hidden rock outcrop.

You can go on organized backpacking safaris such as Waterberg Plateau or Ugab River or take off on your own and really get away from everything. Backpacking is usually incredibly rewarding, as you are taking everything you need to live for several days on your back and become self-sufficient during that time. It can also be quite uncomfortable or dangerous if you don't prepare properly—Namibia presents some challenges to those living in the great outdoors, which with planning can be overcome.

There are several items which you should probably consider bringing on your hike:

Tents are most useful when it is cold, rainy or where there are mosquitoes or wildlife which might be interested in you. For backpacking a lightweight tent is necessary.

Sleeping bag—usually a lightweight three-season bag will be sufficient, but during the winter months, especially June-August, the temperatures can drop well below freezing, so be prepared to augment a lightweight bag with a tent or blankets.

Insulated sleeping pads—are definitely helpful for a good sleep. You should be able to find a body length insulated pad at a camping store or an auto parts specialty store like Cymot. They keep you insulated from the cold ground as well as providing some comfort against rocks and bumps.

Stoves fueled by kerosene (paraffin) are better than white gas as kerosene is widely available. However, kerosene burns much dirtier and may clog your stove eventually. We used kerosene in our small backpacking stove that was built to burn almost any fuel including kerosene. It worked OK for a while but clogged after a few weeks. We were advised to try benzene (bensien) and it worked like a charm. You can buy it in some hardware stores, grocery stores or gas stations, but it's not as widely available as kerosene. Check the stoves that burn methylated spirits—they are simple to use.

Flashlights (torches) are essential, especially in the winter months when the days are short and one must start and end the day in the dusk or dark. To avoid hiking during the hottest daylight hours in the summer, it is a good idea to get up before the sun and start when it is still dark. It is a lot easier to hike during the cooler morning and evening hours and rest midday. It saves on precious water as well.

Maps—good topographical maps can be obtained from the Surveyor-General's office in Windhoek in the same building as the main post office downtown. A very helpful man runs the map department and will get you what you need. Standard scale 1:250,000 and 1:50,000 maps cost from R5-R7. You may also order maps through the mail by writing the Surveyor-General, Private Bag 13182, Windhoek.

Food—should be lightweight for backpacking. In Namibia food which requires little water to cook is preferable. Suggestions include: combinations of dried meats such as salamis, biltong and dröewors (see food section), muesli, crackers and bread, dried fruit, and some freeze dried meals which require only a little water to cook.

Backpacks need to be lightweight but strong—a backpack or rucksack with several compartments is ideal. Internal frame packs with adjustable hip belts and shoulder straps seem to work the best for us. They also tend to mold to the back better than a metal external frame backpack, although personal preference and comfort should guide choice.

Water

Water bottles are a necessity as in some wilderness areas there is simply no water and you must provide enough for all your drinking, cooking and washing for the entire trip. Lightweight bottles are obviously imperative when hiking and 2-liter plastic water bottles are well suited. You can also bring a larger collapsible plastic container. These have the added advantage of taking up less room when empty. Canvas water bags are nice, especially when hung on the outside of your vehicle when traveling. The evaporation of the water on the outside of the bag cools the water on the inside, providing something more refreshing than water warmed by the sun. Keep in mind that **1 liter of water weighs one kilogram.** You should, depending on the temperature and your own needs, bring **at least 2 liters of water per person per day, preferably more.** This tends to shorten most backpacking trips, so check in advance if water is available on the trail and remember to boil it thoroughly (10 minutes) if you are at all unsure of its purity. Water found near any human habitation is suspect as are watering places frequently used by animals.

Water and the lack of it in many places is the main difference between backpacking in Namibia and elsewhere. If you are on a four- day hike through the Brandberg area, you will need for yourself a minimum of 8 liters—about 18 pounds—not including the containers! Knowing where to find water could help considerably. Dehydration and exposure in a remote area can be dangerous and life threatening. Check locally for water sources before starting on the trail and if in doubt, hire a guide who knows the area and where to find water.

Heat

Extreme temperatures in Namibia can pose a serious danger for the unprepared. Water usage will increase with temperature and the two liters per day/per person may double in extreme conditions. Be aware of this when you are planning your trip. It may make the difference between a hot but pleasant trip and a dangerous one. Often it's better to hike in the cooler hours—from first light until 10-11:00am and from 4:00 until sunset, using the hotter hours to rest in the shade. Wearing a hat is a must to stay a little cooler and avoid sunburn. Sunscreen should be used as sunburn and exposure are additional dangers to the backpacker. Hiking on the north slope of a mountain is usually hotter as it receives sunlight at a more direct angle than the south slope. This is the reverse of what North American and European hikers are accustomed to in the Northern Hemisphere.

Animals

While wild animals are rarely a problem for backpackers or hikers, you should be informed of the possible dangers so you'll know what to expect should you run into them in the wild. Most wild animals try to avoid confrontations with humans and usually problems only occur when animals are startled, surprised, stepped on or threatened. Beware of where you place your feet, especially in tall grass that can hide some of Africa's venomous snakes. Snakes will most likely slither away if they sense your approaching footsteps.

Elephants very rarely kill or injure people. When it does happen, it is usually when villagers are protecting crops from damage. It is probably most important to remember not to run when faced by an elephant. If you come across an elephant in the wild, freeze, and if you are near a large tree, slowly get behind it. Their eyesight is not good, so if you do not move, it may have trouble seeing you. If an elephant comes at you with its ears spread out and trunk up in the air trumpeting, it is most likely a mock charge meant to scare you. Slowly back away and it should stop. During a real charge ears are back and trunk down under the chin. Get behind a large tree, but don't run.

Rhino are not equally dangerous. Apparently the larger white rhino is not as dangerous as the smaller black rhino, which is more common in Namibia. White rhino are not found in the wild, whereas black rhino are found in Etosha, Waterberg Plateau Park and in the wilds of Damaraland and Kaokoland. You aren't very likely to come across one, but if you do there are certain things to remember about these often misunderstood beasts. First, their eyesight is very poor and they will often charge at a noise or something in motion. If you can climb about 2 meters up a tree, then you should be safe. If you are hopelessly close and find yourself being charged by a rhino, then it is possible to avoid being impaled by flinging yourself aside at the last moment as it approaches. It may also charge close by and miss you entirely as it can't see very well. It's better not to run the risk of a charge because although this advice sounds OK, actually doing it is a different story.

Lions can easily run you down, so again it is important not to run. They most often will retreat if they see or hear you coming. If you see one closeby, freeze, then retreat very slowly. When angry, a lion will drop into a crouch, flatten its ears and grunt and growl while flicking its tail quickly from side to side. The tail jerks up and down just prior to a charge. If you find yourself with a lion on top of you and a limb in its mouth, and you still have your wits about you, bonking it on the nose may distract it enough to leave you.

Hippos are found only in permanent water in Namibia's

northern rivers (the Kunene, Okavango, Cuando-Linyanti-Chobe and Zambezi). They can be very dangerous especially if you find yourself between a hippo and the water which is its sanctuary. A hippo will run towards the water when frightened, but if you are in the way it will come for you, and at one to two tons with an impressive set of tusk-like canines and incisors, it's best to dive out of the way or get behind or up a tree. They look fat but can outrun you. Look out for cows with calves and solitary bulls as these can be particularly dangerous.

Buffalo can be dangerous if injured but be wary of them in any case. They charge nose up and can easily outrun you. As they are only found in the north of Namibia, mostly in the Caprivi, there may be a tree around to climb or hide behind near. People have been known to walk through herds untouched but it's best to treat them as any potentially large dangerous animal.

Leopards, nocturnal cats, are very rarely encountered and are quite shy, withdrawing from potential encounters. If trapped, wounded or threatened they can be very dangerous. If you encounter one, retreat slowly sideways and away rather than directly backwards. Avoid staring it in the eye as this can be taken for a sign of aggression. They apparently have been choked to death by humans under attack who still had their wits about them. In most attacks people are mauled but not fatally.

Cheetah have not been known to attack humans, however don't be tempted to provoke one.

Hyena, especially the brown hyena, appear to be harmless and attacks by the spotted hyena occur rarely, mostly on people asleep on the ground after a meaty meal around the campfire.

Crocodiles ("Flat Dogs") may grab people who are wading in crocodile infested waters. Their jaws are extremely powerful when biting down, however if you can clamp their mouths shut, the muscles to open them are weak. If you are grabbed, stab at the eyes with anything you can get your hands on.

Crocodiles are hard to spot and are very fast on land and in water. They are fairly abundant in all of Namibia's border rivers except the Orange.

A guide who takes mokoro (dugout canoe) safaris along the Cuando river in the Caprivi gave us some tips on traveling by mokoro through croc and hippo infested waters. First of all it helps to know where the beasts usually stay. You must paddle right next to the shore so if something comes after you, it's easy to jump onto land. The crocs leave if they hear you coming (at least during the day), so make noise as you paddle.

Note: None of the aforementioned recommendations concerning wild animals are infallible; wild animals are often unpredictable—so please travel with care.

CHAPTER 4

Wildlife

Fauna

Mammals

Traveling to Namibia presents an opportunity to see wildlife in a unique way. The desert climate and the low density of human population combine to allow the traveler a more natural and free experience than in the more densely populated and heavily vegetated countries of southern and eastern Africa.

There are several mammals which are rare and found only in Namibia. These include Grant's golden mole, the Namib longeared bat, and the Setzer hairyfooted gerbil. These creatures are nocturnal, so you are not likely to see them. Those which you may run across are the striped tree squirrel in Kaokoland, and the dassie rat in the rocky areas of the Namib Desert.

Outside population centers, it is easy to spot animals if you are looking for them and not driving too fast. In fact, if you are thinking of driving at night, please be very cautious. Often large wild game jump into the road without warning and can do serious damage to your car. Kudu are among the most frequently hit and it is their shape you see on the warning signs posted along the road. These beautiful gray-brown antelope with vertical white stripes have a distinctive hump at the base of the neck. Adult males have enormous spiral antlers. These, as well as many other antelope, live in families of a dominant male, four to six females and their calves, known as a harem. Adolescent males leave the harem

and travel in small groups or independently until they are strong enough to challenge a dominant male and acquire a harem. If you see a kudu on the road, watch out for the others in the group.

Warthogs can often be seen along the roads in northern and central Namibia. A gray pig-like creature, the warthog can have large ferocious looking tusks. They also travel in family groups of females and young or male groups.

The springbok is an animal commonly seen on the road in most parts of the country, especially the desert areas. This dainty antelope is tan on the back and white on the belly with a dark brown stripe separating the two colors. Both males and females carry a lyre- shaped rack of antlers. They run gracefully, but their most distinctive trait is the spring jump in which all four feet leave the ground and pull together swiftly as the animal goes straight up and forward to avoid danger. The smallest antelope in Namibia is the Damara dik-dik, which can sometimes be seen along the roadways. It is only 38 centimeters at the shoulder, and has a yellowish-gray upper body and light belly. Further identifying marks are stripes within its ears, a crest of long fur on its forehead, and dark "tear drops" at each eye; rams have short straight ant-lers. Currently, there is a study to learn more about the distri-bution of the dik-dik.

The animal which graces the official crest of Namibia, the oryx, can be spotted along the road around Sesriem and in many desert areas. This large antelope is more commonly called the gemsbok, its Afrikaans name. It is as large as a cow with a magnificent set of long straight, black antlers set at an angle towards the back. The oryx has distinctive black mark-ings on its face and near the upper legs. The upper body is gray and the belly white. You may see a solitary individual or a herd of four to fifteen. The oryx can exist in this hot and arid environment because it has a large mass of blood vessels below the brain which help to decrease the temperature of that vital organ and allow the animal to tolerate high body temperatures.

Frequently, you may notice the small antelope called a steenbok watching you from the side of the road in the central region. The steenbok looks like a tiny deer and blends well with the roadside grasses because of its golden color. The large ears are distinctive and the males have short straight antlers.

Throughout Namibia you may see the black-backed jackal. It looks like a dog with long ears, a fox face, a back that is mottled black and white, and a tan lower body. Jackals are known as scavengers but they are also good hunters. They can be spotted running through the fields where the grass is short or along desert roads and even beaches.

In areas where there are rocky outcroppings, look for das-sies, also called hyrax. This animal has the shape of a small rabbit but lacks the large ears and tail. Both the dassie and the dassie rat have the habit of urinating over the edge of their rocky dwellings. If you see a small cave marked by white-wash at the entrance, you will know that dassies live there.

The baboon is a creature which will attract your attention if there is a troop by the roadside. Baboons look like large monkeys with dog-like faces. They live in large family groups

NAMIBIA

	CAPE CROSS	CAPRIVI	DAAN VILJOEN	DAMARALAND	ETOSHA	HARDAP	KAUDOM	MAMILI	MUDUMU	NAMIB-NAUKLUFT	SKELETON COAST	WATERBERG
AARDVARK		P	P	P	P	P	P	P	P			P
AARDWOLF		P		P	P	P	P	P	P	P		P
ANTELOPES												
Black Faced Impala					P							
Blue Wildebeest		P	P		A		A	P	P			P
Bushbuck		P						P	P			
Common Duiker		P	P	P	P		P	P	P			P
Damara Dik-dik				P	P							
Eland		P			P	P	P					P
Gemsbok		P	P	P	A	P	A			P	P	
Impala		P						P	P			
Klipspringer		P	P									P
Kudu		P	P	P	A	P	A	P	P	P		P
Lechwe		P						P	P			
Red Hartebeest		P	P	P	P	P	P					P
Reedbuck		P					P	P	P			
Roan Antelope		P		P			A	P	P			P
Sable		P						P	P			P
Sitatunga								P	P			
Springbok			P	P	A	P				A	P	P
Steenbok		P	P	P	P	P	P	P	P	P		P
Tsessebe		P					P	P	P			P
Water Buck		P						P				
BABOON		P	P	P	P	P	P	P	P	P		P
CAPE BUFFALO		P						P	P			P
CATS												
Caracal		P			P		P	P	P	P		P
Cheetah		P		P	P		P	P	P			P
Leopard		P		P	P		P	P	P			P
Lion		P		P	P		P	P	P		P	
Serval		P		P	P		P	P	P			
P=Present A=Abundant												

	CAPE CROSS	CAPRIVI	DAAN VILJOEN	DAMARALAND	ETOSHA	HARDAP	KAUDOM	MAMILI	MUDUMU	NAMIB-NAUKLUFT	SKELETON COAST	WATERBERG
DASSIE			P	P	P	P				P		P
ELEPHANT		P		P	A		A	A	P			
FOX												
Bat Eared		P	P	P	P		P	P	P	P		P
Cape				P	P					P		P
GIRAFFE		P		P	A		P	P	P			
HIPPOPOTAMUS		P						P	P			
HONEY BADGER		P		P	P		P	P	P			P
HYAENA												
Brown Hyaena	P			P	P		P			P	P	
Spotted		P		P	P		P	P	P	P		
JACKAL												
Black Backed	P		P	P	P	P	P			P	P	P
Side Stripped		P										
MONGOOSE		P	P	P	P	P	P	P	P	P		P
PANGOLIN		P			P		P	P	P			
PORCUPINE		P	P	P	P	P	P	P	P			P
RHINOCEROS												
Hook-lipped				P	P							P
Square-lipped												P
SEAL, CAPE FUR	P										P	
SURICATE				P	P	P				P		
VERVET MONKEY		P					P	P	P			
WARTHOG		P	P	P	A		P	P	P			P
WILD DOG		P			P		P	P	P			P
ZEBRA												
Burchell's		P			A		P	P	P			
Mountain			P	P		P				P		
P=Present A=Abundant												

of many males, females and young of all ages. During the time of estrus the rear of the female is swollen and red, obvious to both you and their suitors. You can sometimes hear their loud crow-like scream piercing the air.

If you are coming to Africa to see the famous big game, you

will be able to find them living in the national game parks, on smaller private game farms and also in the wild. Take advantage of guided game drives when you first arrive in order to learn something about the animals and how to spot them. Although many game animals are huge, they are often very well concealed. After you have had some practice spotting game, go off on your own with a knowledge of their habitat and appearance.

National parks in the Caprivi consist primarily of wetland and savanna. Some of the species which require abundant water such as cape buffalo and hippopotamus only live here. Hippo are apparently responsible for more human deaths than any other of the wild animals, so be careful when viewing them. Never get between the water and the hippo.

You will find several antelope which are unique to the wetland. The sitatunga has spiral antlers and a long shaggy coat. It is semi-aquatic, swimming to deep water to avoid danger. The lechwe is also semi-aquatic but is larger than the sitatunga and sports a lyre-shaped set of antlers. The waterbuck is seen only on land and can be easily identified by the white bull's–eye circling its tail. The reedbuck is smaller and has short straight antlers. The only cat which is unique to the wetland habitat is the small spotted serval. It cannot be confused with a leopard or a cheetah because of its smaller size. The only true monkey living in Namibia, the vervet monkey, is found in the wetlands and is unmistakable because of its brilliant blue scrotum. Elephants are found in greatest numbers in the wetlands but their range extends into the Etosha pan and into the drier western areas.

In Namibia it is possible to find a small number of elephant as well as Hartmann's mountain zebra, giraffe, cheetah, and even a few hook-lipped (black) rhino living in a truly wild state. Elephant can be dangerous, so use caution; do not approach too closely and be ready to retreat. Elephant form herds of up to a thousand individuals but are commonly seen in smaller groups of cows and calves or entirely male groups. The African elephant will eat almost the entire day, consuming up to 300kg of grass, leaves, branches and even the bark of trees. This can result in severe local deforestation caused by overpopulation in some areas. Elephant scat is very large and round, composed of undigested wood fiber. They drink large quantities of water and also need water to bathe. You may see male elephants at a water hole greeting each other by putting trunks into the mouths of the newcomers. Ordinarily an old elephant will die when the last of its three sets of teeth wear out.

Cats are elusive and often difficult to spot in the tall grass. You may be unable to find any or you may find a pride of lion or several cheetah lying by the side of the road in Etosha. In some of the game farms the owner will keep cats on his land by feeding them raw meat. This is usually done in a place where you will be able to observe them. Lions naturally hunt at night—the females usually do the hunting, the males getting first bite—but during the day prides of up to fifteen lion may be found sleeping under a tree close to the road. If you remain in your car as the rules of the park stipulate, the lions will pay little attention to you. You will be able to drive very close to them for extraordinary photos. The females and the cubs will be found together with the male of the pride usually somewhere near. Cheetah are rare, but the Namibian population is the largest in the world. They hunt during the cooler hours of the day when you may see several running across the plains. Etosha is a good place to spot them—we saw five cheetah near the road one day. Leopard are the most difficult to spot, being primarily nocturnal and good climbers; they often jump out of a tree to capture prey and then drag it back up the tree. A leopard can be distinguished from a cheetah by its spots. The cheetah has round black spots whereas the leopard has a rosette of black spots surrounding a brown one.

Hyena are odd creatures which have a dog-like face and a sharply sloping back with hind quarters lower than the front. They are known as scavengers, however they are actually very good hunters. The old dethroned male lion may well fall prey to hyena. Their diet ranges from insects to large mammals such as giraffe. They can be heard making loud eerie groans and howls in the night. Hyena droppings are characteristically white. The two species, spotted and brown, are usually found in the northern part of the country, though the shaggier brown hyena can be seen in coastal areas.

Wild dog is a spotted animal which can be distinguished from the spotted hyena by its large ears and flat back. It is much rarer and found only in the Etosha and the northeast.

There are also some strange animals which seem to be a mix of species. The aardvark is a round hairy animal weighing about 35 pounds. It has a long snout like a pig and large tubular ears, a long tail and strong legs. The scaled pangolin may be seen in western Namibia. When in danger it curls up and looks more like a desert flower than an animal. In the dry regions, you may see the suricate or meerkat. It will remind you of a squirrel but has dark piercing eyes and stands on its hind legs using the tail for balance.

Birds

Many people visit east and southern Africa to see the wildlife. Namibia's Etosha Park is famous for herds of elephant, prides of lion and troops of giraffe. Visitors soon notice that there is much more to see if they begin to notice the birdlife. Experienced bird watchers come from all over the world to enjoy the spectacle of color and variety in southern African birdlife. Any visitor who seeks endless entertainment need only begin looking at birds.

Binoculars are necessary, otherwise most birds will appear as dark shapes against the sky. With binoculars you can easily see the colorful beauty of the bee-eater or black-collared barbet. The markings of eagles can usually only be seen well with magnification. Another essential item is a field guide so you can identify what you are looking at. An excellent way to learn identities is to go on a guided drive with an experienced bird watcher. Going with a friend adds to the enjoyment and increases the possibility of seeing different species.

Blackbellied Korhaan - Namibia
(Longlegged Korhaan)

Soon you'll be pleasantly surprised to find birds where you never noticed them before.

Of the 900 species listed in *Newman's Birds of Southern Africa*, 580 occur in Namibia. The most abundant bird populations are found in the Caprivi strip, along the Kunene River, the coast near Swakopmund and Walvis Bay and Etosha National Park. In the summer months (Oct.—April) there are more species present than in winter. Many species come with the rains and are found where water is present. Walvis Bay has a huge colony of flamingos in the dry season whereas in the wetter months many can be found in Etosha. In summer the lilac breasted roller can be seen inhabiting telephone poles in the north, and hornbills and gray louries are seen around the country swooping between trees and bushes. In the north, there is a summer spectacle of colorful bee-eaters on the roadside. Francolins and guinea fowl can always be

Carmine Bee-eater, Namibia

seen running alongside the road. In the northeast, the honey-guide is known to lead humans to bee nests!

Some birds are exceptional in that they put on a display primarily to attract a mate, but they are interesting for us to watch as well. For example, the red crested Korhaan will fly

Crowned Crane (Kenya)
Namibia

straight up, circle and plunge towards the ground as if shot, recovering at the last moment!

The black bellied Korhaan will puff out its feathers, pull its neck in and let out a loud pop. Male ostriches will kneel, waving their head from side to side with wings spread, or inflate their neck dramatically.

Birds are most active in the early morning and at dusk. You must move quietly and slowly to avoid scaring them away. Viewing with the sun at your back is best to see the colors. As you gain experience you will begin to recognize distinctive calls and flight patterns, though often a noisy bird is not so colorful, while some beautiful birds move about silently. A good way to view birds is to chose a spot with suitable habitat (trees, bushes or bodies of water), get comfortable and wait to see what comes your way.

Seventeen birds are listed as rare in southern Africa by Newman's guide (seen 10 times or less in a year) including the Palmnut vulture, Baillon's crake, Peregrine falcon, Sousa's shrike and the Redshank.

There are several birds which, although not rare, are found almost exclusively in Namibia within the southern African sub-region. In the northwest they include Rüppell's parrot, Monteiro's hornbill, the rufous-tailed palmthrush, white-tailed shrike, chestnut weaver and cinderella waxbill. In the north and northeast, there is the black cheeked lovebird, Gray's lark and Sousa shrike. In the central region, the Violet Woodhoepoe and rockrunner, in the southwest the dune lark and throughout the country, except Caprivi, the rosy faced lovebird is found. The national bird of Namibia, the crimson breasted shrike, can be seen all over the country.

Some of the more interesting birds that we've spotted are the Jackass penguin on Halifax Island near Lüderitz, the beautiful Knysna lourie at the Zambezi lodge in Katima Mulilo, wattled cranes in Linyanti swamp, the crested crane and secretary bird in Etosha, ostriches seemingly everywhere in the Namib desert, paradise flycatchers at Popa Rapids and rosy faced lovebirds on top of the Brandberg.

Note: For more information about bird watching, try the Namibia Bird Club at (061) 25372.

Flora

As you travel around the country you will no doubt notice the vegetation (or lack of it) as in some places there is little else to look at. Several plant species are so unique they are worth a trip to see. One of the most unusual plants in Namibia is the *welwitschia mirabilis*, simply known as the Welwitschia.

It is only found in the gravel plains in the eastern Namib desert from Swakopmund to southern Angola. Its twisted foliage is actually only two leaves that are split into several sections. Specimens over 1,000 years old can be seen on Welwitschia Drive in the Namib-Naukluft park.

In the southern Namib near Rosh Pinah you will find the Elephant Trunk or Halfmens. It is a strange, spiny un-branched stem up to 2.5 meters tall with a head of crinkled green leaves that always points to the north. The dunes of the Namib are the home of the Nara plant, a member of the cucumber family that produces melon-like fruits on a spiny vine that snakes along the dune sand. The Topnaar Khoi-Khoi people harvest them to eat fresh or dried.

The Namib is known for its many species of lichens, which are fungi and algae living in a symbiotic relationship. The fungi live off the fog's moisture which regularly bathes the desert and the algae photosynthesizes the sunlight providing food for the organism. They cover large areas of rocky desert plains adding a colorful hue to an otherwise barren land-scape.

Euphorbia species are adapted to the gravel plains of the Namib as well as to mountain areas. They usually appear as a round bush of leafless green stems and, though highly poisonous to humans, some are a highly nutritious food source for elephants and rhinos.

Some tree species have adapted to the harsh desert climate by storing water in their trunks, which appear swollen and bulbous. The beautiful moringa is a fine example with its smooth, shiny copper colored trunk and leaves crowded at the end of the branches or not present at all. Several com-miphora species have swollen trunks with an aromatic sap and are often leafless with a smooth, papery bark that peels off in sheets.

The butter tree is not a tree at all but a vine of the vitaceae family. It has a thick yellow trunk and peeling bark with many green leaves in summer that are covered with fine hairs. The desert contains many aloe species which are characterized by

VEGETATION ZONES OF NAMIBIA

1 Northern Namib Desert
2 Central Namib Desert
3 Southern Namib Desert
3a Desert and succulent steppe (winter rainfall)
4 Semi-desert and savannah transition (escarpment zone)
5 Mopane savannah
6 Mountain savannah and karstveld
7 Thorn-bush savannah (tree and shrub savannah)
8 Highland savannah
9 Dwarf shrub savannah
10 Saline desert with dwarf shrub savannah fringe
11 Tree savannah and woodland (northern Kalahari)
12 Camel-thorn savannah (central Kalahari)
13 Mixed tree and shrub savannah (southern Kalahari)

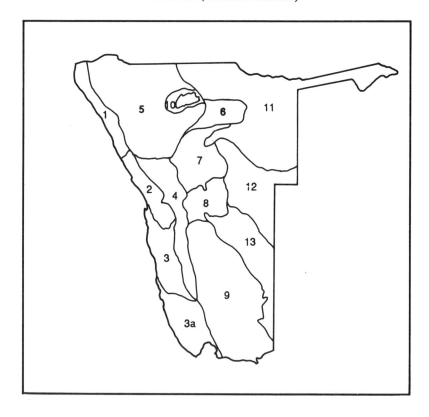

Kokerboom trees, Kokerboom For-   *Flora of the Brandberg.*
est.

tough, fleshy, spiny leaves known to hold water. Some of these plants have beautiful flowers on tall stalks.

In most of the vegetation zones you'll find the ubiquitous acacia species or thorn trees and bushes. Their deep root system helps them adapt to dry climates such as Namibia's. Often occurring in dense thickets, they are found in ranching areas, Etosha National Park, dry river beds and many places you might wish they weren't. Their thorns come in all shapes and sizes, their leaves are usually small and flowers are white to yellow in color. The typical flat top tree, associated with the African veld, is the acacia. Himba tribespeople use acacia bark to make curdled milk, one of their main foods. The gummy sap is used for chewing gum, glue and candy; the wood of certain species pounded and used for medicines.

A common tree is the tamariskia, a feathery leafed species occurring frequently in dry river beds.

In the northeast in zones 11 and 12, trees dominate the flora and are tall and lush due to abundant rainfall. The terminalia develops beautiful purple to rust colored seed pods and the marula tree produces a fruit which is made into preserves or liquor. The shepherd's tree serves as food for birds and animals and humans have used powdered root as a preservative.

The mopane tree is common throughout northern Namibia and is known by its wing shaped leaves while the nut of the makalani palm is carved into interesting curios.

If you are tempted to collect plants you should know that many are protected species and it is illegal to gather them. The Department of Nature Conservation has issued a pamphlet listing and describing the numerous protected species. Obtaining a field guide to plants of Namibia will help you to identify different species and make your observation of Namibia's unique flora more enjoyable.

CHAPTER 5

Windhoek Area

This area includes the city of Windhoek and the immediate surrounding area out to a radius of approximately 50 kilometers.

About Windhoek

The capital of Namibia, Windhoek is really the only place in the country that can be considered a city, with tall, modern buildings, downtown traffic and a steadily growing population of 160,000. Situated 1,700 meters (5,600 feet) above sea level in the center of the country, it is surrounded by low mountains and scrubby hills, yet boasts crystal clear air most of the year. It's also a convenient spot to start a trip to just about anywhere. You'll find many things available here that you just won't get anywhere else in the country.

Windhoek centers on Independence Ave. (formerly known as Kaiser St.), which runs past several high rises, and countless curio shops, restaurants, grocery stores, banks, hotels and government offices. Its combination of German colonial and modern architecture creates a distinctly European impression. The sidewalks are crowded during the day and Namibia's diverse mix of people is evident during a stroll downtown. Herero women in particular, in their large colorful Victorian dresses and triangular hats, stand out among the throngs of well dressed Windhoekers. The city center is generally very clean and has a bright feel to it, especially the Post Street Mall, right off Independence Ave., where modern ar-

NAMIBIA

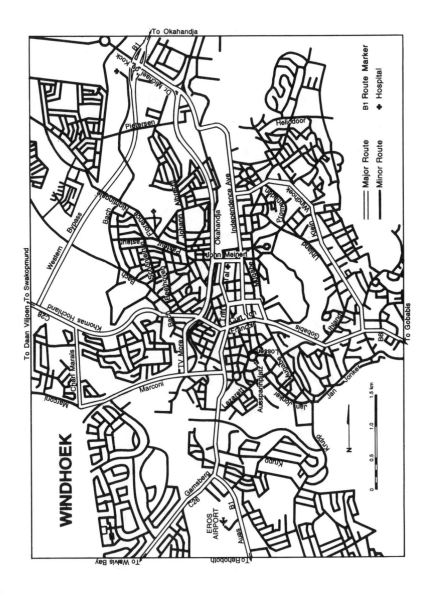

chitecture and brightly painted buildings and kiosks give a fair-like atmosphere to the promenade.

The city center is surrounded by neat neighborhoods of houses, most of them with the property fenced. Further out to the north and south are the so-called industrial areas where light industry and many wholesale supply stores are located.

The areas of Khomasdal and Katutura, formerly reserved for coloreds and blacks, respectively, sprawl out to the west and northwest of downtown. Many of the city's hot night clubs are located there.

The name Windhoek comes from the mid 1800s when the Nama leader Jan Jonker Afrikaner settled here, calling it Winterhoek after his birthplace in the Cape province in South Africa. Eventually this became Windhoek in Afrikaans, meaning "windy corner," though it's not a particularly windy place. In fact, it has a very agreeable climate throughout the year.

German colonial control of the country from the late 1800s until World War I is evident in the architecture throughout the city. Major Curt von François built the Alte Feste fort above the center of town in 1892 and today it serves as a museum and restaurant.

The city still largely retains its segregated population that was enforced under apartheid and is changing slowly with most blacks living in the Katutura section, most colored people in Khomasdal and whites in Windhoek and its suburbs.

Where to Stay

Deluxe Hotels

Kalahari Sands—Tel. 222300; Independence Ave.

Namibia's only Four Star hotel, the Kalahari Sands stands out as the only truly international hotel with all the extras in the country. If you can't imagine staying in Windhoek without room service, exercise room and rooftop pool, plush restaurants, large breakfast and lunch buffets and an elegant

WINDHOEK CITY CENTER

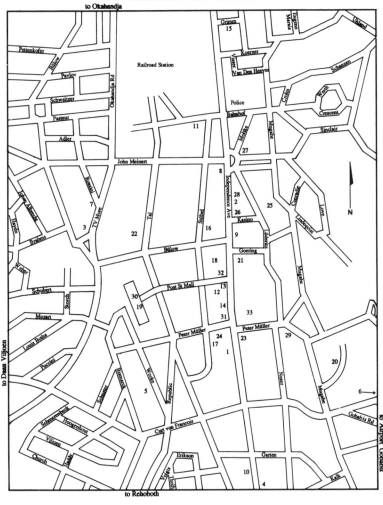

MAP KEY	12. Kaiserkrone	24. AAA Namibia
1. Kalahari Sands Hotel	13. Le Bistro	25. Museum
2. Continental Hotel	14. Gathemann's	26. Ministry of Home Affairs
3. Furstenhof Hotel	15. Joe's	27. DNC Reservations
4. Tucker's Tavern & Hotel	16. Micado	28. DNC Information
5. Pension Steiner	17. The Cave	29. Estorff Reference Library
6. Kapp's Farm	18. Central Cafe	30. Wernhil Park Mall
7. Pension Handke	19. Mike's Kitchen	31. Sanlam Center
8. Hotel Thuringerhof	20. Alte Feste	32. Tourist Information
9. Grand Canyon Spur	21. Post Office	33. Zoo Park
10. Sardinia	22. Vegetable Market	
11. Café de Paris	23. Airport Bus	

doorman in a longcoat covered with pins collected from all over the world, then this is the place for you.

Approximate Rates: Single R308-366; Double R350-422; Room only

Safari—Tel. 38560; Republic Rd.

Namibia's largest hotel by far (452 rooms), it is situated on the south side of town near the Eros airport. There is a nice outdoor pool, an outdoor and indoor patio where you can have lunch, and a restaurant and bar & grill. It is a step down from the Kalahari Sands but has a more outdoor feel to it, though it is less centrally located.

Approximate Rates: Single R222-278; Double R278-333; B&B.

Continental—Tel. 37293; Independence Ave.

Located in an alley off Independence Ave., this is an international hotel (as the flags outside suggest) just a step down from the Kalahari Sands. The rooms are not as nice, but it is comfortable and centrally located. The price includes breakfast, unlike the Sands, and it is a bit more personal. There is a cozy little bar and a large lounge area.

Approximate Rates: Single R130-210; Double R260; B&B

Hotel Thüringerhof—Tel. 226031; Independence Ave.

Part of the Namib Sun chain, this hotel is a deluxe lodging with German flair.

Approximate Rates: Single R210; Double R287; B&B

Fürstenhof—Tel. 37380; Romberg St.

This lovely hotel is located just outside the city center and is a bright, friendly place to stay. Its European influence is evident with warm quilts on the beds and a first rate menu. The Fürstenhof has an elegant dining room with a wide selection of food and wines. The chef is internationally acclaimed. A very comfortable place to stay with more personal attention than the other large hotels.

Approximate Rates: Single R170; Double R240; B&B

Mid-Range Hotels

Tuckers Tavern & Hotel—Tel. 223249; Independence Ave., Ausspanplatz

Centrally located on Independence Ave. south of the Kalahari Sands Hotel, this used to be known as the Hansa Hotel, until it recently changed hands and its name. It is now destined to become one of Windhoek's best night spots with three bars, a restaurant and small attached hotel of 12 rooms, which are fairly standard and decently comfortable with air conditioning and some private baths. Some are close to the pub, so plan on staying up late (midnight to 2am) if you're a light sleeper.

Approximate Rates: There are two dormitory style rooms reserved for backpackers and budget travelers for R60 per bed, 4 beds per room. The rest of the rooms are Single R115 w/o bath, R125 with bath; Double R160 w/o bath, R182 with bath; all B&B.

Pension Steiner—Tel. 222898; Welcke St.

The thing that struck us most about the Steiner was how European it looked and how immaculately clean it was. Situated close to downtown next to the Chinese embassy, it has 10 rooms, swimming pool, telephones in room and a nice lounge.

Approximate Rates: Single R125; Double R195; B&B

Pension Handke—Tel. 34904; Rossini St.

Run by a very fastidious German woman, this is a quiet place to stay near the center of town, though not quite the value it used to be.

Approximate Rates: Single R105; Double R145; B&B

Hotel Kapps Farm—Tel. (061) 34763 or 36374

Out on the Gobabis road 20 kilometers east of Windhoek, this small roadhouse hotel brings in an interesting mix of people. It is popular with international travelers coming from the airport late at night as well as local travelers heading in and out of Windhoek. The hotel is a little run down and seemingly in constant renovation but it is one of the cheaper and more available places to stay when Windhoek's' hotels are full due to conferences and meetings. There is a friendly little bar that will serve you dinners of wild game dishes as well as drinks. The rooms can get quite cold at night in winter as there is no heating, but there are plenty of blankets. Approximate Rates: Double with toilet R150, slightly less with communal toilet.

Aris—Tel. 36006

Located 25 kilometers south of Windhoek on the Rehoboth road, the Aris hotel is a cozy roadhouse inn with a warm bar and restaurant and not so warm rooms in the winter. There are racks of kudu, springbok and oryx decorating the walls of the whole place. The menu looks excellent, but our oryx steak had been sitting in the fridge a little too long. For most people it's a stopping place on the way into or out of Windhoek and a popular spot, especially on weekends. Approximate Rates: Single R86-110; Double R150-172; B&B.

Budget Accommodations

Backpackers Lodge—Tel. 228355; Best St.

This dormitory style lodge is only for backpackers. There are a total of 14 beds in fairly close quarters with shared toilet, fridge and cooking facilities. It's a great place to stay cheaply in Windhoek and meet others, to share transportation, arrange rides and find out about inexpensive places to stay around the country. A must for those backpacking on a budget. There is a swimming pool here as well. They are closed from 10:00-4:30 and you must leave during these times, but if you want to check in and drop a backpack during these hours they'll watch it until you come back. Approximate Rates: R25 per person—no tents, alcohol or smoking—quiet after 10:00 and lights out at 11:30.

El Dorado Youth Hostel—Tel. 213630; Austin & Sterling Sts., Khomasdal

This is Namibia's only youth hostel and if you bring your card you receive a small discount. It is small but cozy with shared rooms of 4-6 people. There is a cooking room, washing room and a place to keep your luggage locked up. A good place to get information about other budget accommodations.

Approximate Rates: R22 per person without Youth Hostel card, R20 with card.

Southwest Star Hotel—Tel. 213205; Chrysler Rd., Khomasdal

Next to a popular night spot, so consider the noise level, especially on weekends.

Rates: Single R45-50; Double R75-80; Room only.

Bed & Breakfasts in Windhoek

In Windhoek and some other towns in Namibia, there is a growing movement to provide inexpensive accommodations for budget and other travelers by residents wishing to open up their homes to paying guests. If you arrive in Windhoek and are surprised at the lack of decent, inexpensive accommodation you're not the only one.

Often we've found hotels full, camping has disappeared and there is little option but to stay in one of the more expensive hotels that have a lot of rooms.

The Bed & Breakfast Association currently has 20 or so members who rent rooms mostly by word of mouth to travelers in the Windhoek area. They don't advertize, as rules and laws for people wishing to rent extra rooms haven't been established yet.

The association is trying to set standards for their members so that travelers can be reasonably assured of decent facilities. It has been our experience that the accommodations are generally good, fairly unstructured and provide a chance to meet Namibians as they live at home. They are usually not the posh residences you find in the U.S. that charge more than hotels, but are clean, priced lower than most hotels and will accommodate singles and doubles in addition to five people in a room or tent space in their yard. Some owners have kids and pets wandering around, some work and are away most of the day, and some manage on a full time basis—it varies widely.

Central Windhoek skyline.

Most are not located downtown so transportation is some-times a problem, but some people will pick you up at an arranged time and some will quote rates on a case by case basis depending on number of persons or length of stay, so talk it over with them.

By the time this book is published, Bed & Breakfasts may already be an institution in Windhoek and other areas and there may be advertising and booking with tourist offices. Check with the Windhoek tourist office about 50 meters from the clock tower on the Post Street Mall. They can probably point you in the right direction.

Approximate Rates:—Usually from R30-60 per person, again depending on the circumstances.

Call Marie Harlech-Jones for further information-Tel. 51787; 156 Diaz St.

Camping in Windhoek

There used to be a camping ground next to the Safari Hotel, but this has closed and currently the closest camping is at

Daan Viljoen, or possibly at some of the Bed & Breakfasts around town. Some people have camped at the stadium across from the Safari, but possessions have been stolen there so it's not recommended.

Where to Eat

Grand Canyon Spur—Independence Ave.

An American-style South African chain of popular restaurants, they specialize in huge Busta-burgers, steaks of all different sizes and types, Mexican food (they need a little work), pizzas, a nice salad bar and other novelties. We felt like we were back in the States for a moment. Try getting a lunch table outside on the second floor to see central Windhoek's busiest street corner in front of the CDM building. There is quite a lot going on and it's fun to watch all the people.

Sardinia—Independence Ave. south of the Kalahari Sands

This little eatery has great Italian-style pizzas and serves Italian ice creams to passersby from a small window facing the sidewalk. A reasonably priced lunch or dinner spot, this is a must for those who crave Italian food.

Seoul House—Rehobother Rd.

A classic oriental restaurant, with standard western style tables and place settings and good Korean and Asian food. This a nice place for something different than Namibia's standard menus of meat and seafood. You can get well prepared food here at a reasonable price. Worth a try.

Kaiserkrone Cafe—Post St. Mall

A nice relaxing spot to spend a sunny afternoon with a beer shandy and a light meal. Located off the mall; there is also occasionally live entertainment here.

Le Bistro-Clock Tower—Independence Ave.

This eatery at the clock tower is a wonderful place to eat and watch the crowd. A quick breakfast can be had for R6-10 and lunch and dinner are inexpensive, especially when you order from the Big Pan, a huge wok-style pan where you get whatever is the special of the day, which is usually very tasty.

Gathemann's—Independence Ave.

Another fine restaurant overlooking busy Independence Ave., Gathemann's is a marvelous spot for a sunny lunch. The food here is wonderfully prepared and the quality is evident upon first taste. The prices are reasonable, and the service excellent. German specialties are the norm here.

Tuckers Tavern—Independence Ave., Auspannplatz

This tavern, unique for an English pub atmosphere, with rugby regalia decorating the walls and Namibian style pub grub, is destined to become an institution. With three bars and a pub, you can wander through the spacious interior, roll dice and have a Guinness in one bar, have a quieter drink with friends in another, or dance to African rhythms inside or outside in yet another. This pub definitely has a more mixed crowd than other bars and can be a very entertaining place no matter what your tastes.

Owned and run by the father-son team of Robert and Kevin Tucker, its central location means you don't have to travel far if you're staying downtown. In fact, they also have 12 rooms available (see lodging). The restaurant serves good food at very reasonable prices (hardly anything over R20) and meals come with a "veggy bar" where you can help yourself to delicious cooked vegetables to add to your main course. In the pub, sports are shown on a wide screen TV and there is live music on Wednesdays and Sundays. Check out the "trivia night" where you compete for prizes—usually meals at the pub!

Joe's—Grimm St.

An extremely popular spot just north of the center of the city, Joe's features an outside beer garden and an indoor section as well. Mostly a drinking establishment, it also has a limited but good, inexpensive selection of roasted meats. You can get a half chicken for R10 and other dishes for up to R15. They have live music in the beer garden and serve some unusual beers as well. A very mixed crowd hangs out here and you can meet all sorts of people. Recommended.

The Roxy—Uhland St.

Just a block away from Joe's, this is another popular place, especially for pizzas which are the best in Windhoek. You can sit down in the warehouse-style restaurant-bar decorated in the finest American-pop motif and listen to live music or order delicious pizzas take out. The greek salads are large and good for R10 and pizzas big enough for two run from R10-25.
Alte Feste—Robert Mugabe Ave. (Formerly Leutwein St.), Tel. 226840

A nice way to spend an afternoon in Windhoek is to tour the museum near Christ church, the large church that looks down over central Windhoek, and have lunch outdoors at the Alte Feste restaurant. It is reasonably priced with lunch or dinner entrees at R10-20 and light meals around R10. They have a good selection of game and stews and some imaginative salads. There is also a pub that's open noon-midnight Mon.-Sat. On Sundays, the Alte Feste features a braai; they are closed for dinner on Tuesdays. Lunch noon to 3, Sundowner 5-7, Dinner 7-11, Sunday Braai-noon-7.
Micado—Stübel St.

Serves typical German food with a few surprises like bacon & banana sandwiches! Lunches and dinners for R10-20. The disco music at lunch was kind of bizarre and the service a little slow but worth a try.
The Cave—Gustav Voigts Center

The Cave has a large variety of international dishes on an impressive menu. Located in the Gustav Voigts center near the Kalahari Sands, downstairs from and outside the main escalator area. Entrees R20-35
The Gourmet's Inn

The Gourmet's Inn is one of Windhoek's best kept secrets. Despite its bizarre location next to the public pool on Jan Jonkerweg that gives diners a view of the miniature golf course below, the cuisine is creative, deliciously prepared and visually elegant. Focusing on seafood and wild game with a German flair, you can enjoy ostrich, springbok, guinea fowl, oryx and other Namibian delicacies in addition to beef prepared in a variety of original ways. The menu contains an

excellent appetizer selection and smaller meals are available if you're not starving. It's not cheap but worth every dollar.
Sam's—Gobabis Rd.

A popular spot for lunch and after work, Sam's has decent but not particularly outstanding food. Eat indoors or out.
Central Cafe—Levinson Arcade

A great spot for a sidewalk cafe breakfast or lunch, this extremely popular diner is often crowded and a good spot to watch the people of Windhoek.
Café de Paris—Bahnhof St.

Just down the street from the train station is Windhoek's only French restaurant with a nightclub attached.

Things to Do in the Windhoek Area

Museums

There is a museum next to the Alte Feste restaurant (see restaurant section) that is worth seeing as it has an excellent display on the independence process as it occurred in Namibia. It gives you a feeling for what was going on in the country during that hectic time. There is also a musical instrument display and a multi-cultural exhibit showing artifacts of many of Namibia's distinct groups. There is no entrance fee at this time, but a donation of a few rand is appreciated. M-F 9-6, Sat.& Sun. 10-12:30 & 3-6.

The State Museum—near the public library on Leutwein St. features the natural history of Namibia with ethnology exhibits of some of the different peoples of the country. Exhibits are so life-like that they disturb some people! M-F 9-6, Sat. & Sun. 10-12:30 and 3-6.

Swimming Pool—and miniature golf are open to the public on Jan Jonkerweg between Krupp and Centaurus Streets. They have a platform, high and low diving boards and large diving and swimming pools. They charge R1.50 (R3 on weekends) and are open M-F 10-8 and weekends 10-6. Popular with kids.

Cinema—The only indoor movie house in town plays many

first run American and European films. They are located on the corner of Omuramba and Klein Windhoek Rds.

Theater—There are plays, modern dancing and music put on by local and visiting professional groups at the Warehouse theater on Tal St. or Windhoek Theater on John Meinert St. Check the newspapers or posters around town as they are well advertised.

Shopping

Post Street Mall—is probably the most colorful place to shop, but possibly a bit expensive. An outdoor/indoor series of shops and eating places in purple, pink, blue and green decorative structures with a fairyland atmosphere, it's a fine spot for a walk or to sit with a rock shandy and watch people go by. Starting at the clock tower on Independence Ave. and ending in the Wernhil Park indoor shopping mall, it is a favorite of both locals and tourists because of its clean, bright feel.

Curio Shops—There are several curio shops around Windhoek, most of them on Independence Ave. They sell a variety of locally made products including painted and carved ostrich eggs, animal skins and rock and wood carvings. Check with the owner or your embassy for prohibitions on shipping things like animal skins. An excellent place to check out local arts and crafts is the Namibia Crafts Center on Tal St. near Curt von François St. You'll get to meet many of the artists as they create and sell their work there in the building.

News—For all your news needs, try Frewer's in the Levinson Arcade (next to the Trip travel office on Independence Ave.). They have an excellent selection of newspapers and magazines from around the world as well as stationery and writing supplies.

Open Air Market—During November through March-April there is an open air fruit and vegetable market where the farmers from Stampriet sell fresh produce. It is located on Tal St. just past the Wernhil Park shopping mall next to the bus depot and parking lot. The hours are usually from 7-7. The watermelons are incredibly sweet and delicious!

Used Bookstore—If you are surprised at the price of books in bookstores—R30 for a paperback!—then try Uncle Spikes Used Book Exchange on Tal St. They offer cheaper, if less current options.

Travel Preparation/Aid

Visa Extensions

If you want to extend your visa, go to the Ministry of Home Affairs on Independence Ave., a block north of the Main Post Office. It's the building with the huge lines out front in the mornings, which are for Namibian I.D. and other documents. Use the opposite door where there is usually no line.

Travel Agencies

TRIP—travel agency, located on Independence Ave. at the front of the TRIP arcade is a large concern with offices in Windhoek and Swakopmund and can help you with practically any of your domestic or international travel. They can book hotels, Nature Conservation camps, guest farms or their own safaris. Car rentals with Avis and Budget are cheaper here than at rental offices. They stress it is almost always cheaper to travel in groups, so plan ahead. Tel. in Windhoek (061) 36880, Swakopmund (0641) 4031.

Ritz Reise is located below the Grand Canyon Spur Restaurant on Independence Ave. and will arrange tours throughout the country, often working with the larger tour companies. Tel. (061) 36670.

Welwitschia Travel—on the Post St. Mall, just 50 meters from the clock tower, will specially design tours and can sometimes find lodging when everything is booked because of their extensive travel connections. Tel. (061) 226134 and 226102/3

Top Travel will arrange any travel, but they specialize in Windhoek city tours. Tel. (061) 51975

Namib Travel Shop—34 Omuramba Rd., Eros., Tel. 225178 or 226174.
Trans Namib Travel—Gustav Voigts Center (Kalahari Sands), Tel. 34821

Offices and Embassies

Windhoek Tourist Office, Tel. 391-2050

The tourist office for the Municipality of Windhoek is located on the Post St. Mall about 50 meters from the clock tower. They are very helpful in finding accommodation and you can put notices up on a board for getting traveling partners to remote regions or lifts around the country. They are open from 7:30-4:30 and are usually open during lunch.

Namibian Tourist Office, Tel. 284-9111

Located on Independence Ave. between the Post Office and Kudu statue, this excellent office is run by the Ministry of Tourism and has considerable information about hotels, guest farms, safaris and attractions throughout the country.

Department of Nature Conservation (DNC) Reservation Office Tel. 36975 (reservations) or 33875 (information)

Located in the green and white building up the street from the Kudu statue on Independence Ave. You can make reservations for any government rest camp or tourist facility here. **Tourist Information Center**, Tel. 221225, has opened on the ground floor of the Sanlam Center (the large modern blue building at the corner of Pieter Müller and Stübel Sts.)

Airline Offices

South African Airways—Independence Ave. near Kalahari Sands Hotel, Tel. 31118 or 31179
UTA (Air France)—Sanlam Building, 154 Independence Ave., Tel. 227688
Lufthansa—Sanlam Building, Independence Ave., Tel. 226662

Air Namibia—at the Gustav Voigts Center entrance on Independence Ave., Tel. 38220 (Eros airport) or 229630 Windhoek
Zambia Airways—Independence Ave., Tel. 223623

Safari Companies

There are several safari companies that offer a wide range of tours from one day to three weeks and longer. The following is a list of tour and safari companies currently operating in out of Windhoek.

African Adventure Safaris—Tel. 34720, Fax 230001
They have some interesting 2-4 day tours to Sossusvlei, Etosha, and the coast as well as longer expeditions to Kaokoland, Botswana and Zimbabwe. Also offered is a self-drive 4X4 guided tour.

African Extravaganza—Tel. 63086/7/8, Fax 215356
In addition to covering Namibian destinations, they will arrange tours to most southern African countries.

Bushtrail Safaris—Tel. 43006, Fax 41473
Bushtrail specializes in fishing, hunting, horseback riding and custom designed tours.

ERMO Safaris—Tel. 51975
Fly-in safaris to their camp at Epupa Falls and around Kaokoland.

Kaokohimba Safaris—Tel. 42633
Specialized tours for small groups of 3-7 people in Kaokoland.

Oryx Tours—Tel. 217454, Fax 63417
One of Namibia's largest tour companies, they have package tours; you see their buses on roads everywhere.

Otjimburu Trails—Tel. 32748, Fax 228461
Mostly short tours within central Namibia.

Southern Cross Safaris—Tel. 37567 or 51553, Fax 225387
If off-road camping safaris to Kaokoland or Botswana is what you're looking for, they offer pricey overland tours.

SWA Safaris—Tel. 37567; after hours Tel. 223702, 227483 or 32739, Fax 225387
Another large bus package tour operator.

TransNamib Tours—Tel. 2982388/9, Fax 223056

The national tour company offers standard packages on large buses around the country.

TRIP Travel Safaris—Tel. 36880

The TRIP travel agency has its own pricey fly-in tours as well as booking for other tour companies.

Embassies, High Commissions and Missions

United States—14 Lossen St., Auspannplatz, Private Bag, 12029 Tel. 221601, Fax 229792

Germany—11 Uhland St., Klein Windhoek, Box 231, Tel. 229218/9, Fax 222981/92

Sweden—10 Stein St., Klein Windhoek, Box 23087, Tel. 222905, Fax 22274

Angola—4th Floor Ausspan Corner House, Ausspanplatz 3, Box 6647, Tel. 227535 or 35364, Fax 227535

France—1 Goethe St., Tel. 229022 or 229023

Italy—Anna St., Tel. 228602, Fax 228602

Spain—Room 206 Kalahari Sands Hotel, Box 21811, Tel. 223066, Fax 223066

Zimbabwe—Grim St., Box 23056, Tel. 228134/ 227738/ 227204, Fax 226859

Zambia—22 Curt Von Francois St., Box 22882, Tel. 37610, Fax 228162

Britain—116 Leutwein St., P.O. Box 22202, Tel. 223022/ 221293/ 228874, Fax 228895

Botswana—Tel. 41961/ 41359/ 41639/ 41140

South Africa—On Klein Windhoek Rd., near Gobabis Rd. (The tall blue building) Tel. 227771

Namibian Government Offices

Ministry of Home Affairs—Independence Ave. & Casino St., Private Bag 13200, 1 block from Main Post Office. For visa extensions and residency permits, Tel. 398-9111

Ministry of Health & Social Services—Harvey St., Private Bag 13198, Tel. 203-9111

Namibian Police—EMERGENCIES ONLY-10111

Ministry of Trade & Industry—State Building, Private Bag 13340, Tel. 289-9111

Ministry of Wildlife, Conservation & Tourism—State Building Private Bag 13346, Tel. 284-9111

Reservations for Government Game Parks and Resorts—Write to: Director of Tourism Reservations, Private Bag 13267, Windhoek; or phone (061) 36975 Reservations, or (061) 33875 Information:

Reservations office hours: M-F 8-1 & 2-3
Information office hours: M-F 8-1 & 2-4:30
Cashier hours M-F 8-1
NOTE:—This office is sometimes very busy. Let the phone ring a while!

Camping Rentals—In addition to some of the 4-wheel drive car hires that rent camping equipment, Gav's Camping Hire rents everything from cutlery to 12 volt fridges. Gav's is located in a residential section of Windhoek called Olympia. Tel. (061) 51526 for info or directions.

Laundromat—Near corner of Klein Windhoek and Gobabis Rds. there is a laundromat .

Outside of Windhoek

Daan Viljoen Game Park

Situated only 20km from Windhoek, this is probably one of the closest opportunities to see wildlife and one of the few public places in Namibia where you can take your own walking safari. Follow Curt von Francois St. out of the center of town in a westerly direction. It becomes Gammans Rd. which you take out of the city and through the hills following the signs to Daan Viljoen. You sign in at the gate then drive on to the office where you register.

They provide rondavels with communal toilets or you can camp with a caravan or tent, though it can be very cramped and noisy. Reservations must be made through DNC Windhoek; they seem to be busy weekends as many Windhoekers find it a nice place to get away. The rondavels come with cookplate and teapot, fridge, braai area and sink. There is a small reservoir with many bird species including Egyptian geese, cormorants, herons, guinea fowl and francolins. Baboons and kudu are particularly active here. Red hartebeest, oryx, springbok, kudu, eland and wildebeest roam the surrounding hills and occasionally the campsites. The restaurant serves three meals daily and overlooks the reservoir. Try bringing your own braai meat and having an evening cookout!

There are trails in the surrounding hills where game can be viewed on foot. The 9 km. Rooibos trail goes from the swimming pool through the hills and along the ridges where some of the aforementioned beasts and birds may be seen. It then follows a small dry riverbed and on up to the dam and restaurant. There is also a shorter 3 km trail and a longer overnight camping trail. Daan Viljoen is a great place to stay if you want to avoid staying in Windhoek yet remain close to the city to do necessary shopping or planning for longer trips. Day visitors are allowed to picnic here but must arrive before sunset and leave by midnight—call in advance!

Rates: 2-bed bungalows R46, Campsite R25; Day visitors picnic site R25 + R5 per adult and car.

Khomas Hochland Road

From Windhoek to Swakopmund or Walvis Bay, you have the option of taking the tarred road to the coast through Okahandja and Karibib or the gravel Khomas Hochland Rd.

To start, take the road to Daan Viljoen Game Reserve and continue on past it through low rolling hills that stretch for miles. After 65 km. you'll notice a National Monument sign and a small deteriorated stone building on the right where Curt von Francois had a drying out station in the 1890s for German troops who had drunk too much.

The hills gradually turn into mountains as you come to Bosua Pass which shouldn't be attempted with a caravan. From here you wind down into the Namib desert and Namib-Naukluft Park as the land around gets dryer by the kilometer.

It's a 350 km. trip from Windhoek to Swakopmund and takes about 4-5 hours. Be careful on the curvy portions of the road—slow down!

Windhoek Area Guest Farms

Finkenstein—P.O. Box 167, Windhoek, Tel. (061) 34751

Located 20 km. east of Windhoek on the road to the airport. March-April is very busy, book 6 months ahead; other times 1 month ahead.

Rates: R120 per person, B&B; R180 per person full board

Hochland—P.O. Box 22221, Windhoek, Tel. & Fax (061) 32628

Head out of Windhoek towards Daan Viljoen (follow Curt von François St.) and keep going east until you come to D1958. Turn right and continue on until you see the sign. Situated west of Daan Viljoen Park in the Khomas Hochland, this 4,500 hectare farm hosted by Margot & Günther Garbade offers a solar heated swimming pool, sport and gymnastic facilities, horseback riding, mountain biking, donkey cart and walking trails, hunting and photo safaris in addition to five well appointed rooms. Lots of game can be seen here including cheetah and leopard.

Rates: R220-270 per person per day with full board

CHAPTER 6

Central Region

This region covers the very center of the country except Windhoek, Swakopmund, Walvis Bay and Namib-Naukluft Park. Here you will find many guest and hunting farms situated in thorn tree and bushy savannah puncuated with mountain ranges.

Rehoboth

The first town south of Windhoek on the main B1 highway is Rehoboth, home of Namibia's Baster community. After driving 87 km. from Windhoek, first over some scenic hilly territory then an incredibly straight road, you arrive here. Most of the town is on the east side of the highway. The people of Rehoboth are primarily Basters, which sounds derogatory, but it is the name these descendants of mixed European and native blood call themselves. Originally coming from what is now the Cape Province in South Africa, they migrated across the Orange River and moved slowly northward, eventually settling at the hot water wells called Rehoboth. They elected their own leaders called kapteins and had autonomy for a time when Southwest Africa was under German control. This autonomy was lost until the Odendaal commission decided that the Rehoboth area would become a homeland under apartheid law and was granted self-governing status in 1976. Since Namibian independence control has fallen to the central government.

You will find a delightfully mixed population in Rehoboth where the people are among the friendliest we have encoun-

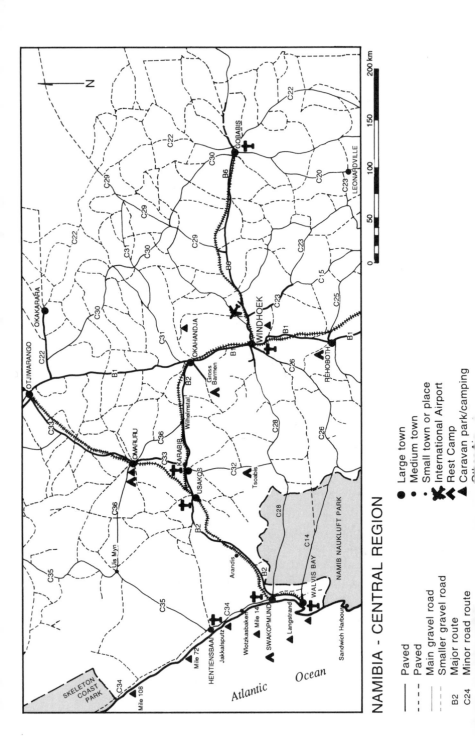

NAMIBIA - CENTRAL REGION

Paved
Paved
Main gravel road
Smaller gravel road
B2 Major route
C24 Minor road route

● Large town
• Medium town
·∙ Small town or place
✳ International Airport
✕ Rest Camp
▲ Caravan park/camping

tered. Rehoboth is also famous for the Reho-spa, a tourist complex with natural hot springs. Rehoboth is a mix of tarred and dirt roads beginning and ending in a somewhat haphazard fashion around town. There is a supermarket and 24 hr. petrol, but for ice, take outs and other groceries try the Dolphin store just off the highway near the south end of town.

Places to Stay and Eat

Reho-Spa—Tel. (06271) 2774 (Book at this number)

Off the main highway turn east at the Total gas station and drive past the church, taking the first road to the right. Follow the main road as it winds though the neighborhood for a short distance and you'll see the church-like buildings of the spa. Opened in 1985, the Reho-spa is a modern tourist resort on the southeast side of town that offers a huge indoor thermal pool, where soothing water jets feel great after a day driving. There is also a huge outdoor pool where cool waters are for hotter days. The modern buildings are a little incongruous compared with the rest of the town and it seems a little cut off, being fenced in like a compound. It is now run by the DNC and the interiors are mostly standard government issue though the stucco exteriors are a bit different than most other government resorts. Suites are not deluxe but comfortable, however, with fridges, stoves, linen, braai pit and large sitting rooms that double as second bedrooms. The restaurant is not currently operating, so bring your own food or eat in town. It may open again soon.

Rates and Hours: 4-bed bungalows R58; 5-bed bungalows R58; 5-bed bungalows (1 bedroom) R70; 6-bed bungalows (2 bedrooms) R104; camp or caravan sites R15. Day visitors R5 per person; R2.50 students of any age.

Office is open 8-7 though you can come in after these hours. Spa is open 9-noon and 2 to 9. You must pay R2 for each session in the spa morning or afternoon. Outdoor pool hours 8 to 7.

Reho Monte Hotel—A place to stay if the Reho-Spa is full, Reho Monte has 10 decent rooms, though they are dark inside. Meals upon request; attached bar and off-sale liquor store as well.

Rates:—R50 single and R60 double; breakfast R12 extra.

Sudwes Hotel—If everything else is full and you really need to stay in Rehoboth, another option is the Sudwes Hotel. Drop by and see if they have a room available, although weekend discos make it noisy. Rate: R50 per room.

Siggi's Restaurant and Beer Garden—is on the main tarred road in town parallel to the highway across from the Sentra supermarket. A friendly place that offers breakfast, lunch and dinner, this is the first place we would try in town. The a la carte dinners are reasonable at R10-20 and they have take outs and a bar as well. The beer garden is actually just an outside dining area. Open Mon.-Sat. 8:30-10, Sun. 8:30-4.

Museum—There is a small museum next to the post office that has displays on the history of the Baster community and examples of traditional houses of the Nama, Damara and Kavango people. Open M-F 10-12, 2-4 and Sat. & Sun. 1-12.

Bus—You can take an Eagle Express or Bailey's bus from Windhoek to Rehoboth. They leave from the bus parking lot next to Wernhil Park shopping center in Windhoek.

East to Gobabis and Botswana

Traveling east towards Botswana on the B6 road out of Windhoek takes you through cattle farming country with low scrub and a few trees dominating the sometimes hilly landscape.

Witvlei—is the first town you come to along the road. The Witvlei hotel has a bar and will serve meals on request. They have a few single rooms for R50 and doubles for R90. You can get petrol here as well.

Gobabis

Lying about 200 km. east of Windhoek, Gobabis is one of the cattle farming centers of Namibia, as the large Brahma bull at the town's entrance announces. There are a couple of hotels, 24 hr. petrol, banks and several shops here. This is the last town you'll see on the way to Botswana.

The tarred road currently ends 15km. east to town, but there's a good gravel road to the border at Buitepos, about 110km east. If you're going through to Botswana, check on road conditions first with the AAN or locally as we've heard the road is a little bumpy and sandy, possibly requiring a 4-wheel drive vehicle.

Where to Stay

Central Hotel—Tel. (0681) 2094

The first of Gobabis' two hotels is plain but reasonably priced and serves meals.

Rates:—Single R75, Double R100

Gobabis Hotel—Tel. 2568

Just down Voortrekker St. the second of Gobabis' two hotels is a little more active, and has cable TV and phones in the rooms. They also serve meals and have a bar.

Rates:—Single R80, Double R110

Welkom Bungalows—Tel. (0688) 12213

About 20 km. east of town is the Welkom farm and Bush Life rest camp which has 5 bungalows on 5,000 hectares. They offer trophy hunting but have no restaurant and you must bring all food and drink to the fully equipped bungalows. To get there take the B6 east towards Botswana and after 15 km. turn left and go 5 km. further where you'll find it on the left.

Rates:—R70 per 4-bed bungalow.

Okahandja

Okahandja is a good size town with surprisingly little to do. There are only two places to stay and one restaurant. Okahandja is Herero for "the place where two rivers meet," referring to the Okakongo and the Okahandja. Okahandja is the capital of the Herero people and they have a large Herero Day here every year. Every August, the whole town celebrates in a festival atmosphere highlighted by the women's colorful costumes indicating their tribal affiliation, and military parades honoring war dead. The Hereros wear modern military uniforms unlike most tribes. There are graves of war dead from all sides in Okahandja—ask at tourist information if you're interested.

Okahandja is the first large town north of Windhoek where the highway splits into the B2 to Swakopmund and the B1 to Otjiwarongo, Etosha and north. To go to Swakopmund just stay on the B1 as it bypasses town and changes into the B2. To continue on the B1 you must enter town at one of the exits and follow the main street north out of town.

Places to Stay

Okahandja Hotel—With 13 very basic but clean rooms, this is the only hotel in town and it doesn't offer much in the way of food. It's downtown on Main St.

Rates: Single R45, Double R80-120, Family R180

Reit Club—Tel. (06221) 2678

This is the German club in Okahandja and they also have 5 rooms they'll rent to tourists. It is the site of horse shows that take place June-August at a showground behind the club. The building was built in 1908 and it's an interesting place to stay. There's a bar and restaurant, pool tables, a badminton court and beer garden. Dr. Gerhard Fock, the man responsible for helping free Okahandja of malaria, lived here.

Rates: Single R50, Double R 60, bathroom downstairs.

Places to See

Kavango Woodworks—has a huge selection of wood carvings. Look for it at the side of the road after you take the last exit into town from the highway and start heading north. Not much bargaining, but give it a try; there are some nice pieces. **Von Bach Dam**—is just a few kilometers south of Okahandja on the B1. It supplies some of Windhoek's water. There are 22 very small, rustic stone and wood huts with bunk beds overlooking the lake that you can rent here for R30. There are braai pits, sinks and an ablution block. You can also camp for R25. Cars, boats and people all cost R5 to enter. You can fish here as well.

Gross Barmen, a government-run resort, is 25 km. southwest of Okahandja. Take the Gross Barmen turn-off at Okahandja on the B1 where you follow the paved road 25 km. to the entrance. Famous for natural thermal springs, Gross Barmen attracts many visitors from Namibia as well as overseas. It is inexpensive and the natural hot pool is a welcome relief after hours on the road or on a cool winter morning.

"The Eye" of the spring is next to the outdoor pool. Some of the naturally occurring elements are listed next to the 65°C water. The depth of the spring is 2500 meters and the flow 6700 liters per hour.

The indoor thermal pools' sulphur waters hover around 40°C and the outdoor pool stays around 23°C year round. There is a large reed lined pond facing the bungalows that contains many aquatic waterfowl including the strange purple gallinule, sometimes visible lurking among the reeds.

Gross Barmen has many amenities: government issue bungalows equipped with toilet, shower, fridge, camping spaces and braai pits, a nice restaurant, filling station, tennis courts, a playground for kids, a store where food and other essentials can be bought, a kiosk and a path around the reed lined pond where thousands of birds make their home.

Indoor baths are open from 8-1 and 2-6 and on Friday and Saturday until 9. Day visitors are allowed until 11.

Rates: Admission to grounds is R5 per car or caravan plus R5 for adults and R2.50 for kids; mineral baths R2 per session for adults, R1 for kids. Bungalows, 5-bed R104; 2-bed or rooms R46; camping or picnic sites R20 per day.

Karibib

Karibib is a hub for small-scale mining, and with the opening of the new Navachab gold mine, some large scale efforts as well. It offers a bit more than Usakos to the west as it has experienced rapid growth due to the new mine.

Where to Stay and Eat

Hotel Strublhof—Tel. (062252) 81, Fax 240

At the east end of town on the highway, the Strublhof has 11 rooms with private bath, a swimming pool, billiards tables, a bar and a restaurant. Dancing on weekends; closed Mondays unless you book ahead.

Rates: Single R75, Double R130, B&B

Hotel Erongoblik—Tel. (062252) 9, Fax 95

Also known simply as Number 9, the Erongoblik has 34 rooms and an owner who plays in the band Friday nights, which is probably the most fun thing happening in Karibib. The owner will also set up tours, including a guided mining tour where you can actually dig (for a price) on someone's claim for tourmalines, quartz, beryl and other stones. The rooms are clean and spacious and there's a pool, sauna (which you don't need in summer here!), squash court and gym. He'll put 4 people in a double room if you're on a budget and if you want to camp, he'll set you up. There's a conference room for up to 40 people and he's trying to arrange cheaper car rentals and tours to the gold mine. Located just off the main road.

Rates: Single R45-80, Double R90-150, includes continental breakfast

Karibib Bakery—is inside the old Schulte bakery building (a national monument), famous for its brötchens and coffee. Open 7-1 and 3-6

Things to Do Around Karibib

Marble Works—The marble works on the west end of town produces granite and marble for export and also fashions it into locally finished products. Visit their showroom where marble tables, ashtrays, plates and other pieces are displayed. Their marble is all locally mined and if you're in a group of 10 or more, phone ahead for a tour of the factory. Showroom hours are 8-12 and 2-5.

Navachab Gold Mine—Discovery of low grade ore in large quantities led to the opening of the Navachab gold mine here in 1991. There are tours the first and last Thursday of the month but more regular ones are planned. Call #75 for more information or ask at the tourist office.

Gem Shop and Tourist Information—People are surprised when they walk in to the gem shop in Karibib. Most comment "what's this place doing in Karibib?" It looks like it belongs in Windhoek or another large city. A family business for 35 years, it doubles as the tourist information office. You'll see an incredible selection of precious and semi-precious stones, especially tourmalines of all colors, beryl, quartz crystals and aquamarines. They also sell curios, wood carvings and jewelry. Free tea and coffee whether you buy or not! Open 7 days 8-5 and sometimes later.

Municipal pool—On a hot day, go to the municipal offices during business hours and get a day card for the pool.

Webschule—is the local weaving school where they comb, spin and weave wool. Worth a visit.

Tsaobis Leopard Park—Tel. (062252) 1304

About 52 km. from Karibib is a unique park. Take the C32 south out of Karibib about 50 km. until you cross the Swakop river; .5 km. later turn right and follow signposts. Tsaobis is known for dealing with problem and injured animals more than the leopards, which, although roaming the area, are difficult to see. They have taken animals such as cheetah that were to be shot because of conflict with farmer's stock and reared them in enclosures. An assortment of cheetah, wild dog, caracal, bat-eared foxes as well as an aardwolf breeding program are featured here. Hiking is possible. There are several chalets and a swimming pool.

Rates: R85-105 per 2-bed bungalow; extra beds R20. Some are equipped and some are beds only—you must supply your own food.

Usakos

Pronounced *oó sa kos* or *eé sa kos*, this small town lies on the Windhoek–Swakopmund road and the rail line about 30 km. west of Karibib. The tourist information office is near the Usakos bakery but there isn't a whole lot to do here except go out to the Ameib guest farm outside of town. There are two 24 hour petrol stations here, a small supermarket and a hotel.

Where to Stay and Eat
Usakos Hotel
They have 8 basic, clean rooms all with private bath and a flat which is rented on a case by case basis. All the rooms have A/C and phones in them. A la carte meals are available any time of day. There's a bar with lots of beer labels on the wall and it's usually quiet.

Rates: Single R50, Double R100, flat rentable for any length of time-the more you spend at the bar, the cheaper the room! Breakfast R12.50 extra.

Ameib Guest Farm—Tel (06242) 11
A well organized guest farm 30 km. out of Usakos, they welcome day visitors who come to see Philip's cave with its rock paintings, including the white elephant and rock formations. The cave is an hour walk, so during the summer it's best to do it early in the morning unless you love heat. It is a game farm as well with the usual desert game plus a few giraffe and wildebeest, though you don't always see them. What you do see often are the warthogs that come to drink near the house and the cheetahs in a cage out back. There are trails of different lengths among the Erongo Mountains and you can camp but not with a caravan or motorcycle. They are busiest May-November; day visitors are welcome from 8-5.

Rates: R150-200 per person depending on how many meals you want. Camping is R25 per person and day visitors are charged R8 each.

Omaruru

This small town about 2 1/2 hours from Windhoek is a convenient stopover for those on the way to the Damaraland area. After taking the B1 north out of Windhoek to Okahandja, stay on the highway as it curves west toward Swakopmund. Do not take the Okahandja exits as they will lead you north towards Otjiwarongo. Past Okahandja about 65 km. or so turn right onto the Wilhelmstal road, which is a good graded dirt road to Omaruru which is shorter than the tarred road through Karibib. Along the Wilhelmstal road, you can often see kudu (be careful!) and steenbok by the side of the road.

You will find a couple of banks and various stores selling furniture and hardware. There are a few well stocked markets and take outs and two hotels—The Central and The Staebe. A small private rest camp sits on the north edge of town as well.

Places to Stay and Eat

The Staebe—Tel. (062232) 35

Located across the river east of town, this quiet efficient place is often frequented by tour groups. There is a comfortable pub, restaurant and swimming pool. The Staebe was built at the turn of the century. Dinners run about R30-35.

Rates:—Single R105, Double R145, B&B

The Central Hotel—Tel. 30

Located "downtown" on the main north-south highway, this place at first looks as if it may not be open, but actually there is a bar and restaurant, a large dance hall open occasionally and 10 rooms and 2 rondavels for rent. The rooms are fairly standard but the rondavel we saw was fairly spectacular, definitely out of place in comparison to other rooms in country hotels. It looked more like a suite in the Hilton, complete with TV, very plush bedding and furniture. The real double bed was a shocker as most double beds are two singles pushed together. At R100 per night you might want to reserve a rondavel in advance. There is also a small swimming pool and meals can be ordered.

Rates: Single R75, Double R95, Rondavel R100—breakfast not included.

Omaruru Rest Camp—Tel. 337

On the right hand side of the road as you are leaving town going north, there is a rest camp with 3 bungalows, 1 "luxury" bungalow and room for camping. A warning: you must bring your own bedding or sleeping bag even for the "luxury bungalow" as none will be provided. There are braai pits and the office can be contacted 24 hours a day.

Rates: Camping R10 plus R1 per person—some electrical outlets; Bungalows R22 for 2 beds plus wash basin and communal bathroom. "Luxury" bungalow with 3 beds, toilet and shower R44.

German Cafe

There's a cafe across from the pink mini-mart that serves sandwiches on fresh baked breads as well as pastries, cakes and other sweets that are delicious. The woman who runs the place with typical German efficiency will create a nice lunch for the road or for eating inside or outside. Worth a stop if you're hungry!

Dinosaur Footprints

One of Namibia's lesser known attractions, the famous dinosaur footprints are really worth visiting only if you have time to spare or are an avid paleontologist. They look vaguely like large reptilian spoor of some sort. The drive out is nice but the site itself is unremarkable. If you must go, follow the D2483 west of the B1 south of Otjiwarongo (the road to Mt. Etjo) to the junction of D2414, then turn left and follow the signs. Alternately, take the D2414 from Kalkfeld for a shorter dirt road. Ask at the small farm there for directions—they might be able to put you up for the night as well.

Hyrax Rocks

If you're traveling west from Omaruru towards Uis on the main road after about 20 km. you come to small piles of rocks on both sides of the road around a small bridge. If you look closely, the Hyrax or dassie can often be seen lounging about in the early morning or late afternoon. A small rodent-like creature, the Hyrax is the closest living relative to the elephant-though it's hard to imagine after seeing them.

Central Region Guest Farms

Gobabis Area

Hetaku—P.O. Box 2656, Windhoek, Tel. (061) 36674, Fax 227841

Hetaku is just 2 hours east of Windhoek. Take the B6 past Windhoek International Airport towards Gobabis, and 55 km. east of Omitara, turn onto the D1658 and go 50 km. past 5 gates to Hetaku. It has an attractive Cape Dutch style farmhouse with comfortable rooms in log cabins! SEM Senior is the host. Very rich in game including wildebeest, oryx, and hartebeest which you can view from an open truck or along game trails on foot. You can also take horse cart rides and view game from special platforms near waterholes. Reserve 1 week in advance.

Rates: R195-235 per person/day, full board

Ohlsenhagen—P.O. Box 434, Tel. (0688) 11003

Take the C22 just east of Gobabis north towards Drimiopsis and about 22 km. later you'll arrive at Ohlsenhagen. They are busiest April-June and least busy November-February, but call a week or so ahead any time of the year. Ohlsenhagen Guest Farm features excellent meals, wildlife viewing and a swimming pool.

Rates: R195 per person Double, R210 Single

Steinhausen—P.O. Box 23, Omitara, Tel. (06202) 3240

Karibib Area

Albrechtshöhe—P.O. Box 124, Karibib, Tel. (062252) 230 or (061) 223994

26 km. east of Karibib on the Windhoek-Swakopmund tar road, turn south at the sign to Albrechtshöhe just 2 km. further.

Albrechtshöhe is hosted by Paul-Hein and Ingrid Meyer and is primarily a hunting farm. They are busiest during the hunting season. However, an advance booking of only two days is usually necessary.

Game-viewing and trail-walking are also easily accommodated, or just relaxing by the swimming pool.

Rates:—R222 per person full board

Audawib—P.O. Box 191, Karibib, Tel. (062252) 1631

Okahandja Area

Haasenhof—P.O. Box 72, Okahandja, Tel. (061) 32748 or (06228) 82131, Fax (061)228461

From Okahandja take the D2110 northwest for 62 km., then turn right and drive 6 km to the farmhouse. Haasenhof or Otjombuindja (place of the ibex, as it called in Herero) lies about 140 km. from Windhoek near Okahandja. Hosts are Hans-Peter and Hildegard Haase. There are driving and walking tours available and mountains on the farm where you get spectacular views. Five rooms available. June and July are the busiest months—reserve 60 days ahead; November to March, 30 days ahead.

Rates: R88.80 B&B or R166.50 per person full board; 25percent deposit required.

Otjisazu—P.O. Box 149, Okahandja, Tel. (06228) 81640, Fax (061) 37483

Take the D2102 south of Okahandja for 27 km. to the gate. Hosted by Hagen and Allison Detering, Otjisazu (place of the red cattle, in Herero) is a guest and hunting farm (hunting season from Feb. 1- Nov. 30) located just outside Okahandja. Its three star rating assures you of comfortable accommodations. Horseback riding, game drives, conferences and private functions are available here. Nine double bedrooms with full facilities and a swimming pool make a stay relaxing. Usually 4 weeks advance reservations necessary.

Rates: R220 per person/day full board; Single R175, Double R165 B&B

Otjisemba—P.O. Box 756 Okahandja Tel. (06228) 82103

Wilhelmstal-Nord—P.O. Box, 641 Okahandja, Tel. (06228) 6212 or 6321

J&C Lievenberg—P.O. Box, 66 Okahandja, Tel. (062252) 3112

Matador—P.O. Box 214, Okahandja, Tel. (06228) 4312

Omaruru Area
Mt. Etjo Safari Lodge—Tel. (06532) 1602

Mt. Etjo can be reached by taking the B1 highway about 70 km. south of Otjiwarongo, then taking D2483 about 40 km. west. The way is well marked. It's also reachable from Kalkfeld taking the D2414.

This well-known lodge caters to wildlife viewers and hunters alike. Part of the property is for game viewing safaris and part is for big game hunters. Since we are not big game hunters, we only saw one half of the farm. What we saw was well worth the trip. Mt. Etjo also features a "pet" cheetah, Felix, that wanders around as you're eating breakfast. (Whatever you do, don't pet him under the chin—slowly brushing the top of his head is OK, though.)

The accommodations are fairly deluxe and a little expensive but worth it. You can even stay in the Presidential Suite, where the president has stayed, which is quite unbelievable with a large diorama complete with stuffed game and birds in a natural setting as you enter; it has a huge conference room and extra large bedroom.

There are game-viewing safaris twice a day in the morning and afternoon. There is also leopard viewing at night from behind a blind. You get a good spotlighted view of the leopards attracted to a slab of meat nailed to a tree. It's rather touristy, but it is rare to see these animals feeding. During the day safari you see every antelope imaginable and often some of the bigger game. We had a good view of a black mamba from about 3 meters. He arched his body up to about half his height (which was a good 2 meters) then moved very quickly up a tree.

The food here is excellent, far more than guests can eat, and served in an open rondavel; the staff is very helpful and friendly. There is a lovely swimming pool, a great place to relax in style in a unhurried atmosphere.

Rates: Single R183, Double R161 per person, full board.
Erindi Onganga—P.O. Box 20, Omaruru, Tel. (06532) 1202 or (061) 32624

From Omaruru take the D2334 northwest towards Omatjette just west of town. After 31 km. turn right onto D2351 and follow it for 27 km. where you'll see a sign. Turn right and 6 km. later you'll reach Erindi Onganga. Here you can experience the everyday life of farming in Namibia. You can tour the farm by foot, donkey cart or 4X4. Be sure to see their organic garden, or relax in the swimming pool or sauna.

Rates: Single R133.20, B&B and 194.25 full board; Double R105.45 per person, B&B and R166.50 per person full board; 15 percent discount to pensioners.

Immenhof—P.O. Box 250, Omaruru, Tel. (06532) 1803

From Omaruru take the road towards Uis, then after a few km. turn right towards Omatjette. Turn right later onto D2337 and proceed for 21 km. From Otjiwarongo, take D2337 north of Omaruru for 21 km. to Immenhof. The Immenjof guest farm, hosted by Freddy and Ria von Seydlitz, has 7 double rooms with private bath and a variety of activities. In addition to rock paintings and engravings on the farm, there are "singing rocks," horseback riding, amethyst and rosequartz sites, tours by car and light aircraft, and gameviewing as well as superb birdwatching. April and June-August book 3 months ahead, October-November, a phone call is usually enough.

Rates: Single R122 B&B and R183 full board; Double R111 B&B and R167 full board/person.

Schönfeld—P.O. Box 382, Omaruru, Tel. (06532) 1831, Fax (061) 227021

Take the paved highway north 40 km. to D2337. Turn left and go 13 km. further. Or take the Uis road towards Omatjette, then 25 km. later take D2337 till you're there—a total of 32 km.

Your trilingual (German, Afrikaans, English) hosts, Hartwig and Elke von Seydlitz, are out to make your stay an easy one. They have 2 single, 2 double and 2 triple rooms with private bath and toilet, and if you stay 2 days or more they'll do your laundry for free! They have waterholes where you can see game, including cheetah, and drives to see game as well as rock engravings nearby. They have a swimming pool and will take you on safari practically anywhere in Namibia. Busy months are June-October when you should book 2 months ahead, while during Feb.-May and Nov-Dec. 2 weeks or less is enough.

Rates: Single R160 B&B with dinner, R190 full board; Double R130 per person B&B with dinner; R160 per person full board

Boskloof—P.O. Box 53, Omaruru, Tel. (06532) 3231
Okosongoro—P.O. Box 324, Tel. (06532) 1721
Otjandaue—P.O. Box 44, Tel. (062232) 1203 or 255
Otjumue-Ost—P.O. Box 323, Tel. (062232) 1913

Usakos Area

Ameib Ranch—See *Usakos*
Wüstenquell Desert Lodge—P.O. Box 177, Usakos, Tel. (062242) 1312

Other Central Region Guest Farms

Hope—P.O. Box 21768, Windhoek, Tel. (0628) 3202
Kamab—P.O. Box 3873, Windhoek, Tel. (061) 31614 or (06228) 5313
Karivo—P.O. Box 11420, Windhoek, Tel. (0628) 1321
Kuzikus Game Farm—P.O. Box 13112, Windhoek, Tel. (0628) 3102
Monte Christo—P.O. Box 5474, Windhoek, Tel. (061) 32680
Okapuka Ranch—P.O. Box 5955, Windhoek, Tel. (061) 34607 or 227845
Silversand—Private Bag 13161, Windhoek (06202) 1102

CHAPTER 7

Southern Region

The vast southern region is often dry with widely spaced towns and hot summer temperatures. It covers the lower portion of the Namib—Naukluft park including Sossusvlei and the Naukluft mountains as well as the Fish River Canyon. Namibia's diamond mining areas are found here as well as the windy port of Lüderitz.

Mariental

A small farming community about 260 km. south of Windhoek on the main north-south highway, Mariental gets its irrigation water (rare in Namibia) from the Hardap dam, located about 20 km. northwest of town. Maize, lucerne (alfalfa), cotton and grapes are grown here, and this is where Namibia's fledgling ostrich industry got its start with two of the largest operations closeby. Mariental is also the center of Namibia's Karakul sheep farming industry which earns substantial foreign exchange as the prized pelts are shipped overseas. There are some Karakul farms nearby. You can visit the Welbedacht farm 54 km. out on the road to Gochas where they also do weavings that you can buy. If you call ahead, you can arrange a tour. Check at the tourist office for more details.

Domesticated Ostrich Products may offer tours if you call ahead (Tel. 350). They raise young chicks and eggs for export, mostly to the U.S. There are a couple of banks, one hotel, three restaurants, a tourist information office and several stores, including a large new Spar supermarket on the north end of

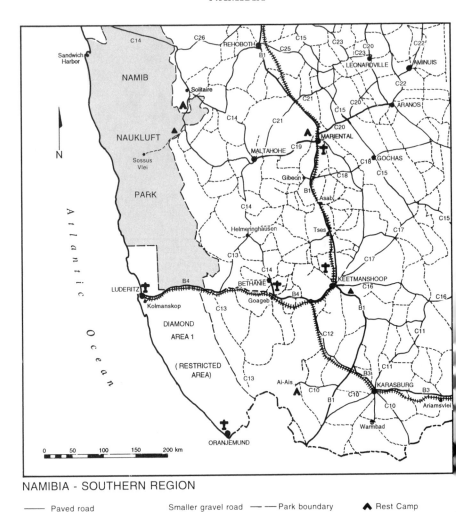

NAMIBIA - SOUTHERN REGION

—— Paved road	Smaller gravel road	—— Park boundary	▲ Rest Camp
- - - - Paved road	B3 Major route	● Large town	▲ Caravan park/campir
under construction	C11 Minor route	● Medium town	✚ Airport
Main gravel road	·········· Railroad	· Small town or place	

town. The town is split in two by the main railroad track
through Namibia.

Places to Stay

Hotel Sandberg—This is the only hotel in town since the
Mariental Hotel has closed and is for sale. There is a nice bar

and restaurant serving three meals and a dirty-looking pool we're not sure is ever used. They are busier weekdays than weekends. Many people stay at Hardap dam north of town.

Rates: Decent rooms with air conditioning for Single R90, Double R135 and triple R167. Rooms with no a/c are about R20 less.

Places to Eat

Hotel Sandberg—pizzas for R12-25 and a typical dinner menu of meat and fish for R15-30.

Bambi restaurant and take-away—at the Mobil station at the north end of town on Marie Brandt St. (the main street); hamburgers, hot dogs, toasted sandwiches and a small dinner menu.

Gugluft restaurant—named after a German sponge cake, the Gugluft has a bar and serves fish, steaks and chops for R17-25, as well as take-aways. It's one block off Marie Brandt St. on Park St.

Tourist Office

Open M-F 8-12 and 1—5, the tourist office on Marie Brant St. has information for tourists and business people interested in the area.

Ostrich Farming in Namibia

An industry currently booming in Namibia is ostrich farming. This has occurred since independence has given Namibia an opportunity to export ostrich products that formerly were under South African control. South Africa, currently the world leader in ostrich farming and ostrich products has an industry centered in Oudtshoorn in the northern Cape Province. The industry is based on selling the hides, feathers and meat of the world's largest bird which is domesticated there. Export of live birds or eggs from South Africa is banned.

Upon independence, some Namibian farmers decided to start raising domesticated ostriches in an independent Namibia, free from the controls of the South African industry.

Ostrich farm in Mariental.

Ostrich chicks.

Adult ostrich "inflating"its neck..

A clutch of wild ostrich eggs.

The industry in Namibia has an entirely different market—one based on the export and sale of eggs and small chicks—which fetch a high price on the world market. Most of the eggs and chicks are shipped to the United States, where ostrich farming is a booming industry as well and the demand for new stock is high. This is what is known as a breeders market where eggs and chicks are sold to produce more eggs and chicks for sale until the price comes down enough to where the market shifts to a skin, feather and meat market.

For example, a farmer in South Africa can get about R1000 for a bird going to slaughter, while a Namibian farmer can get R600 for <u>one</u> egg, R2000 for a chick less than 3 months old and R20,000 for a breeding adult. An average laying female can produce up to 80 eggs a year, making ostrich farming very profitable indeed. After being airfreighted to the United States and incubating there, a 3-6 month old chick will sell for US$ 4,000 (R12,000)!

A good percentage of eggs shipped won't hatch due to infertility and there is also a high mortality rate among young chicks, but the prices are drawing farmers and business people into the game all over the world. Critics say that Namibian farmers are cutting their own throats by shipping away their breeding stock so that other countries can create their own industries in competition with Namibia. Farmers say that the world market will settle down to a skin and meat market within a few years so they might as well draw farmers in Namibia into ostriches while the money is good and then capitalize on the relatively low cost of labor and land which will give them an advantage over other countries.

The Namibian ostrich industry started around Mariental but has spread all over central and southern Namibia where the domesticated birds enjoy warm temperatures and dry weather. The birds are fenced off in family groups that vary widely according to the farmer. A typical family group may consist of one male and two females or two males and four females or a larger group of, say 8 males and 25 females. The females generally lay during the drier months from June-January. Males mate at 3 years of age and females at 2 years of age, and produce more eggs as they grow older. Removing the eggs causes the female to lay more—up to about 80 per laying season.

How long this boom will continue is anyone's guess, but farmers are starting to realize that perhaps they should restrict exports, possibly to prolong the current breeders market and high profits for existing farmers.

Hardap Dam

Hardap is 24 km. north of Mariental. Take the B1 north out of town and follow the Hardap Dam signs. Don't take the route marked Hardap Skema.

Hardap is the largest dam in Namibia with a capacity of over 320 million cubic meters and an area of 25 sq. km. The height of the dam wall is 39 meters (129 feet). The presence of so much water in the middle of some of the driest country is wonderful to behold, especially after you've been driving through the Kalahari or Namib deserts and have scarcely

NAMIBIA

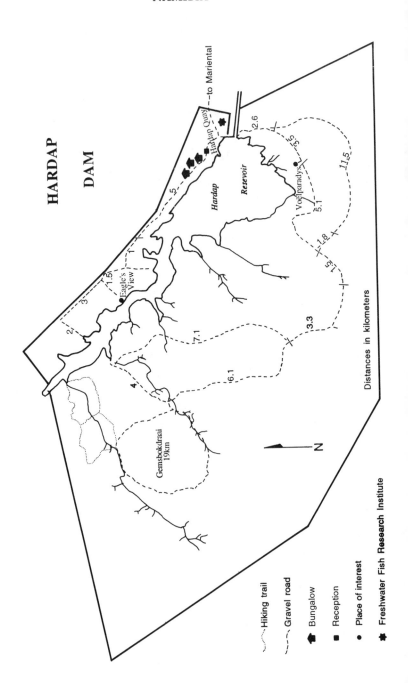

HARDAP DAM

to Mariental

Hardap Quay

Hardap Resevoir

Voëlparadys

2.6
3.5
11.5
5.1
1.8
1.5
3.3
Eagle's View
1.5
5
3
2
7.1
6.1
4
Gemsbokdraai 19km

Distances in kilometers

N

········· Hiking trail

– · – Gravel road

■ Bungalow

■ Reception

• Place of interest

✦ Freshwater Fish Research Institute

seen a drop! It is situated on the Fish River, the longest river totally within Namibia and is a popular place for fishing (license required—you can get one at the tourist office) and water sports such as windsurfing, sailing and boating. It is also an important wildlife and bird refuge as well as an area to preserve Namibia's freshwater fish. Go to the Freshwater Fish Institute where they are breeding and harvesting fish in a controlled program. There is also an aquarium next to the tourist office, where a selection of Namibian fish are kept. It is the only freshwater aquarium in Namibia. Endemic fish include large and small mouth yellowfish, mud mullet, mud-fish, carp, blue kurper and barbel. Hardap has quite a large bird population including pelicans, flamingos, fish eagles and goliath herons. There is a game park on the southern side of the lake where kudu, springbok, zebra, oryx, hartebeest, and ostrich can be seen. As of October, 1992 the drought had caused the level of the dam to drop severely so that it stood at only 13 percent of capacity.

On the southeast side of the lake are standard bungalows found throughout Namibia's government rest camps, though here they are beautifully situated near a cliff above the lake. There are some nice grassy campsites and day visitors are allowed to stay until 11pm but are admitted from sunrise to sunset only. There is a restaurant, which has a standard menu, perched on the cliffs above the lake where you can have a drink on a circular patio overlooking the water. It is open the usual hours and there's a well-provisioned store for between meal times. A swimming pool (closed in winter) and tennis courts are available and you can even rent a boat house for your boat! Hardap is very busy during school holidays, so book well ahead (often 3-4 months). It is sometimes deserted during the day as many people coming from South Africa use it as a convenient stopover point on their way into Namibia, often arriving in the late afternoon and leaving in the morning.

For hikers, there is a trail through the game park which

leads down to an inlet on the lake that is 15 km., or a shorter version of the same route that's 9 km.

Rates: Bungalows R50-104; dormitory room R30 (2 beds) or R50 for 10 bed group room; camping or picnic site R25.

Kalkrand

Located on the B1 190 km. south of Windhoek and 70 km. north of Mariental, at Kalkrand you can get petrol as well as take-away food from the Kalkrand Hotel which also has a small restaurant. The Aurora restaurant has fish & chips and other take-aways. This is a one street town and everything is located on the highway.

Asab

A small roadside town about 125 km. north of Keetmanshoop on the B1 highway, Asab has one hotel with a bar/restaurant, 24-hr. petrol and a small store. The Asab Hotel has rooms with bath for R85, a 3 person room with bath down the hall for R60 and a 4 person flat for R95 with breakfast extra. The store is open 8-1 and 3-6.

Gibeon

The chief town of the Nama people in southern Namibia, Gibeon, a 10 km. detour from the main road, may give you an idea of what the Namas live like today.

Brukkaros Volcano

Take the B1 north from Keetmanshoop to the town of Tses, where you turn west and head towards Berseba. Just before Berseba is the D3904 that takes you to the crater. Brukkaros is an extinct volcano 1586 meters high, with a crater about 2 km. in diameter. It dominates the surrounding area as you're driving along the highway. There was a solar research station here used by the Smithsonian Institute in the 1930s. There's a road up to the crater rim that's negotiable by 4-wheel drive though you can get most of the way up with a 2-wheel drive.

Mukorob (Finger of God)

Quickly being removed from the tourist itineraries since it fell over in 1988, this narrow finger of rock sticking 34 meters up into the air was similar to the Vingerklip in Damaraland. Its fall has been attributed to windstorms, the Armenian earthquake and an act of God. If you want to see what's left of it, it's located about 20 km. east of Asab.

Maltahöhe

(For those of you wondering how this is pronounced, try *mahl tah hyuh'*, which is as close as we can come in English.) It was named after Malta von Burgsdorff, the wife of the German commander at Gibeon and it's German for Malta heights. A stopping point for those on the way to Lüderitz or Sossusvlei, there is 24 hour petrol as well as a decent reasonably priced hotel here. Maltahöhe is a Karakul sheep farming community of about 2,500 people, many of whom come into town when supplies arrive. Archies Café on the west end of town has take-aways, snacks and cool drinks.

Maltahöhe Hotel—Tel. (06632) 13

The only lodging in town is the Maltahöhe Hotel with 26 rooms, built in 1912. The older part of the hotel is built of stone and has cages where a flock of rosy-faced lovebirds flew in one day and have remained. The newer part of the hotel is not as attractive but all the rooms are comfortable and nicely furnished and have their own toilet and bath or shower. There is a small swimming pool for hot desert days and two very well stocked bars. You can ask the owner about camping. Meals are available as are fans upon request— no A/C.

Rates: Singles are R65 and doubles R95.

Duwisib Castle

The roads to Duwisib are decent. From Maltahöhe, take the C14 towards Helmeringhausen about 38 km. to D824 where you turn right. Keep an eye out for the road signs. After 12 km. turn left onto D831 and go 16 km. where you'll see a turnoff to your left, which you ignore and go straight another

NAMIBIA

20 km. to the castle. From Helmeringhausen, take the C14 north towards Maltahöhe 62 km. to D831. After 27 km. turn left at the T and go 20 km. to the castle. This is an interesting diversion and a chance to camp next to a castle in Namibia. Its presence on the edge of the Namib desert is a testimony to one man's dream and a bizarre landmark of German colonial times in Namibia.

It was built in 1907-1909 by Captain von Wolf who was later killed in World War I. Constructed of sandstone blocks, it is furnished with some 18th century pieces and has interesting fireplaces. Today it is run by the DNC. You can camp or picnic outside here but there is only water, a toilet and a little shade.

Hammerstein Rest Camp—Tel. (06632) 5111

This rest camp is situated on highway 36 a few kilometers west of D827 fairly close to Naukluft Park. They have 5 bungalows where you can do your own cooking, or order food.

Rates: 2 beds R120, 4 beds R160 with dinner; R120/ person B&B

Southern Section of Namib-Naukluft Park

This huge park and conservation area is the largest in Namibia and the fourth largest in the world with an area of 49,768 sq. km. (19,130 sq. miles). It was proclaimed in 1907 with the Naukluft mountains and a section of Diamond Area 2 added in 1979 and the rest of the Diamond Area added in 1986.

There are four areas of the park: Sandwich Harbor, the Northern section consisting mostly of gravel plains, the Sesriem-Sossusvlei area with its incredible sand dunes and the Naukluft Mountains.

The southern section of Namib-Naukluft Park covering Sesriem, Sossusvlei and the Naukluft Mountains is in this section.

NOTE: To find out about the northern section of the park

including Welwitschia Drive and the Namib desert see the Coastal Region section of this book.

Naukluft

From Windhoek, take the B1 south to Rehoboth, then the C24 until you reach the D1206 turnoff, where you turn right. When you come to the C14, turn left and soon after right off the C14, following the signs to Naukluft. You enter the gate about 12 km. before you reach the office.

From Maltahöhe take the C14 north to Büllsport then left on D854 to the gate. From Walvis Bay take the C14 through the northern section of Namib-Naukluft Park and continue straight past Solitaire, avoiding the turnoff to Sesriem-Sossusvlei. At Büllsport, go right onto D854 to the gate.

This section of Namib-Naukluft Park covering the Naukluft mountain range contains a small remote camp which should be booked well in advance. The 4 campsites are spaced very close together, providing little privacy. For hikers, there are two day-long hikes, a 10 km. and a 17 km., through the Naukluft mountains. The 17 km. Waterkloof trail follows a perennially flowing stream for the first 6 km., welcome after traveling in the dry Namibian climate. It is a beautiful, relatively lush area, with birdlife, groups of kudu wandering about the hillsides and a refuge for Hartmann's mountain zebra. The trail then leads to the dry highlands over a pass and down to the Naukluft river valley where pools and relative lushness return for the last few kilometers before reaching the campsite. CAUTION: Look for baboons that inhabit the area—they will take any food that you leave out in your tent or campsite.

There is also an 8 day hike that covers 120 km. through the Naukluft range; water is available at convenient intervals so you don't have to lug it along. A shorter 4 day version of this hike also exists. There are huts and shelters for camping at convenient intervals, though they don't always coincide with the water sources. The trail is only open from March 1 to October 31 because of high summer temperatures; you must start on the 1st or 3rd Sunday and Wednesday of each month. Group size must be 3-12 people. Once you know when you are going, you must pay R30 per person which includes a stay at the farmhouse at Naukluft on your first and last days.

Call the DNC office in Windhoek for more information or restrictions.

Solitaire

A tiny, but friendly, outpost where you can get petrol and some food, Solitaire has a store which is open 24 hours. The owners also have a mountain house to rent for R30 a night about 8 km. from town. Plans are for campsites and improved facilities.

Sesriem and Sossusvlei Region

Sesriem

From Windhoek, take the B1 south to Rehoboth, then the C24 west, following the right fork towards Solitaire and Remhoogte pass. When you come to the C14, don't go to Solitaire, but instead cross the road onto the shortcut which takes you to the road to Sesriem. On the way to Sesriem you cross a corridor for migrating game such as springbok, oryx, kudu and ostrich.

Sesriem is a clean popular group of 20 campsites that is the base most people use for seeing Sossusvlei and Sesriem canyon. It must be booked through the Windhoek DNC office, though there is some room for overflow camping. Toilets, showers, petrol, cold drinks and postcards are available though the office is open from sunrise to sunset only. Each campsite has its own water and thorn tree. The staff is very efficient and friendly though reservations don't always come through from the DNC office in Windhoek so you might find yourself without one you thought you had!

The Karos Sossusvlei Lodge is opening mid-1994. It is a 45 room luxury lodge which should help accommodate the many people that visit this area.

Sesriem Canyon

Only 4 km. from the campsite at Sesriem, this marvelous little canyon appears out of nowhere. Formed by the Tsauchab river, the same one you follow to get to Sossusvlei, Sesriem Canyon is merely one kilometer in length and you can actually step across the top of it in points as it narrows to underground caves near the road. There is a small trail down to the bottom and there are pools, which after rains provide a refreshing swim! Sesriem is Afrikaans for "six straps," referring to the six oxhide straps that early travelers used to lower the water bucket into the canyon. Sesriem Canyon is an interesting place to explore for an hour or two to see the geology and to look for bats that are found in the canyon caves.

Sossusvlei

This spectacular desert area is truly one of Namibia's most incredible natural wonders, inspiring artists and photographers and gracing tourist brochures and post cards as well. The peach colored sand dunes towering over 300 meters above stark white dry lake beds that become pools when enough rain comes is one of the sights that deservedly brings fame to this area. The relative difficulty of getting here adds to the adventure of climbing the dunes in the still morning when perhaps a lone oryx wanders by.

Get up early to arrive at the dunes by sunrise for a spectacular "shadow show" as the morning light gradually works its way across the sharply creased dune ridges. Ask the park personnel when the gate will open in the morning so you can get out there. It takes about an hour to drive and another hour to walk, or alternately, if you have a 4-wheel drive about an hour and a quarter to drive to Sossusvlei. The road follows the Tsauchab river, which is also responsible for the Sesriem canyon. The only facilities here are toilets and picnic tables, so bring water and everything else for what should be a day long trip. There are countless dunes and vleis to explore, and depending on the time of year, you might want to do more strenuous climbing during the early morning or late afternoon hours.

For an otherworldly experience, walk across a few sets of dunes to the Deadvlei. On the south side of the 4-wheel drive parking area there is a small sign which points in the general direction of the dead vlei, or you can just proceed towards the tall, steep dune that dominates the area south of the parking area. After a short hike you find yourself looking out over a large stark white *vlei* that ends abruptly at the bottom of the giant dune. There are a few scraggly trees and bushes here and the extremely photogenic view is positively science fiction. Cross the dead vlei to the base of the mammoth dune and try climbing straight up from there. When rain falls here the vleis fill up creating an entirely different but no less magical effect of an oasis in the middle of the sand sea. Each dune offers a different vantage point for incredible views and photo opportunities. Bird and animal life is quite abundant here with goshawks, ostrich and oryx frequent residents. There is no other place quite like Sossusvlei in the world.

Balloon Trips

For the ultimate upscale adventure, try taking a balloon ride over the dunes of the Namib! Flight includes an hour long ride and a champagne breakfast—afterwards, of course. For details contact Namib Sky Adventures, P.O. Box 197, Maltahöhe, Tel. (06632) 5703

Keetmanshoop

Pronounced *kate mahns hoo'op* after Johann Keetman, a wealthy German who sent money for the Rhenish mission to build a church here in the 1860s, this is also known simply as Keetmans by many Namibians. It is the first town of any size if you're traveling from South Africa and is a focal point for southern Namibia. It is also a convenient spot to stock up on supplies if you are traveling to Fish River Canyon or Ai-Ais. Both Fish River and Ai-Ais are within a few hours drive of Keetmanshoop.

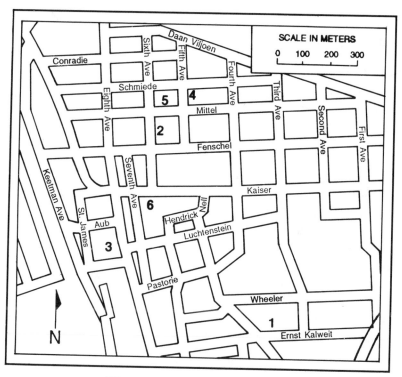

KEETMANSHOOP

1- Canyon Hotel

2-Travel Inn

3-German Club

4-Lara's Restaurant

5-Balaton

6-Museum

The tourist information office is located next to the central park on Fifth St. and they are very helpful. Keetmanshoop gets very hot in the summer months, so you might want to consider the swimming pool in town.

Your choice of places to stay in town are limited to one expensive hotel, one moderately priced hotel, possibly the German club, the municipal campsite, and 13 km. out of town the Kokerboom forest, where there is a guest house and camping.

Places to Stay and Eat

Canyon Hotel—Tel. (0631) 3361, Fax 3714

The Canyon, southern Namibia's nicest hotel (three stars), is right off the highway as you come from Lüderitz and its 54 air-conditioned rooms make a stay comfortable any time of year. The Canyon has a nice clean swimming pool, restaurant and bar and has conference facilities for up to 100 people.

Rates: Single R184, Double R288, Triple R320, Quad R380; breakfast included.

Travel Inn Hotel— Tel. (0631) 3344/5/6, Fax 2138

Formerly the Hansa Hotel, this is less expensive than the Canyon, but not quite as luxurious. Located downtown on Sixth Ave. between Mittel and Fenschel Sts., all the rooms are A/C with telephones. Alas, there is no pool and no TV in the rooms, but you can borrow a TV. The restaurant serves three meals and room service is possible. They will wash your car for free with an overnight stay!

Rates: Single R82 without bath, R115 with bath; Double R165; Triple R209; Family R209. All rates include English breakfast. Restaurant dinners are reasonably priced at R15-20 for entrees.

German Club—Tel. (0631) 3400

Established in 1899, this is not a real hotel but has a few rooms for a R51 single and R62 double. English breakfast is an extra R12.50. The Schutzenhaus is the popular restaurant/bar that serves meals at R15-25. Sometimes they'll cook special stews for R10. The restaurant is open 10-10; the club opens at 5. The German club is just down the street from the Municipal campground.

Municipal Campground—Tel. (0631) 3316 or 147

Located at 8th and Kaiser St., this is the place to stay if you're on a budget. It's small compared with other campgrounds and close to downtown. There is some grass to camp on and they have showers, toilets, braai pits and even a washing machine. You can iron if you bring your own iron.

Rates: R5 per car; R7 per caravan plus R5 per person.

Places to Eat

Lara's—At 5th and Schmiede Streets is Lara's, where most Keetmanshoopers eat. They serve standard Namibian fare and are open until 11 for 3 meals a day.

Balaton Hungarian Restaurant—For a taste of the unusual, try Keetmanshoop's (and Namibia's) only Hungarian restaurant located downtown on Mittel St. Hungarian dishes are only R10-15 and other dishes R20-30. They're open 7 days M-Sat. 800-7:30, Sun. 10-7:30.

Things to Do

Keetman's Museum—For a view of Keetmanshoop's history, check out the museum at 7th and Kaiser Streets. It's open M-F 8-12 and 2-6 and on Saturdays 8-12.

Naute Dam—If you'd like to fish or go boating near Keetmanshoop, then a trip to Naute Dam might be on your itinerary. It's also worth a stop on your way to Fish River Canyon as the road to the dam is actually a short cut to the canyon.

Kokerboom (Quiver Tree) Forest—About 13 km. northeast of Keetmanshoop is the famous Kokerboom or Quiver Tree Forest. Take the B1 highway towards Windhoek and within 2 km. you'll see the signpost where you turn right on the way to Köes. The way is well posted from here. Guest house Tel. (0638), ask for 11302.

The forest is actually a stand of about 250 trees, including some rather large specimens that are over 200 years old and up to 9 meters high with a base trunk diameter of 1 meter. These trees are actually a type of aloe plant, *aloe dichotoma*, that get their name from the early San inhabitants who used the bark and branches to make quivers for their arrows. The forest was declared a national monument in 1955.

The Kokerboom forest is located on a farm that is responsible for maintaining the area which has a guest house as well as campsites next to the forest. The guest house has a stone exterior and a bizarrely modern interior with 8 rooms with baths.

Singles R90, Doubles R140 B&B. Some of the double rooms have actual double beds, not the two twins beds pushed together. The owners will serve lunch or dinner with some advance notice for about R20 for a set meal.

The campsites next to the forest have solar hot water, toilet and table for R5. They'll make you meals if you're camping as well. There is an entrance fee of R5 per person to visit the forest and the adjoining attraction, the Giant's Playground.

Giant's Playground—a little over 4 km. from the Kokerboom forest is the Giant's Playground, an aptly titled series of rock formations with kokerboom trees scattered about. You must pay the entrance fee of R5, which is good for both the forest and the Giant's Playground, before entering. The rocks are seemingly stacked upon one another in large blocks, as if some giant (or giant's children) was making a sculpture of sorts. This site is as interesting as the Kokerboom forest.

Kalahari Desert—if you're heading east from Keetmanshoop towards the Kalahari desert and Kalahari-Gemsbok Park in South Africa, you can't enter at Mata Mata, but must cross the border at Rietfontein and get to the park from there. There is very little as far as accommodations in the Namibian Kalahari, but you could try the Donkerhoek guest farm (see guest farms in this chapter) or the Kalahari Game Lodge, near Mata Mata off the C15. They charge R120 per person for a chalet or tent (everything provided) or R200 per person full board. Telephone (06662) 3112.

Seeheim—listed on some maps as a medium size town, this is nothing more than a railway stop where there is no lodging, no petrol and not much of anything else.

Helmeringhausen—This small town, which is really just a farm with amenities attached has a nice hotel which runs safaris, an open air museum and a petrol station. There are San rock paintings 40 km. from town and some beautiful desert scenery nearby as well as the Konkiep river to explore.

Helmeringhausen Hotel—nice, clean rooms available, 5

double and 1 single. The hotel has safaris to the surrounding desert, sheep farms or Sossusvlei. They are open 8-6 Mon.-Sat. and closed Sundays. All meals can be prepared by the hotel. This is a quiet place to relax.

Rates: Single R70, Double R130 B& B

Bethanie—Located 25 km. off the Lüderitz-Keetmanshoop road north of Goageb, this is a fairly well-to-do Karakul farming community judging by the size of the church and the tarred road into town paved by the farmers themselves. There is a 24-hour Cal-Tex petrol here and the Bethanie Hotel—closed Sundays—featuring "The Ugly Inn." Strangely, only clean and well dressed people are allowed inside The Ugly Inn—by order of the manager—so look neat!

Lüderitz (Lüderitzbucht)

This desert port on Namibia's desolate southern coast seems like a real outpost from the rest of the country and for this reason alone is worth a trip. Save at least a few days to visit the town of Lüderitz itself and the surrounding peninsula as there is much to see and to get a feel of the town takes more than a few hours. You may also want to go when it is not windy as it is very different here on a calm sunny day! The windy season is generally from October—March but it's often fine the rest of the year. Lüderitz, or Lüderitzbucht (German for Lüderitz Bay), as many of the locals and tourists call it, is named after Adolf Lüderitz, a German merchant who started businesses here in the 1800s. The German character of this town is unmistakable in the architecture of many of the buildings. It owes much of its current success, however, to the Consolidated Diamond Mine (CDM) presence with its mining operations in nearby Elizabeth Bay and offshore.

Lüderitz is also famous for its fishing industry, most notably crayfish (also known as lobster). The often windy, rocky coastline attracts unique wildlife such as Namibia's only penguin colony on nearby Halifax island, until recently a South African possession. In fact, South Africa owned all the islands off the Namibian coast, even though some of them

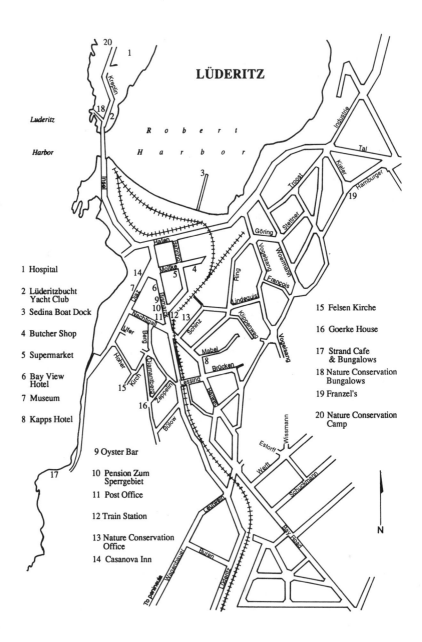

LÜDERITZ

1 Hospital

2 Lüderitzbucht
  Yacht Club

3 Sedina Boat Dock

4 Butcher Shop

5 Supermarket

6 Bay View
  Hotel

7 Museum

8 Kapps Hotel

15 Felsen Kirche

16 Goerke House

17 Strand Cafe
   & Bungalows

18 Nature Conservation
   Bungalows

19 Franzel's

20 Nature Conservation
   Camp

9 Oyster Bar

10 Pension Zum
   Sperrgebiet

11 Post Office

12 Train Station

13 Nature Conservation
   Office

14 Casanova Inn

like Halifax are a stones throw away! This has changed however with the recent South African-Namibian negotiations. (See Walvis Bay section) For excellent information in English, German or Afrikaans, the first stop should be the tourist information office on Bismarck St. They can help you find private accommodations as well as book a Kolmanskop tour. Office hours are M-F 8:30-12 and 2-4 and Sat. 8:30-12.

Places to Stay

Bayview Hotel—Tel. (06331) 2288

The largest hotel in town with 30 rooms, this is a nicely furnished place centrally located (as are all the hotels) with a courtyard setting that is a protection from the wind. There is a small swimming pool and a restaurant which will serve outside guests if they're not full.

Rates: Single R115, Double R178. Breakfast R9-12.

Kapps Hotel—Tel. (06331) 2701 or 2916

Run by the same people who own the Bayview, the 25 rooms are a little less expensive and there's no pool. The restaurant menu is the same as the Bayview and they will also serve non-guests.

Rates: Single R100, Double R145 room only.

Zum Sperrgebiet Hotel—Tel. (06331) 2856

A more lively place than the other two hotels, although they have only 10 rooms and no pool. The bar is off the main street and is quite popular at times. They feature an all-you-can-eat breakfast for R12. Mon.-Sat. 7:30-11 and Sun. 8-11.

Rates: Single R89 with private bath or R78 without, Double R145 with bath, R120 without, Triple R180 and Quad R220.

The Strand Bungalows—Tel. (06331) 2398 or 2957

Situated on the beach on the south edge of town, there are a variety of bungalows for reasonable rates. This is a former government rest camp that has been privatized.

Rates: 2-bed bungalows R50-80, 4-bed bungalows R60-220 B&B

Nature Conservation Campground

One of the most beautiful campsites in Namibia, it covers

Shark Island and offers impressive views of Lüderitz Bay, the town and the surrounding area. Highly recommended to anyone prepared to camp. You must stake your tent tightly as tents have gone to sea with the wind. Consider using rocks on the floor to hold it down if you leave the area. There are showers and bathrooms—sometimes used by campers whose tents can't handle the wind! Sites are R25 per night.

Other options include 3 bungalows you can reserve at the Nature Conservation office in town or by calling (061) 63131 in Windhoek. They accommodate up to 5 or 6 people and are one of the best deals in town for only R60. The bedrooms are quite small and have bunkbeds, but the kitchen is fully equipped with outstanding views from both windows. They are located across the street from the yacht club just after the causeway to the campground on Shark Island.

Just down the street from the tourist office, Mrs. Looser takes in guests, but she prefers those who stay at least 2 nights and preferably longer. She can accommodate up to 10 people. It's better if you are in a group as the rooms are connected and you might have to go through someone else's room to get to yours. R80 plus R10 per person for up to 10 people and R20 extra for one night stays. Laundry is R6 a bundle and a maid will clean for R12/day for longer stays. Telephone 2630, Fax 2365.

Places to Eat

Franzel's—Out on Tal & Hamburger Streets is what many Lüderitzers describe as the best restaurant in town. We would agree as this was our favorite place. Franzel's serves a variety of different dishes in a cozy atmosphere. The portions are large and not expensive though the wine is a bit more costly than some places. Make reservations as they are sometimes full.

The Strand—Attached to the Strand bungalows, this bay-front diner specializes in crayfish, though at a price that is fairly outrageous for what you get. The food is more expensive here but the wine is very cheap, with some bottles only R8. It has a nice light atmosphere and is recommended.

The Oyster Bar—They serve among other things, oysters, which are also available all over town. Located on Bismarck St., it's a nice place for a snack.

Casanova Inn—We didn't try this place but it is another option, though it didn't look as nice as the other restaurants in town.

On the Rocks—A new restaurant.

Car Rental

For local car rental, call Danie Viljoen at 2054.

Things to Do

Crayfish

If you can't live without rock lobster, or crayfish as it's also called, the only reasonable way to eat it affordably is to catch it yourself. Restaurants charge R30-90 for a crayfish meal and they are usually small with the only decent meat in the tail.

You can buy crayfish at the Seafood Distributors on the shore north towards Agate Beach. A 2.5 kilo tray costs R120 and contains 10-16 crayfish. Call ahead if you want it fresh, but it is almost as good frozen and more available. All commercially caught crayfish are exported to Japan as the Japanese buy the entire 200-ton yearly quota. If you want to have some fun and eat well, catch them yourself. You must get a license, net trap and bait (most people use pilchards) or dive with a mask and snorkel (and preferably a wet suit). The season is from Nov. 1-April 30 and you are limited to 5 per person and 20 per vehicle. The carapace must be over 65mm and no females with eggs may be taken. All of Lüderitz Bay is closed to crayfishing, so try south of Diaz Point on the peninsula. We've seen some big ones come out of that area! Check with the local fisheries office as regulations can change yearly.

Lüderitz Peninsula

One of the highlights of a trip to Lüderitz is the Lüderitz Peninsula southwest of town. It is a beautiful, relatively

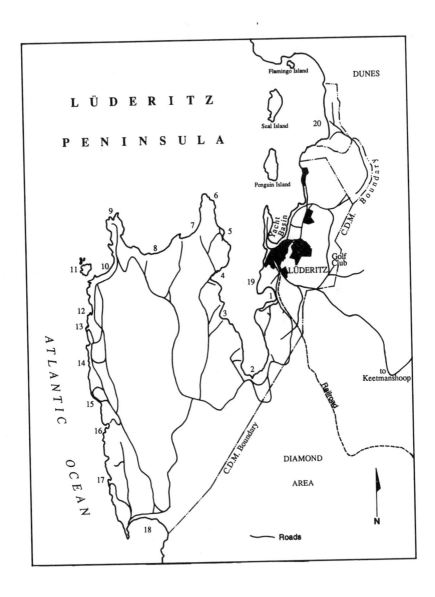

unspoiled area and one of the only places where you can enjoy Namibia's rocky coastline. Try crayfishing south of Diaz Point near the lighthouse or go for a bracing swim in the deep clear pools of the fjord. There are plenty of secluded spots to picnic, have a braai or fish from the rocky shoreline. Flamingos frequent the bays on the peninsula and the sight of low-flying pink and black flocks against the tan dunes and barren moonscape is breathtaking. Spend at least a day or two here, for this is a truly unique part of Namibia. No camping is allowed on the peninsula.

Some of the most interesting places on the peninsula include the following:

1) **Radford Bay**—the first lagoon you come across frequently has flamingos feeding and is a good place for fishing.

2) **Second lagoon**—a good spot for sailing or windsurfing as well as viewing flamingos and other shore birds when the tide is right.

3) **Bay**—beautiful sandy beach, good bird watching and good fishing.

4) **Griffith Bay**—a broad rocky bay unsheltered from the wind.

5) **Angra Club beach**—a lovely sandy beach with small secluded coves on either side.

6) **Angra point**—this tip of land is best explored on foot!

7) **Sturmvogelbucht**—a long windswept sandy beach where in 1914 Norwegians built a whaling station; the remains can still be seen. There is a braai pit but the toilets are locked. The Lüderitz Rotary maintains small cabin facilities for visiting youth groups. If you are interested in using the facility, write the Lüderitz Rotary Club at P.O. Box 146, or call the Deutscher Schuleverein at Tel. 2246.

8) **Shearwater Bay**—the west end of the large sweeping beach.

9) **Diaz Point**—a rocky home for a colony of seals as

well as a lighthouse important for ships approaching this rocky, foggy coast. In 1488 Bartholomeu Diaz erected a cross on this point of land where the first Europeans landed in the area, calling it Angra Pequena. In 1988 the present replica of the original cross was placed here.

You will find a toilet here as well.

10) **Guano Bay**—a sandy beach with large expanses of rock at either end. This is a good area for crayfishing as well as bird watching.

11) **Halifax Island**-—off the rocky point at the end of Guano Bay lies Halifax Island where a colony of Jackass penguins live. You can see them from the tip of the point at low tide with binoculars though they are a little far away for a decent photo.

12 & 13) **Knochen Bucht and Witmuur**—two rocky points of land jutting into the sea.

14) **Essay Bay**—the sea meets the bay more gently here, with tidepools providing good crayfishing and angling. You will also find a well used braai shelter and toilet here.

15) **Eberlanz' Hohle**—at high tide this formation creates a blow hole. The vertical rock edges lie very close together and when the sea crashes in, the water is forced up through the crevasse, spouting like the blowhole of a whale. The view of the hole is about a 10- minute walk from the road. Keep left of the pinnacle rock on the way down.

16) **Fjord**—One of the most beautiful (and most used) places on the peninsula. Litter is sometimes a problem here so please keep it clean. The beautiful clear water provides excellent swimming or snorkeling on a sunny day.

17) **Kleiner Bogenfels**—a tiny version of its larger cousin farther south, this is a good picnic spot.

18) **Grosse Bucht**—a south facing sandy beach good for fishing and swimming. The rocky point which

protects it from the Atlantic is a good spot for cray-fishing. There is a toilet here. This is the furthest south you are permitted to go without incurring the wrath of CDM.

19) **Swimming**—Beach in front of the Strand bunga-lows is close to town.

20) **Agate Beach**—as far north as CDM allows you to go, this long smooth strand has braai shelters that protect from the wind. Here is a chance to find dia-monds among the agates, but even if the ore is very rich you'll have to sift through some 2 tons of sand and gravel and lots of look-alikes to find a small dia-mond! On the drive out look for the oryx, springbok and ostrich that live in the area. Quite often you'll see small herds along the road.

"Sedina" Cruise

You can take a trip on the 42 foot steel-hulled schooner "Sedina" anchored at the harbor. The friendly owners have done a lot of sailing in various parts of the world and will take 8-10 people on a 3-hour round trip to Diaz Pt., and (weather permitting) Halifax Island, where Namibia's pen-guin colony roosts. Along the way, look down into the water at the bow of the boat and see the Benguela Dolphins frolick-ing so close you can almost touch them. Seals also hang out on the rocks along the way, making this trip a real coastal safari! On Halifax Island penguins waddle among the old houses and it's one of the few places in the world where flamingos and penguins stand side by side! African black oystercatchers pick the rocks for food and with any luck you'll spot a whale spouting offshore. The "Sedina" leaves the dock at 7am sharp and charges R30 to Diaz Pt., and an extra R10 for Halifax; it is often too windy to go there. To book, call 2919 or the tourist office or hotels will book for you. DRESS WARMLY!

Kolmanskop Tour

Another must for visitors to Lüderitz, Kolmanskop is a

former diamond mining town that the desert and wind have taken over so that it is now just a shadow of its former self. Ever since April, 1908, when August Stauch told the workers who swept the railway clear of sand to look out for anything interesting found along the tracks, the Lüderitz area has never been the same. A diamond was found by Zacharias Lewis and the diamond rush started. By September of that year, the German colonial government declared the "Sperrgebiet" a forbidden area that stretches from the Orange River northwards to latitude 26°S and 100 km. inland. Only those who had claims were allowed to continue mining and over 5 million carats were removed before World War I.

The town flourished and the white miners lived as they would in Europe, importing all their goods, many of them luxurious. In 1928 much larger diamonds were found on the banks of the Orange and Kolmanskop lost its importance. For a while it served as a way station for goods going south to Oranjemund, but by 1956 the last people moved out, leaving a ghost town to the mercy of the elements. In 1979 CDM started looking for ways to preserve the town and it was opened to tourists. Since it is in the Sperrgebiet, you must still obtain a permit to go to Kolmanskop.

Fortunately, getting a permit is as easy as buying a tour ticket at the tourist office. Don't go to the CDM office. The tour lasts about an hour and you have another 3 hours or so to wander about the empty houses and buildings. Many of the houses are half filled with sand—the mine manager's house must have the world's windiest bathroom! Be careful as these are decaying houses and some of the wood is not in the greatest shape. Visit the excellent museum for a history of the area as well as a view of some of the current diamond mining operations. There is a nice little cafe next to the museum if you get hungry or thirsty.

Digging for Desert Roses

Desert roses are conglomerations of salt, gypsum and sand that have the appearance and color of a rose. They are formed by changing salinity in salt pans due to tides and evaporation that causes crystallization in this unique form. You will see them for sale in area curio shops. You can dig for them yourself with a Nature Conservation guide and a fee of R10 per person. Stop by the Nature Conservation office ahead of time to plan a 2-hour trip.

Lüderitzbucht Safaris

The only tour operator in town, Lüderitzbucht specializes in local tours. One tour that is off the beaten track is to Koichab Pan in the restricted area northeast of town. Some 120 km. east is the area where the town's water supply originates. Apparently over 10,000 years old, the water source is very pure. You must have a Nature Conservation Guide with you and the tour operator so it can be quite expensive. You must book in advance.

Elizabeth Bay Mine Tours

Tours of CDM's new Elizabeth Bay plant used to draw hundreds of tourists. Changes late in 1992 made a police clearance from your own country necessary to get a permit for a guided tour—waiting time for a permit is 6-8 weeks. The apparent reason for this is new regulations issued by the Namibian police, who are now responsible for security in the diamond areas. Apparently they are worried about someone picking up a parcel or two in the sand while visiting the area. This may change in the future, so inquire beforehand if you really want to go. Call Gino Noli at Tel. 2445 for more information.

Houses—There are some fascinating examples of turn of the century German architecture in Lüderitz, including the Goerke house and the Lutheran church which both overlook the town.

Festival Train—In July and during Easter holiday, there are special overnight trains that ply the route from Keetmanshoop to Lüderitz. Book well in advance at the Southern Tourist Forum in Keetmanshoop, TransNamib in Windhoek, or at the tourist information in Lüderitz.

Skiddle Alley—Similar to bowling, but more difficult, skiddle is a game you might try at the Kapps Hotel for something different. It's supposed to be open 1 or 2 nights a week.

Dancing—There is dancing in some of the hotel bars and disco night in the black township, both of which are interesting. There are also occasional Saturday night dances at the German Club.

Television—You could just relax and watch the tube, but as Lüderitz does not receive television signals, the programs from NBC arrive by plane on videotape a week late so the news, etc., will be dated.

Museum—There's a small museum on Diaz St. that's open 4:30-6 M-F.

Golf—There's a golf course 5 km. out of town that has oil and sand greens, if you're really into golf!

Getting to Lüderitz

Air Namibia has flights to Lüderitz from Windhoek, Swakopmund, Keetmanshoop and Cape Town. The drive over the Namib is a stunning desert experience. Be careful as the winds pick up and blow sand across the road as you approach the Lüderitz area, creating mini sand dunes on the road which are not as soft as they look. Under extreme conditions, sandstorms will remove the paint from your vehicle!

There is a TransNamib bus that is used instead of the train on Saturday and Sunday between Keetmanshoop and Lüderitz. Inquire at the TransNamib office in either town. If you're one of the lucky few arriving by private boat, you can moor your vessel and use their facilities for the first 2 weeks free; then it's R20 a month.

Wild Horses

On the highway between Lüderitz and Aus, you will notice signs on the road that warn of horses. These horses are a group of 150 or so "wild horses of the Namib" that have survived in this inhospitable area for decades. During drought years they seem very lean as the food supply is not plentiful. The DNC has tried feeding them lucerne (alfalfa) but they apparently will not eat it, so the oryx in the area gobble it up. Near the railway stop of Garub you might be able to see them wandering around the desert.

Aus

Aus could possibly be described as Namibia's winter wonderland due to the snowfall received here every several years. Snow has actually stayed on the ground for up to two weeks here recently. Aus (which means *snake* in the Nama language) was the site of a World War I prison camp where German soldiers were interned. It is the only place to stay if you can't make the rest of the 120 km. to Lüderitz. There is one hotel, petrol and a couple of stores here. The electrical lines apparently don't reach Aus and the town is run on generators, most of which are shut off at night.

If you're coming from Lüderitz, the gravel road to Goageb starts here, although they are paving it in the near future.
Bahnhof Hotel—Aus' only hotel is run by Bets Swanepoel, a friendly woman who will show you pictures of the snowfalls in Aus and a collection of black amethyst from the Brukarros volcano. The hotel has 10 quaint rooms and Bets will let you camp on the hotel grounds for a few rand and a few rand more for a shower. She serves meals and take-aways and there is a bar here as well. The hotel is closed Sundays 2-6.

Rates: Single R 60, Duble R50 per person. Breakfast is R12 extra.

Petrol hours: 8-6
Goageb—There used to be lodging here in the form of a small hotel, but the crew building the Aus-Goageb road has taken it over to house employees; there probably won't be any lodging in Goageb for about three years. There is a petrol station here, but petrol isn't always available.

Diamond Mining

As you may have noticed from all the signs warning you not to leave the road into Lüderitz under penalty of death and worse, diamond mining is important in this region. All kidding aside, income from diamonds is a significant part of the Namibian GNP and stealing diamonds is a significant part of crime in Namibia.

Southern Namibian diamonds are thought to have originated from kimberlite pipes in the higher regions of what is today South Africa. Over some 90 million years, these pipes containing diamonds were eroded away and the stones washed down the Orange River and then up the coast towards Lüderitz where they have settled in sands on and off shore. Most Namibian stones are of gem quality since those of poor quality eroded away over the years. The largest diamond ever found here was a 249 carat monster near the mouth of the Orange river.

The mystery and aura of wealth surrounding diamonds has persisted since their discovery at Kolmanskop. (See Kolmanskop section). After the initial diamond rush, small miners formed companies and did well until diamond prices dropped just after World War I. At that time Sir Ernest Oppenheimer bought up all companies to form Consolidated Diamond Mines, or CDM. (CDM is the second largest employer in Namibia after the government.) With the discovery of larger diamonds at the mouth of the Orange River around 1936, CDM shifted its operation to the new town of Oranjemund and the southern coast became the major mining area for the next fifty years.

Dykes have been built and the surfline has actually been pushed back up to 300 meters so the rich deposits below the water line can be mined. Approximately 25 meters of overburden has been removed so that the mining takes place at 20 meters below sea level! Large dykes usually keep the sea at bay but when a storm powerful enough to break through occurs it is a major setback to operations. CDM also mines on the banks of the Orange upriver at Auchas where significant deposits were found. They also opened the Elizabeth Bay plant in 1991 just south of Lüderitz where they hope to produce 250,000 carats yearly, most in the form of stones less than .2 carats. The trend for the future, however, is offshore diamond mining that is done by dredging the ocean bottom in up to 200 meters of water. Sometimes you can see small subcontractors of CDM dredging off the Lüderitz peninsula. Security is a constant concern when one is dealing with something as small and as valuable as a diamond. CDM and Namibia take it very seriously as you may notice. The Namibian police have a special diamond branch that is responsible for diamond security, preventing diamond theft and diamond sting operations. Oranjemund is a town closed to tourists and the police are constantly battling diamond theft and smuggling out of the area. Tales of diamond smuggling escapades are often heard. For example, one unfortunate smuggler loaded down a homing pigeon with so many diamonds it couldn't fly. The police found the poor bird struggling and noticed the sack tied to its body. After a little food and water and being relieved of its burden, it was released and followed home, to an unsuspecting accomplice! To further discourage theft, CDM offers rewards of 70 percent of the diamond value to those who recover stolen diamonds. Whatever you do, don't even think of looking at someone's diamond collection or consider buying from anywhere but a jewelry shop. Your seller could be a smuggler or a police plant and the results may not be in your best interest.

CDM is owned by DeBeers, which controls diamond marketing worldwide. They have bought diamond rights in almost every country in the world (including the former Soviet Union), though areas not under their control are of great concern to them. A current diamond glut and cash flow problems have taken a bite out of their absolute monopoly.

After mining, DeBeers sorts the stones and they are sold to individual buyers, mostly in London. The largest stones are cut in New York, mid-size in Israel and the smaller stones in India; Antwerp cuts stones of all sizes. Diamonds come in a variety of colors (including black) and their natural crystal form is two pyramids with bases attached.

Ai-Ais and Fish River Canyon

Ai-Ais

Ai-Ais is located 714 km. south of Windhoek and 232 km. south of Keetmanshoop. It is famous for natural hot springs and in fact the name Ai-Ais means *burning hole* or *steaming water*. The temperature of the spring water reaches 60°C (140°F) and is cooled (thankfully) before it reaches the thermal bath area. There are bungalows and campsites available.

Rates: Bungalows R64-115, camping R25 per site. Admission for overnight and day visitors is R5 for adults and cars, children are R2.50.

NOTE: It gets incredibly hot here in the summer and for this reason Ai-Ais is closed from Nov. 1 until the 2nd Friday in March.

Fish River Canyon

The Fish River Canyon is one of Africa's great wonders. The second largest canyon in the world after the Grand Canyon in the U.S., it's probably one of the least known natural wonders on Earth. It is 161 km. (100 miles) in length and up to 27 km (17 miles) wide. Depth varies from 457 to 549 meters (1508 to 1811 feet). There is a 90 km. (55 mile) hiking trail along the bottom of the canyon that is only open from May—August due to extreme summer temperatures and possible flash floods.

The massive gorge has been carved by Namibia's longest river, which follows a course over 800 km. from its source near the Naukluft range to the confluence with the Orange river bordering South Africa. The Fish River starts carving its gorge south of Seeheim and at the confluence with the Gaap river the depth is 50 meters. Soon afterwards it enters the deep ravine that is Fish River Canyon. It is the only river in the Namibian interior that has pools outside the rainy season. Even after 5 years of drought there were pools over 5 meters deep in the dry season! The canyon is thought to have started forming 300-500 million years ago by erosion and glacial action which created a valley that the river carved into a canyon.

Hiking the Fish River

Hiking the Fish River Canyon does require a bit of planning with the following conditions:

1) Backpacking is permitted only from May 1-August 31
2) Groups hiking the trail must have a minimum of three and maximum of 40 people.
3) Children must be over the age of 12 and accompanied by at least one adult.
4) A medical certificate completed by a doctor must be handed in at the Hobas rest camp before the hike. This certificate must have been issued within 40 days of the starting date of the hike!

The hike covers 80-90 km. depending on how many shortcuts you take and is usually completed within 4-5 days.

If you still have enough energy to hike the trail after you've taken care of the formalities, you start (preferably after a night at Hobas rest camp) from near the main viewpoint which is well signposted. The first part of the trail is hacked into a cliff and has chains you can hold as it is very steep. After a precipitous hour long climb to the canyon floor you proceed along the trail towards Ai-Ais.

There is plenty of water in the canyon, however check locally whether you must boil it. There are fish, strangely enough, in the Fish River and you can fish with a permit. Yellowfish, barbel, carp and blue kurper are found in the pools.

Please take care to leave only footprints and take only photos of the canyon as it is still in a relatively pristine condition. Use as little wood as possible or, better yet, bring a gas stove to eliminate wood use entirely. Some parts of the trail have very little wood available and seemingly dead trees are not always so. Never bury litter—carry it all out with you. Bury all human waste at least 100 meters from the riverbed in a small hole if possible. Use only existing fireplaces. Most of all enjoy this fascinating natural wonder and leave it as you found it.

Reservations—Book well ahead as this is a very popular hike. Written reservations are accepted 18 months in advance and held on file and confirmed 11 months before your starting date. Telephone reservations are accepted up to 11 months in advance. Write to Director of Tourism, Reservations, Private Bag 13267, Windhoek, Tel. (061) 36975.

Hobas Rest Camp—Open all year, the Hobas rest camp is the place for hikers and others who want to see the canyon. Opened in 1989, there are 12 comfortable campsites that will take up to 8 people each. The campsites are equipped with braai pits, power outlets and water faucets, and there is an ablution block closeby. A small swimming pool beats the summer heat and the staff is very helpful. There is also a small not very well stocked store, so buy what you need beforehand. The camping areas are currently gravel, but there are plans for grass to be planted. Hobas is 10 km. from the main canyon viewpoint, on a road where you can't really see the canyon until you're right on top of it. If you're hiking the trail, you might be wondering how to get back to your car from the end of the trail at Ai-Ais. There are locals who, according to the staff at Hobas, are trustworthy and will drive your car to Ai-Ais for you for R50. Otherwise you must hitchhike or arrange a lift beforehand. Ask the staff also about horse trails from Fishrivermond near the South African border to Ai-Ais (when it is open) that a local farmer offers for R750 per person all inclusive. The gate hours at Hobas are 6am-10pm, but if you arrive after hours and there is nobody around, find a place to pitch your tent (quietly) and you can pay in the morning. The store has regular hours but seems to be open at almost any time if you're polite enough.

Rates: The charge at Hobas is R5 per person and R5 per car to enter plus R25 for a camping spot.

Gaap River Campsite—As Hobas can be full during the hiking season, a new private camping area has been created on a farm on the Gaap River northeast of Hobas. On the C12 to Fish River Canyon, you'll see a sign that points you to Natuurpark just before the settlement of Hoolog and about 7 km. before the turnoff onto D601 to Fish River. Take this farm road through a few gates and after 16km. you'll arrive at the campsite, then the farmhouse.

As of early 1993 there are only 5 basic camping huts in the riverbed near the farmhouse, but there are plans for a full guest farm with luxury bungalows, swimming pool and restaurant. The Gaap river has formed a small canyon of its own close to the Fish River Canyon, accessible a few km. away by 4-wheel drive. You can hike around the area and have a chance to view wildlife including the albino klipspringer that the owner says are on this farm. There are also rock engravings close. You must bring your own bedding as the huts are basic with outhouse and wood-fire heated shower.

Rates: R20 per person and R10 per car.

Getting to Ai-Ais and Fish River Canyon

From South Africa, if you cross at Vioolsdrif, take the D316 after 35 km. or so towards Ai-Ais, then turn left onto the C10 for a short drivee. Crossing at Nakop, take the B3 to Karasburg to the C10 southwest of town. Follow it to the tarred B1 highway, turn right and follow for a few kilometers then turn left back onto the C10, which you follow to Ai-Ais.

From Windhoek, take the B1 south to Keetmanshoop (about 500 km.), then take the B4 west towards Lüderitz. At Seeheim, turn south on the C12. Watch for the sign to Fish River Canyon on the D601. Take this road, following the signs to Fish River or Ai-Ais.

Grünau

In the middle of a sheep farming area, Grünau boasts one hotel and a 24 hr. petrol station with a small store, take-away and showers for truckers. There is a mechanic available round the clock as well. This is where the road splits, with the eastern tarred road going to Karasburg, Ariamsvlei, Upington (South Africa) and Johannesburg; and the southern tarred road to Noordoewer, Springbok (South Africa) and Cape Town. The Grünau Hotel has singles for only R25 without bath or R35 with bath, and doubles for R45 without bath and R60 with bath. There's a bar and a restaurant that serves meals for R15-20. They will also allow camping. They are starting renovations so prices may increase. Call at (0020) 1 for more information. This is also the closest hotel to Fish River Canyon (104 km.), which you can reach by taking the C12 and following the signs.

Karasburg

A sheep farming community that grew up around the railway, Karasburg is a convenient stopover for those on the way into Namibia from South Africa. Situated 53 km. from Grünau, it has a 24 hr. petrol, a couple of hotels, some take-aways, banks and shops, but not much else. The town of Warmbad to the south still has some hot springs but they have fallen into disrepair. Warmbad is the site of one of the oldest communities in Namibia, but the town lost its importance as Karasburg developed.

Where to Stay
Kalkfontein Hotel—Tel. (06342) 172
Just 300 meters off the main road through town, the Kalk-fontein has rooms with from 1-7 beds. The rooms with their own baths have A/C while those without have only fans. It's busier than the other hotel and a little nicer plus it has a restaurant while the Van Riebeeck doesn't. They have set *boerekos* dinners for about R25.
Rates: Single R75-85, Double R95-110 and R35 for each extra bed— room only.
Van Riebeeck Hotel is basically the overflow hotel for the Kalkfontein, but you may want to have a look as it's a few rand cheaper.

Noordoewer
A tiny sweltering border town on the Orange River, Noor-

doewer grows many fruits and vegetables on the banks of the river and is a nice stopover for those traveling north or south. There is a 24 hr. petrol, a bottle shop, mini-market and hotel.
Camel Lodge—Fortunately the only hotel in town has something to offer. All the rooms are A/C and there is a cool, wonderfully clean swimming pool with a bar. When the temperature climbs to 50°C during the summer, these are nice amenities! They have an a la carte restaurant, bar and a real, live disco with large banks of flashing lights. Dinners run about R15-25 and omelettes are only R10. Camping is allowed although there's only a small spot of grass amidst the gravel. There is a live camel is down the road at the BP station.

Rates: Single R77, Double R115, Triple R150, Quad R175 for room only; camping R15 tents, R25 caravans. You can use the pool when you camp.

White Water Rafting on the Orange

At present, there are no Namibian companies running the Orange River, possibly because the border with South Africa was drawn at the northern high water mark, denying Namibia access to the river. The area is currently being resurveyed to dawn the border at the more internationally accepted mid-river point.

The River Rafters of South Africa has a camp in Noordoewer and they offer year round rafting in 2 or 6 person rafts with camping along the way. Call (021) 725094/5.

Guest Farms in the Southern Region

Namtib Desert Lodge—P.O. Box 19, Aus, Tel. (06362) 6640

Nestled in a remote valley of the Tiras mountains, Namtib lodge provides original farm-style accommodations with hosts Renate and Walter Theile. The Namtib Desert Lodge is located on the Namtib farm, 250 km. from both Sesriem and Lüderitz on the D707. From the town of Aus, take the C13 north 50 km. to the D707, which you follow for 47 km to the gate.

Namtib has 5 two-bed bungalows with private showers and toilets. They offer game drives, walking and horseback riding in 16,400 hectares of virtually pristine land. They are busiest during March, April, July and August when you should reserve 1 month ahead. They are least busy during January, February and November when you should reserve 1-2 weeks ahead.

Rates: R135 per person full board

Sinclair Gästefarm—P.O Box 19, Helmeringhausen, Tel. (06362) 6503

Situated in the dreamlike landscape of southwest Namibia between Helmeringhausen and Duwisib Castle, the Sinclair Gästefarm is hosted by Gunther and Hannelore Hoffmann. South out of Helmeringhausen on the C13, take the D407 about 50 km. to the gate; or from Duwisib castle, take D826 southwest to D407 and after 45km., you'll be there. Sinclair has 5 rooms, all with private toilet and shower. You may walk or drive around the farm or they will arrange trips to Sesriem and Sossusvlei and the Namib desert. For geology buffs, there is an old copper mine on the property or you can just relax in the garden. They are busiest March, April, July and August—reserve 2 months ahead—and least busy Jan., Feb. May and June—book a few days ahead.

Rates: R150 Per person/day full board

Burgsdorf Guest & Safari Farm—P.O. Box 28, Maltahöhe, Tel. (06632) 1330, Fax 141

If you take the C14 for 25 km. south from Maltahöhe and watch for signs, your will find Burgsdorf Farm, with hosts Walter and Lindi Kirsten. Burgsdorf is a working farm that has 7 double rooms, all with private bath. They have donkey cart rides, archeological sites, an old German police station—and will provide petrol. They will arrange travel to Sossusvlei, Duwisib castle or to a local ostrich farm. A medicinal plant is produced here known as devil's claw. No credit cards please. In April, July and August book 1 month ahead; Feb, May, June just phone.

Rates: Single R159, Double R135 per person—dinner and B&B; Single R180, Double R156 per person—full board.

Donkerhoek—Private Bag, 2145 Mariental, Tel. (06662) 3113

HOSTS: Piet & Gerrie Scholtz

Located only 28 km. from the Mata Mata rest camp in Kalahari Gemsbok Park is Donkerhoek. This farm hosted by Piet and Gerrie Scholtz is one of the few guest farms in the massive Kalahari desert. To get there take the road east from either Köes or Gochas towards Mata Mata and continue 28 km. Game drives and drives around the farm are included in the price and they promise personal attention unmatched. A 4X4 route on the farm is planned. During June and July book 3 months ahead; Oct. to Jan. 2 months.

Rates: Per person R153 B&B, R235 full board.

Swartfontein—P.O. Box 20113, Windhoek, Tel. (0628) 1112

Located southwest of Rehoboth, Swartfontein has some game such as black and blue wildebeest, kudu, ostrich, hartebeest, zebra, blesbuck and klipspringer on the farm. To get there take the C24 southwest of Rehoboth and then the right fork towards Solitaire after about 35 km. About 60 km. later, past the D1275 turn off, turn right at the sign. There are five rooms, all with bathroom. Hosts Reinhold and Ingrid Granse will organize trips to Sesriem and Sossusvlei with a 4X4. April and August, book 2-4 months ahead, Feb., June and Nov. 2 days ahead.

Rates: R150 per person B&B, R165 per person full board

Daweb—P.O. Box 18, Maltahöhe, Tel. (06632) 1840

CHAPTER 8

Coast Region

The coastal region includes the barren foggy northern strip that is the Skeleton Coast Park, as well as the popular West Coast Recreation Area, the tourist town of Swakopmund, the port of Walvis Bay and the northern section of Namib-Naukluft Park with its fine desert scenery and many campsites.

NOTE: For maps of the Coastal Region, see the Kaokoland-Damaraland Region map and the Central Region map.

Swakopmund

Swakopmund or simply Swakop, as many people call it, is definitely Namibia's premier tourist town. This is especially true during the hot summer months of December and January when Windhoekers and other people living in the interior flock to the cool coast to fish, swim, explore the desert and other surrounding natural wonders—or just relax.

The German charm and friendliness—Gemütlichkeit—excellent facilities, outstanding fishing along the entire coastal area, and cleanliness attract enough people to almost double the population of 20,000 during the summer. In December, probably the busiest month, there are many special events that draw people as well. The palm lined streets and wonderful turn-of-the-century colonial buildings add a quality to this town that is found nowhere else. German style beer is still brewed here according to the centuries-old German brewing laws, and many varieties of delicious pastries can be found in a number of shops.

Lying at the mouth of the dry Swakop River, Swakopmund

Swakopmund's lighthouse.

is surrounded by the vast Atlantic Ocean to the west, sand and gravel plains of the Namib desert to the east and north, and to the south the beginning of the huge sand dune sea that stretches for hundreds of kilometers.

Swakopmund was part of the protectorate of South West Africa under German control in the late 1800s and early 1900s. When it became prosperous as the main port for South West Africa many companies developed and government buildings were built here. After World War I, German South West Africa was taken by the Union of South Africa and port activities transferred to Walvis Bay with its deep water port. Swakopmund then declined and many businesses and people left.

More recently, Swakopmund's economy has been revived by tourism and the discovery of uranium at Rössing, 65. km. outside of town, where the world's largest open pit uranium mine operates today. Swakopmund gets its name from the Nama description of the muddy flood waters of the Swakop River and means excrement.

Tourist Information Office—Tel. 2224

Located on Bismarck St. next to the library, it is in the tall tower-like building called Woermann House.

Places to Stay

Deluxe Hotels

A large deluxe hotel with casino is planned for Swakopund within the next couple of years. For now, the Hansa and Strand hotels provide the only deluxe accommodations in town.

Hansa Hotel—Roon St., Tel. 311

The three star Hansa Hotel is the largest in Swakopmund with 57 rooms. Its rather drab exterior contains a fancy a la carte restaurant and semi-plush rooms. Being situated at the center of town it can be a bit noisier than other hotels.

Rates: Single R210, Double R 322 B&B

Strand Hotel—The Beachfront, Tel. 315, Fax 4942

Situated away from the rest of town on the main beach, this is a popular international hotel. There is a café facing the beach and you can eat outside on a sunny day. The rooms are modern, clean and comfortable with elegant candlelight dinners in the dining room. A helpful staff makes the stay here very pleasant.

Rates: Single R176, Double R232 B&B

Mid-Range Hotels

Pension Avignon—25 Brückenstrasse, Tel. 5821

Managed by Margit Avignon, this is a quiet 10 room B&B a couple of blocks off the main street. Eat indoors or outdoors, very comfortable and a great value for the money. Highly recommended.

Rates: Single R78, Double R133 B&B

Europahof Hotel & Restaurant—39 Bismarck St., Tel. 5061, Fax 2391

This place looks like it belongs somewhere in the Bavarian Alps and its appearance really helps give Swakopmund its German character. A very comfortable place to stay, except when it's foggy and cold, then the unheated rooms are a bit chilly like the rest of the hotels in town. Europahof has one of the nicest restaurants in Swakopmund, if not Namibia, and the service is excellent. The dinner menu has a variety of seafoods, steaks and game complete with a large salad bar and a live crayfish tank.

Rates: Single R111, Double R166 B&B. Dinners entrees R15-50

Hotel Schweizerhaus—Bismarck St., Tel. 2419

Home of the semi-famous Café Anton, this charming hotel is located across from the lighthouse and is surrounded by palms and flowering plants. It is very relaxing to sit in the cafe at any time and watch the fog roll in from the cool Atlantic while smelling the salty air. The rooms are, as most in Swakopmund, unheated and can be chilly during those cool foggy days. On warm days you can eat outside and sample wonderful baked sweets.

Rates: Single R105-178, Double R178-267 B&B

Hotel Atlanta—Roon St., Tel. 2360

Run by an Irishman and a Canadian M.D., this hotel has the popular Fagin's Pub and Restaurant. They have 9 rooms which are reasonably priced and clean.

Rates: Single R60, Double R90, Family R120 B&B

Budget Accommodation

JJ's—Brücken St., Tel. 2909

The cheapest hotel in Swakopmund, if not all of Namibia, JJ's has rooms that are a surprisingly good bargain. Only a block away from the ocean, they also offer a backpackers' room for only R13 per person. Off road parking available. The owner will serve special meals for a reasonable price if you ask.

Rates: Single R16, Double R30 without private bath; R24 and R45 with bath. Outside rooms are nicer.

Swakopmund Municipal Bungalows—Tel. 2807/8 (M-F 8-1 and 2-4)

The municipality of Swakopmund maintains a number of bungalows at the very south end of town. These cater to all tastes, from the spartan fisherman's bungalows to the more luxurious VIP bungalows. They are a good deal for the money as accommodation elsewhere in town can be quite expensive. No towels are included in any of the rooms, but they do all come with a fridge, some sort of cooking device (hot plates to full stoves with ovens), bedding and toilet with shower and sink. They get very full during school holidays and hot summer weekends so book in advance during these periods. No pets are allowed. These bungalows range in price from R30 to R150—something to fit every budget.

Bed & Breakfasts and Holiday Flats

If you don't want to stay in a hotel or camp, the Swakopmund Holiday Flat Association has over 20 members who will put tourists up for a night or longer at rates varying from R25-100 per person. A few of them are bed and breakfast and most houses have 1-5 beds. Amenities vary so check the list at the tourist office.

Places to Eat

Putensen Bakery and Café—Kaiser Wilhelm St.

A popular spot on the main street in town for snacks and drinks and some of the best baked breads and sweets around. You can have bread with butter and almost anything else plus a delectable array of cakes, tortes and cookies.

The Old Steamer—18 Moltke St.

Popular business person's lunchspot, it has decent food though it is a little pricey. Salad bar, fish, steaks and other dishes.

Ron's Hide Away—37 Brucken St.

A new restaurant (formerly Garfield's), they specialize in Italian food such as lasagna and pizzas and have a small salad bar. Pizzas are quite good and reasonably priced.

Napolitana—Breite St.

An interesting combination of Italian, Greek and Mexican—Spanish food. We would probably rank their quality in the order listed here. The pizzas are quite passable with many different toppings. You can order other Italian dishes as well.

Some of the Greek dishes are good too, with the Mexican food coming in last place. For Namibia, it's a decent start. The motif is definitely Mediterranean and a large wood fired stove bakes your pizzas for eating there or to take away.

Erich's—Post St.

The large gourmet menu at Erich's lets you know you'll be in for a haute cuisine experience. Their fish and meat menu is surpassed by no other. Though a little more costly, the quality here is outstanding. Worth a splurge.

Café Anton—next to Hotel Schweizerhaus

Certainly one of Swakopmund's best places to watch the fog, the scenery or the people. They serve breakfast, lunch and dinner in a small café. Stop by one sunny afternoon and check it out. Connected to the Hotel Schweizerhaus.

Fagin's—Roon St.

With an English Pub atmosphere, this is a decent place for a meal any time of day that won't set you back a lot of money. The pub grub is quite good in this informal spot to eat or drink. Recommended for anyone, especially if you're on a budget.

Bayern Stübchen—Garnison St.

For a taste of authentic German food à la Swakopmund, this is the place to go for lunch or dinner. Sausages, wienerschnitzel and other German favorites are reasonably priced and the meals are filling if a bit heavy sometimes.

Die Kelder—Moltke St.

Described as a family restaurant, this is more like one of the finer gourmet spots in town. The food is finely prepared and presented in large portions. The baked camembert with youngberry jam is excellent for R10. They really seem to take care that everything is prepared well and though it may take a few minutes longer, it's worth it.

Kücki's Pub Restaurant & Take-aways—22 Moltke St.

Reportedly good seafood and friendly atmosphere. For a quick pizza, you can order take-aways at the window on the street. At R5-7 it's passable.

Kentucky Fried Chicken—Roon St.

The colonel has made it all the way to Namibia with his finger lickin' good recipe, complete with mashed potatoes, cole slaw and barbecued beans!

Green Grocer

Hopley's—sells fresh fruit and vegetables with an excellent variety not found in the supermarkets. They are located on Woermann St., a block off the main drag (Kaiser Wilhelm St.). Stock up here for long trips.

Ice Cream Parlor

The Milky Way—favorite hangout for ice creams, sundaes, hamburgers and all sorts of cold concoctions. Located half a block off Kaiser Wilhelm St. on Moltke St.

Laundry

Swakop Laundrette on Swakop St. has washing machines, dryers and irons. You can do it yourself or have them do it for you.

Things to Do

Tour & Safari Companies

Charly's Desert Tours—Tel. (0641) 4341, Fax 4821

Charly's is a popular operator in Swakopmund, offering half and full-day tours of the Namib desert, Sandwich Harbor, Cape Cross and Spitzkoppe, as well as camping safaris in the Namib, Sossusvlei area and Damaraland/Kaokoland.

Desert Adventure Safaris—Tel. (0641) 4459, Fax 4664

DAS runs 4-wheel drive tours throughout the remote, rugged northwestern part of Namibia and has their own rest camps at Palmwag in Damaraland and on the Kunene River on the border with Angola. They have fly-in safaris to these locations as well.

Westcoast Angling Tours—Otavi St., 9 Tel. (0641) 2377, Fax 2532

If fishing is your game, they will take you on a beach fishing tour with 4X4s, an inshore trip fishing just beyond the surf, deep sea fishing for snoek or yellowtail, or shark fishing for the huge Namibian coppershark (Nov.—May). All equipment is provided for a charge of around R150 per person per day.

Historical Buildings and Sites in Swakopmund

Swakopmund is an excellent place to gain an appreciation for the German colonial architecture of Namibia. The buildings have been thoughtfully preserved not only as museum pieces but as useful municipal offices, homes and shops. Eleven of them have been designated national monuments. What follows are highlights of some of the buildings and other places of historical interest. Consult the map key for locations.

1) **Martin Luther**—a steam engine was ordered from Germany in 1896 to haul goods from Swakopmund to the interior. The engine broke down 2 km. from town and the costs to repair it were too high, so here it stands. The name Martin Luther was given to it after the breakdown as the engine reminded people of Luther's famous statement "Here I stand; God help me, I cannot do otherwise."

2) **Scultetus Heim (Kramersdorf)**—built in 1912 as a residence and subsequently used as a joinery and smithy, it was later converted into a hostel by Major Scultetus and thus bears his name. It was declared a national monument in 1977.

3) **Prison**—this lovely building was erected in 1909 and is still used as the local jail though declared a national monument in 1977.

4) **Villa Weise**—this turn-of-the-century residence gives you an idea of what the average settlers' home was like.

5 & 6) **Otavi Bahnhof and O.M.E.G. house**—in the early 1900s there was a narrow gauge railway to the copper mine in Tsumeb. This station was used for the line until 1914 and today it is a private residence. The O.M.E.G. house was a storage building and is now used as a research center for the study of

SWAKOPMUND

African history by the Swakopmund Society for Scientific Development. This building was declared a national monument in 1973.

7) **Railway station**—one of the most beautiful railway stations built by the Germans in Namibia, it was declared a national monument in 1972 and is still in full service today.

8 & 9) **Evangelical Lutheran Church and Parsonage**— the stone church was consecrated in 1912, six years after the founding of the Lutheran Congregation in Swakopmund. The parsonage was completed in 1911.

10) **Villa Wille**—a residence built in 1911, the turret roof is covered in copper and the balcony and other

ornate features make this a landmark in Swakopmund.

11) **Dr. Schwietering house**—these two residences were built in 1910 with the corner house used as a medical office.

12) **Litfass Säule**—before radio and TV, most advertising was done by posters. This poster pillar is the last of its kind in town.

13) **Altes Amtsgericht**—built as a school but finished as a Magistrate's office, this eventually fell into disrepair. Restored in 1976, this functions as municipal offices today.

14) **Marine Denkmal**—monument erected in 1908 to honor German soldiers killed in action.

15) **Lighthouse**—this is the symbol of Swakopmund. Built in 1903 and 11 meters high, the light can be seen 35 km. out to sea. Now automatic.

16) **Die Kaserne**—this beautifully decorated structure looks like a fort but was built as a barracks in 1905 and converted to a school in 1927. It was declared a national monument in 1973.

17) **Prinzessen Rupprecht Heim**—built in 1902 as a hospital, this serves today as a private hotel.

18) **Woermann & Brock House**—the public library, art gallery and tourist information office are all housed in this exquisite building. It is open to the public during business hours. Built in 1894 by the Damara-Namaqua Trading Co. and extended in 1904 by the addition of the Damara Tower, it was used as a water tower as well as navigation aid for ships off the coast. In 1909 Woermann & Brock bought the building and thus it bears their name. It became a school hostel in 1921 and slowly fell into disrepair. It was saved from demolition by the people of Swakopmund who raised sufficient funds to restore it to its former beauty and usefulness.

19) **The Mole**

20) Tannery
21) Bayern Stübchen Restaurant
22) Café Anton
23) Die Kelder Restaurant
24) Erick's Restaurant
25) Europahof Hotel & Restaurant
26) Ron's Hide-a-Way
27) Napolitana Restaurant
28) Kentucky Fried Chicken
29) Kücki's Pub
30) Ol' Steamer
31) Palmen Café
32) Putensen Café Treffpunkt
33) Western Saloon
34) Milky Way Ice Cream
35) Hopley's Produce
36) JJ's Hotel & Restaurant
37) Hotel Atlanta & Fagan's Pub
38) Hansa Hotel
39) Strand Hotel
40) Hotel Adler
41) Hotel Avignon

Museum

The museum in Swakopmund is quite interesting and worth a visit. You can observe stuffed wildlife of all sorts, historical artifacts, gemstones and minerals, ethnic displays, the mutated horns of oryx and springbok and the Rössing display on the operation of the world's largest open pit uranium mine.

Hours: 10-12:30 and 3-5:30; admission: R4 Adults, R2 Students, R1.50 Kids

Rössing Uranium Mine Tour

Every Friday (except during the holiday season) at 8am, tourists can take the Rössing uranium mine tour which starts below the Café Anton. You go in a Rössing bus to the mine, 45 minutes from Swakopmund through the Namib.

The name Rössing comes from General von Rössing, who

never visited Namibia, but charted the railway line from Swakopmund to Usakos using contemporary maps. The mountain to the west of where the mine is presently located was named after him, and the mine named after the mountain. Uranium was discovered here in 1928 but it wasn't until 1976 that uranium oxide was first produced from the mine. It is the largest open pit uranium mine in the world, currently measuring 1 by 3 km. and 250 meters deep, and producing some 2,500 tons of uranium oxide annually. That is half its intended production, which has lagged due to an abundance of uranium on the international market, largely due to production of the former Soviet Union.

To mine uranium, the ore is first blasted then loaded with huge scoopers into massive trucks which are assisted out of the pit by electrical overhead wires to cut on fuel consumption. A scanner measuring radioactivity looks at each truck-load and decides whether to process the ore or throw it away. The ore is then crushed in a series of crushers and processed with acids and solvents until the end product of uranium oxide is reached. It is then packed into drums and shipped. Rössing boasts about many safety awards and shows you how mine workers receive about the same exposure to radiation as the general population, but the emergency showers near the mine entrance made us wonder. The trip ends with a look at Arandis, the mining town built in the desert by Rössing for lower wage scale (black) workers. It's a modern and clean town with solar water heating on every house. Arandis is now a municipality after being handed over to the Namibian government on the second anniversary of Namibian independence March 21, 1992. Tickets for the tour can be purchased for R5 at the Swakopmund museum. The tour lasts approximately 4 1/2 hours.

Welwitschia Drive—(See Namib-Naukluft Park section)
Salt Works Tour—Tel. 2611 or after hours 4015 or 2810

If you're interested in seeing how salt is produced, call the salt company for a tour of the salt pans and bird paradise. The tour lasts about 1 1/2 hours.

Shopping
Tannery—sells kudu hide leather shoes and other game skins and leather goods. Located near the corner of Leutwein & Otavi Sts.
Art Galleries—Woermann house, Die Muschel, Hobby Horse and Reflections.
Brewery tour—Tours of the Hansa brewery conducted for groups of not less than 10 when the bottling process is operating. Make an appointment Tel. 5021.

Public Library—Mon.—Thurs. 9-12 & 3-7, Fri. & Sat. 9-12.
On Bismarck St. next to Tourist Information office.

Horseback Riding—Tel. (0641) 2648 or 2799
Okakambe Trails has horse riding trails, tours and lessons for R30/hour or R50/2 hours. You can take the horse onto the beach or on excursions of varying lengths up the Swakop River.

Skydiving
If you are interested in taking the plunge—try the Swakopmund airport on weekends where the local skydiving club will give you lessons.

Swimming
You can swim in the ocean in the mole basin where it is calmer and safer. There is a great beach there for getting a tan or just relaxing. There is also an Olympic size swimming pool next to the beach across from the Strand Hotel. It has a retractable roof and and is heated with saunas down below. You can pay a daily entrance fee or buy a long term pass.

Camel Rides
There is a camel farm 12 km. east of town where you can ride camels through the desert.

Annual Events

August: Carnival

September: Swimming gala

December: Carols by Candlelight, Seasonal fair, Walvis Bay to Swakopmund sailing regatta, Coastal tennis championships and squash championships, Practical shooting tournament, Dune marathon and ski boat angling competition

Transportation

Car Rental

Avis—38 Kaiser Wilhelm St., P.O. Box 1216, Tel. 2527

Imperial Car Hire—P.O. Box 748, Tel. 61587

Swakopmund Caravan Hire—P.O. Box 3497, Tel. 61297

Trip Swakopmund—11 Post St., Box 882, Tel. 4031

Getting to Swakopmund

From Windhoek—The Mainliner luxury bus operates between Swakopmund and Windhoek three times a week. See under Transportation in the Getting Around chapter.

Trains—There are TransNamib trains to and from Swakopmund and the interior and Walvis Bay. Check the train schedule in the transportation section.

Airport—There are frequent flights to Windhoek via Air Namibia as well as flights to Cape Town via Lüderitz and Oranjemund.

If you're driving from Windhoek, take the B1 north to Okahandja and stay on the highway past Okahandja where it curves west, becoming the B2 and is tarred all the way to Swakopmund.

Walvis Bay

Walvis (whale) Bay was until recently part of the Republic of South Africa.

Walvis Bay is surrounded by the dunes of the Namib desert on three sides and the Atlantic Ocean to the west. Its strategic importance as the only deep water harbor on the Namibian coast has played a role throughout history, with it changing

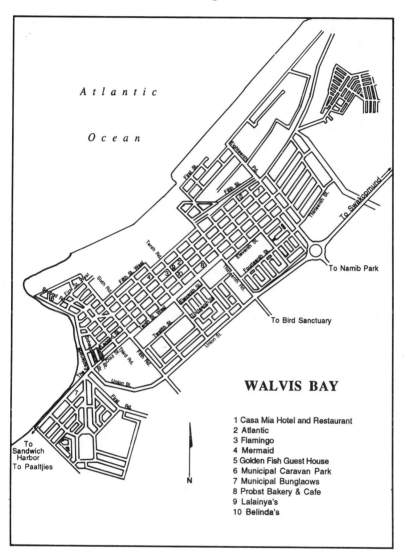

WALVIS BAY

1 Casa Mia Hotel and Restaurant
2 Atlantic
3 Flamingo
4 Mermaid
5 Golden Fish Guest House
6 Municipal Caravan Park
7 Municipal Bunglaows
8 Probst Bakery & Cafe
9 Lalainya's
10 Belinda's

hands several times over the centuries. It is also a vital feeding ground for flamingos and shorebirds in southern Africa. The Walvis Bay Wetlands and Nature Reserve is a wonderful place for bird watchers and the proximity to Namib-Naukluft Park make it an ideal place for those wishing to explore the natural wonders of this area. Walvis is also frequented by anglers who fish off the long, often deserted stretches of beach.

History

Bartholomeu Dias discovered Walvis Bay in 1487 but not much interest was taken in the area until some American whalers used the bay in the late 1700s. Soon after, the Dutch raised their flag here for a couple of years until Britain, realizing the importance of safe passage for ships sailing around the cape, seized control of the area and eventually annexed it in the mid-1800s as Germany began to assert its influence in southwestern Africa. It became part of the Cape Colony and was administered from the Cape until 1922, when administration was transferred to South West Africa—a territory that the League of Nations mandated to South Africa.

Realizing that Namibia was soon to become independent, Prime Minister Vorster of South Africa reverted the enclave to control of the Cape Province in 1977.

When Namibia became independent in 1990, South Africa retained control of the Walvis Bay colony (which includes the islands off the coast of Namibia) over Namibain objections. Walvis Bay is Namibia's only deep water port and is vital to the economy of the country. Sovereignty of Walvis Bay shifted in late 1992 when, after negotiations, it came under a joint South African-Namibian administration. This was one of a series of steps designed to eventually give Namibia full control. On March 1, 1994, Walvis Bay officially became part of Namibia, ending South Africa's control here.

The mainstay of Walvis bay's economy is fishing and port activities, which are sometimes evidenced by the stench of canning factories when the wind blows the wrong way.

Tourist Infromation—Tel. 5981

Inside the large municipal building at 12th Rd. and 10th St. is the tourist information office, which can set you up with lodging and tell you about all the sites around Walvis. They are open from 8-1 and 2-5 M-Th. and Fridays 8-1 and 2-4:30.

Places to Stay

Hotel Casa Mia—Tel. 5975/6 7th St. between 17th and 18th Rds.

The Casa Mia consists of 23 semi-luxurious rooms with TVs and telephones. They have a good restaurant and bar and are very busy— book ahead, especially during holidays.

Rates: Single R143, Suite R221; Double R186, Suite R264. All B&B.

Atlantic Hotel—Tel. 2811 7th St. between 10th & 12th Rds.

One of the Namib Sun chain of hotels, they have 18 deluxe rooms and a restaurant/ bar.

Rates: Single R109, Double R191 B&B.

Flamingo Hotel—Tel. 3011 7th St. & 10th Rd.

Good, clean rooms with TVs and phones. Restaurant with meals at R20-35.

Rates: Single R95, Double R130, Family R118 plus R48 for extra beds. B&B.

Mermaid Hotel—Tel. 4862 6th St.

There are 26 basic but clean rooms and a restaurant. TV R10 extra. Rates: Single R55, Double R82, Family R136 sleeps 5 B&B.

Golden Fish Guest House—Tel. 2775 7th St. between 16th & 17th Rds.

This rather plain and clean lodging is a good deal if you have more than a couple of people to share the cost. Some suites have sitting rooms and very large showers! Breakfast is an extra R15 on request.

Rates: They have a variety of rooms, from R50 to R90 depending on bath facilities.

Municipal Caravan Park—Tel. 5981 1st St. near lagoon

Located a stone's throw from the lagoon and the Esplanade, there are also tennis courts and a swimming pool next door which you can use for a nominal fee. You can take your wash to the laundromat at the Municipal Bungalows if you need to. They are quite busy Dec.-April with lots of anglers coming to the area.

Rates: Camp or caravan sites R10 plus R1.50 per person; electrical hookup R1.65.

Municipal Bungalows—Tel. 6145 or 5981

The municipality maintains 21 5-bed and 5 7-bed bungalows south of town on the Esplanade overlooking the lagoon. They are attractive and very well equipped. A R100 deposit may be required.

Rates: 5-bed bungalow R88, 7-bed bungalow R121

Places to Eat

Probst Bakery and Café—Tel. 2744 9th St. & 12th Rd.

This is the place to lunch inside or outside with a fantastic bakery and good German food. Very popular and recommended.

Lalainya's—Tel. 2574 7th St. between 10th & 11th

A fine dining establishment that specializes in seafood dishes at R20-55. It is owned by the same people that run the Flamingo Hotel.

The restaurant at the Casa Mia Hotel—Tel. 5975/6

This has been given great reviews by townspeople and often requires reservations. They serve seafood and a variety of other dishes for R15-50 with R50 dishes including crayfish.

Belinda's—Tel. 6455 8th St.

If you want pizza (R15-20), hamburgers, snacks or breakfast, try this small eatery.

Lion's Den—Langstrand resort

Located halfway between Walvis and Swakopmund, they reputedly have enormous portions for a reasonable price.

Things to Do

Tour and Safari Companies

Levo Pleasure and Fishing Tours—Tel. (0642) 7555

An upmarket tour company based in Walvis Bay that specializes in fishing tours and has their own guest house in Langstrand.

Gloriosa Safaris—Tel. (0642) 6300

Small group tours around Namibia.

Cinema

There is a movie theater on 10th St., but the drive-in is now closed.

Walvis Bay Lagoon and Promenade

Most of the lower half of the Walvis Bay area is the Wetlands and Nature Reserve which is one of the two best places in the world for flamingo watching along with Kenya's Lake Nakuru. The lagoon supports 66 percent of southern African population of Greater Flamingos and 82 percent of the Lesser Flamingos. Greater Flamingos are whiter and have a pink beak, while Lesser Flamingos are a bit smaller, pinker and have a dark-red beak which appears black. They eat by filtering out tiny organisms from the mud and sand—watch them as they dip their heads below the water. Flamingos don't actually breed here, but its importance as a feeding ground for them and other intra-African migrants is unequaled. Just one of the excellent places to birdwatch is the Promenade, a 4 km. long walkway that follows the lagoon shore.

Bird Watching Area

At the end of 13th St. past the waterworks take a left on the dirt road to the bird sanctuary where you'll see flamingos, pelicans, Egyptian geese and many other species in the small ponds. There is also a viewing tower for a better look.

Dune 7

The largest dune in Walvis Bay at 95 meters. People sometimes paraglide and ski down this dune although they say skiing down it is very dangerous. To get there follow the Rooikop road out and you'll see it on your left.

Pelican Point

There is a 4-wheel drive track out to the lighthouse and seal colony on Pelican Point. Be very cautious of the tides if you plan to go and check locally on conditions.

Paaltjies-Fishing

Pronounced *paal' kees*, this is a popular fishing spot on the coast south of the Salt Works. You can get here with a 2-wheel drive but don't go past it without a 4-wheel drive.

Langstrand (Long Beach)

A popular resort halfway between Walvis Bay and Swakopmund, this 99-site camp/caravan park gets full on the Christmas holidays. Activities here include fishing, swimming in the cement tidal pools (though the water is a bit cold) and walking along the beach. A reputedly excellent restaurant here is called the Lion's Den. There are few bungalow or guest house accommodations if you're not set up for camping, but ask at the office as they may have something during slower times.

Rates: Camping R11 per site plus R1.50 per person; electrical hookup R1.50. There is water and a braai pit at each site but no other cooking facilities. A laundromat and ablution blocks are close by.

Bungalows—There is one 4-bed flat for R88 and a 2-bed flat for R50 fully equipped except for towels. Day visitors are charged R2 per vehicle and R2 per adult.

Office Hours: M-F 8-1 and 2-5, Sat.& Sun. 10-11 though there is someone available other hours
Restaurant—The Lion's Den is closed for dinner Sun. & Mon. and only has lunch during the holiday seasons and on weekends.

Dolphin Beach (Dolfynstrand)

This is a water fun place for kids of all ages situated a few kilometers south of Langstrand. There are pools, a long water slide and many picnic areas.

Getting to Walvis Bay

From Swakopmund, take Breite St. south and you'll come to the Swakop River bridge within a few hundred meters. The main tarred road continues south for about 30 kilometers to Walvis Bay past beautiful sand dunes which are the beginning of the huge sand sea that stretches south along the coast.

This is a beautiful drive along a desolate coast, so stop and enjoy the beach or the dunes closeby.

Travel Onward

There are flights from Walvis to Cape Town, Windhoek and Joburg, as well as buses that go to Windhoek.

Namib-Nauklauft Park
(Northern Section)

NOTE: Sandwich Harbor and the northern section are covered in this chapter, while Sesriem, Sossusvlei and the Naukluft Mountains are covered under Southern Namibia.

Sandwich Harbor

Situated about 40 km. south of Walvis Bay, this area was once used as a whaling station by American whalers. You must have a 4-wheel drive vehicle to get here and a permit obtainable from the DNC office, the Hans Kriess gas station in Swakopmund, CWB or Suidwes gas stations in Walvis Bay.

To get to the harbor take 10th St. south and continue on past the lagoon and towards the salt works. Follow the dirt road and the signs *Sandvis* left past the salt works onto the flat plains of the Kuiseb delta. Do not go off the main track onto the dark oily looking sand because even if you have a 4-wheel drive you will get stuck and stranded until you can get a tow. If you keep to the main track, which gets quite wide in places and becomes 10 lanes or so, you will eventually come to the old border fence. The permit is required beyond this point. Stay on the tracks that are very close to the beach about 20 km. or so, being careful not to drive onto the oily looking sand until you reach the Sandwich Harbor fence where you must stop and park.

The massive sand dunes come right down to the lagoon where there is an abundance of bird life, depending on the time of year. The lagoon stretches on for several kilometers south and much of the birdlife is frequently beyond the first

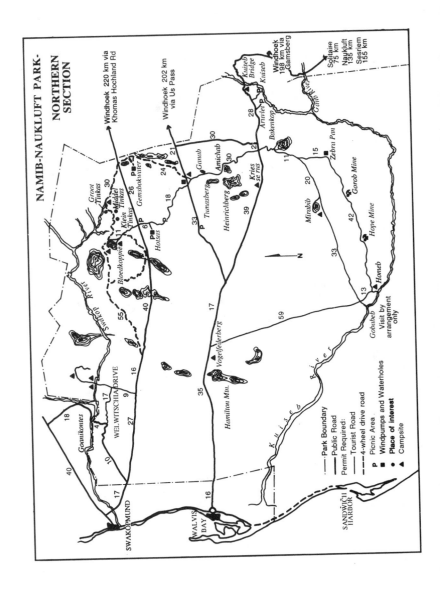

NAMIB-NAUKLUFT PARK- NORTHERN SECTION

lagoon. Jackals can also be spotted pacing back and forth on the beach side looking for food. Walking among the towering dunes is a good way to get an overview of the area and will offer stunning views of the lagoon and the coastline. Water percolating through the dunes from the Kuiseb River helps reduce the salinity of the lagoons so that reeds and grasses grow on the fringes.

Unfortunately, camping is not permitted here as the lagoon area is only open from 6AM to 8PM. If you are very clean about how you camp, you could walk from the last place where vehicles are allowed and hike down the beach and camp, but there are no facilities and you would have to be extremely careful to leave this unspoiled area exactly as you found it.

Fishing is permitted along the beach but not in the lagoon itself as it is a fish breeding area. The fishing season is closed from January 25 to April 15.

The Northern Section

This section of the park is characterized by barren gravel plains through which run desert rivers with a contrasting abundance of plant and animal life. The scenery can change after good rains when seeds blown from inland germinate and with shallow root systems live off the moisture from the fog.

The Khan, Swakop and Kuiseb rivers cross this part of the park and though dry most of the year, support birds, ostrich, oryx and other wildlife. An oryx, for example, can live in the middle of this desert. Though you may see one lying in the open plain with nothing edible or drinkable in sight, it must only walk to the nearest river bed to graze. With its well adapted physiology for withstanding heat, it thrives in this forbidding climate. As for water, ostrich, springbok, oryx, giraffe and zebra can go for months without water, obtaining enough from the plants they consume. Insects, as well, have adapted to this unique ecosystem, using the fog that bathes the western regions of the park to sustain them. Certain species of beetles do headstands in the sand so that the lower body collects the fog's moisture to obtain the water they need.

This park provides a wonderful opportunity to observe true desert life; in fact there is a desert research station at Gobabeb (closed to the public, except by special appointment) that closely studies desert ecology in this unique area.

Be sure to bring plenty of water for the trip as there are few water sources in the park. It's also a good idea to bring spare tires, tire repair kit, pump, jack and tools, as traffic and possible help are sparse in many areas and you could be waiting days for willing passers-by.

Getting There

You can get to the northern section most easily from Swakopmund or Walvis Bay as they are both just a few kilometers from the park border. Entering from Swakopmund, you take the main Windhoek tarred road a few kilometers east of town until you see the turnoff for Namib-Naukluft Park and Welwitschia Drive. You'll soon pass the Swakop River—watch for flamingos and other birds here. After about 15 km. or so you'll come to the Welwitschia Drive turnoff.

Welwitschia Drive

The Welwitschia drive in Namib-Naukluft Park is a way to explore by car many natural and man-made phenomenon of the desert culminating with the largest welwitschia plant we've ever seen. Some of the sights corresponding to the numbered stone markers on the drive are not clearly visible, but the main attractions here are the Swakop River and its strangely beautiful canyon, the desert plains and the large number of Welwitschia plants. At point number 10 is a river-bed campground which you can use (toilets and tables only—no water). Ostrich and springbok are seen frequently near the camping sites. Past this campground is another new campground situated on the windy welwitschia plains that is dug in below the desert surface to give protection from the wind (again toilets and tables only).

The drive ends at the huge 1,500 year old welwitschia specimen that has been fenced off to prevent damage. Permits are needed for this drive and are obtainable at the DNC or tourist offices in Swakopmund and at several service stations in Walvis Bay and Swakopmund.

Below are brief descriptions of each of the numbered markers along Welwitschia Drive:

1) **Lichens**—there is a subtle depression running perpendicular to the road where lichen is growing on the rocks, surviving only on sunlight and the fog's mist.

2) **Dollar bush and ink bush**—the dollar bush with its coin-like leaves and the ink bush can survive on the 20 mm. of precipitation the area receives yearly. You'll see better specimens elsewhere.

3) **Wagon tracks**—these tracks made by ox wagons driving on the desert surface decades ago are evidence of the fragility of the desert and the importance of staying on the marked roads.

4) **An impressive view** of the Swakop river valley, created 460 million years ago.

5) **More lichen**—it appears black, green or orange on the rocks. Pour water on the shriveled black lichen and watch it unfold in slow motion.

6) **Another fantastic view** of the Swakop river valley.

7) Rusted equipment left after WW I. Please do not remove any of the pieces.

8) **Dolerite dikes**—looking toward the yellow hills you'll see a black stripe which is an intrusion of molten rock that pushed up through the sedimentary rock surrounding it. Many valuable mineral deposits are discovered in such intrusions.

9) **Another dolerite intrusion** is visible after you turn towards the river.

10) **The Swakop river** is a dry river bed most of the time though it occasionally floods. There is always water beneath the surface as the plant life attests. You can picnic or camp here. A little farther on is an-

other campsite dug into the ground on the barren, windy plains.

11) **Welwitchia plants** dot the landscape where you leave the valley. The male and female plants are identified for you here.

12) **Huge welwitschia plant** after a long flat stretch of road and a sharp right turn is thought to be 1,500 years old.

13) **Abandoned mine** worked by hand in the 50s is visible if you head back through points 11 through 8 to point 13. Parts of the desert show the ghastly effects of mining. Now there laws pertaining to repair of the landscape when mines are shut down.

Goanikontes—Tel. (0641) 366 or 4434

Things are starting to happen at Goanikontes since Archie "Tortoise" van der Ploeg and his family took over this palm-covered oasis on the Swakop River. There is currently camping and a few strange igloo-shaped bungalows you can rent. The Namib Magic art studio features the van der Ploeg's and other local artists' works. Beside the small pond there may be live music on weekends. A large garden has been started and the whole place is solar powered. Wildlife can be seen along the lush riverbed year round. Camping and bungalows were ridiculously cheap when we stopped by and even if prices are raised it will still be quite an interesting place to visit. Call to see what is currently happening at Goanikontes. To get there start on the Welwitschia drive tour. After you leave the main road and begin the tour you'll come across a road after 10 km. that leads down into the canyon. It's only 4 km. down to Goanikontes.

Northeast Namib Park

After entering the main C28 road from Welwitschia Drive, continue another 16 km. where a 4X4 road goes all the way to the eastern edge of the park. Some of the 4X4 roads are negotiable with a high clearance 2-wheel drive but ask at the nature conservation office about which ones are passable. If you have a 2-wheel drive vehicle, continue another 40 km. to the Bloedkoppie turnoff. Turn left and continue about 10 km. to the campsites surrounding the granite inselberg. Bloedkoppie is a beautiful granite outcrop, koppie or inselberg, (depending on which language you speak). There are many weird rock formations worth investigating and you may see zebra, springbok or oryx as tracks are all over. From the campsites and especially higher up on the Bloedkoppie there are beautiful views of the desert and the Kokerboom trees that grow sparsely on the surrounding plains. There are campsites (just tables and braai pits) and a few toilets around the entire base of the outcrop.

On the right of the main road opposite the Bloedkoppie turnoff is the road to Hotsas and points south in the park. After traveling 6 km. turn right again and it's 2 km. to the waterhole with a viewing shelter. Ostrich and springbok often run away as you approach, so wait for them to come back to the hole to drink.

Groot Tinkas is about 15 km. from Bloedkoppie or 18 km. from the turnoff near the eastern park boundary. There are a few campsites in a rocky valley with tables, braai pits and a toilet. About 1 km. away is a small dam that looks strange in the middle of the desert but it is there to impound flood waters.

A new campsite several kilometers northeast of Groot Tinkas is reachable by a track heading in that direction. At **Klein Tinkas** are the graves of two German soldiers and a nature walk through the surrounding desert and on to **Middel Tinkas.**

Farther east is **Gemsbokwater**, which can be reached by 4X4 about 10 km. from the main C28 road. There is a waterhole fed by a windmill pump and a shaded picnic table here, as well as **braai** pit and toilet. Many desert animals can be seen here including the lappet-faced vulture, which nests in the short trees. Continuing south, you come to the D1982 road which you cross to arrive at Ganab 4 km. later. The desert plains are often full of ostrich running about, but it's hard to get close to these shy creatures.

If you enter Namib-Naukluft Park from Walvis Bay, take Eighteenth St. east towards Rooikop Airport and you will pass Dune 7 on your way. The scenery gets very stark from here on and is punctuated only by a few rocky outcrops. It takes a while to get used to this beautiful barrenness, but you will have plenty of time to think about it as you drive. The first large outcrop you come to near the road is Vogelfederberg or Birdsfeather Mountain where you can camp. Climbing Vogelfederberg or any other koppie (rocky outcrop) gives you a view of the barren gravel plains.

You can either continue straight on towards Kuiseb canyon and the camping spot at the inselberg called Mirabib or turn right (south) towards the Kuiseb river and the beginning of the great sand sea that covers most of the southern Namib desert.

Turning south you will pass close to the Gobabeb Desert Research Station, where scientists are closely studying the unique ecosystem and the life that has adapted to the harsh environment. This research station is closed to the general public but has an open house once a year or so. Descending down the ancient carved gullies to the river, you will come to the Kuiseb and the Homeb camp which has several sites near the small goat farm of a Khoikhoi family. Toilets and picnic tables are provided under the shade of thorn trees. From here you see the beginnings of the massive peach colored sand dune fields on the southern river bank. The contrasts at this natural boundary are fascinating: in the midst of the dry, desolate plains and the sand ocean is the comparative lushness of the Kuiseb with its many bird species. Take a walk in the sandy river bed with your binoculars to observe the birds that live or migrate here.

On the way out of Homeb, there are a couple of abandoned mines, Hope and Gorob, where the remains of operations can be seen. Further on at the Zebra pan, there is water available for both you and the animals. Ostrich and oryx can be seen drinking or lounging nearby.

Kuiseb Canyon

Continuing on from the zebra pan, you'll come to the main cross-Namib road after about 26 km. where you turn right towards the Kuiseb Canyon. There are a couple of viewpoints of the canyon, one of which has a short trail to the rock overhang used by two German geologists during World War II to hide from South African troops. The fascinating story of how they survived the years is told in the book *The Sheltering Desert*. The panorama reminds the viewer of the aeons of erosion needed to form the canyon and the gullies leading down to it.

West Coast Recreation Area

This is a region that is popular with anglers and anyone who likes the lure of the sea. There are several campsites along the beach which are particularly busy during Christmas holidays.

Henties Bay

This small tourist town attracts fisherman from all over southern Africa. The fishing is fantastic—caljoun, cabeljou, steenbras and crayfish. Most people fish right off the beach, though it is possible to take a boat out for deep water fish. Crayfish can be caught on the shallow reefs off the southern end of town, but you need a wetsuit as the water is never too warm. The area can get quite crowded during school holidays and is often full from September to May. During the December school holidays 15,000 people may descend on Henties Bay for the fishing and to escape the inland heat. It can be difficult to find a place to stay during this time, so book ahead.

For other accommodations, contact the few real estate

agents for a weekend house or longer term rental. There are also a couple of take-aways that stay open late for snacks. Henties Bay has a lovely golf course with sand fairways and grass greens situated in the riverbed that divides the town in two. There is at least one 24 hour gas station here as well.

Where to Stay
DeDuine Hotel—Tel. (06442) 1
The only hotel in town has basic rooms and a nice adjoining restaurant with good oysters and fresh fish.

Rates: Single R60-70, Double R 90-100 B&B
Die Oord—Tel. 165 or 239
This group of 15 bungalows is located on the north side of town over the river. The bungalows are fully equipped except for towels and it's just a short walk to the beach.

Rates: Single R55, two bedroom R70, three bedroom R90, extra beds R10
Desert Rose—Tel. 181
For luxury accommodations, the Desert Rose has fully furnished, fully equipped condo type townhouses with verandas overlooking the beach. They can be rented on a short or long term basis. Call for rates.

Where to Eat
De Duine
The restaurant at De Duine Hotel serves excellent fresh fish and oysters as well as meats and has a small salad bar. Next to the dining room there are pool tables, 21 tables and a lively bar.
Spitzkoppe Restaurant & Bar
Here you can get excellent fresh seafood and steaks in a cafe-like atmosphere. They have take-aways on one side of the restaurant and a popular bar on the other with pool, 21 and darts.

Getting to Henties Bay
From Swakopmund, take the C34 north along the ocean about 75 km. This road is a salt road. From Windhoek you

have basically two options. Take the B1 north then stay on the road past Okahandja where it becomes the B2 and follow the road to Swakopmund and proceed from there. Alternately, take the D1918 about 25 km. west of Usakos on the B2, where you'll take a dirt road. There is an opportunity to see the Spitzkoppe Mtn. along this route.

Mile 4 Caravan Park—Tel. (0641) 61781

Just up the beach from Swakopmund, there are campsites with electricity available.

Rates: Sites R10 (Electricity R5), Adults R4, Vehicles R10 one-time charge

Mile 14, Mile 72 and Jakkalsputz Campsites

All of these are beachfront campsites with only basic amenities. Hot showers are R1 each and water is 10 cents/liter. Mile 72 has a petrol station. These are popular fishing spots especially during December holidays.

Rates: R10 per group (Max. 8 people, 2 vehicles and 1 caravan).

Cape Cross

Located about 55 km. north of Henties Bay, Cape Cross is the home of the Cape fur seal. To get there take the Terrace Bay/Torra Bay road north until you see the sign for Cape Cross; then it's a short drive to the office, where you must sign in and pay the entrance fee. If you can handle the stench of the seals, it is well worth the trip. Actually, the smell does become bearable after a while but it doesn't go away, even after you've left Cape Cross—it seems to stick to your clothes. Don't let this deter you, however, as the mass of seals of all sizes is a sight to see.

This is the spot where in 1486 Diego Cão, the Portuguese sailor, first landed, presumably the first European to set foot on the coast of Namibia. Here he erected a cross in honor of John I of Portugal. Two replicas of that cross stand at Cape Cross today, one ordered built by Kaiser Wilhelm in the late 1800s to replace the weathered original and another built in 1980 by the National Monuments Council.

Cape Fur Seals - Cape Cross Namibia

The real attraction here is the seals, however. The seals you see are Cape fur seals that have external ears, as opposed to true seals that lack external ears. These seals do not migrate and are here year round although they do take long trips up and down the coast. There are approximately 80,000 to 100,000 seals here at one time, the number fluctuating as pups are weaned and go out to sea. Adult males come in great numbers around mid-October when they arrive for mating. They form territories and expend a lot of energy defending territory and herding females into harems of 5 to 25. The bulls can weigh up to 360 kilograms but average about half that weight, while the cows weigh about 75 kilograms. Soon after the males arrive, the females, already pregnant from last breeding season, come onshore to give birth to a single pup within the bull's territory. Within a week of giving birth they mate again but the embryo remains dormant for three months before development begins thus making the gestation period 9 months.

Most of the pups are born November-December and suckle for up to a year. They begin to go out to sea to hunt for their favorite foods—pilchards, squid and crustaceans—within their first year. However, approximately 27 percent of the pups don't make it due to predation by jackals and brown hyenas and crushing by other seals.

The fur of the seal has two layers. An inner layer of short, thick fur is kept dry by an outer layer of long, coarse hairs. Blubber and the air trapped in the short fur keep the seal warm in the cold water. Seals eat about 8 percent of their body weight per day, and as in many other countries the commercial fishing industry sees them as competition for food resources. There is no plan to reduce the numbers but the herd at Cape Cross is culled to keep the population constant. Seal skin souvenirs are sold at a little curio shack just north of the office.

Seals are generally disturbed by people and although it is possible to get very close to them behind the wall, it is unwise to try to go over or around the wall to get closer. You might cause a stampede that would injure the seals, especially the young. They are very photogenic and truly interesting.

Fees: Cape Cross entrance fee R5 per Adult, R5 per car. Hours 10am- 5 pm.; closed Fridays. No accommodations.

Mile 108

At mile 108 there is a Nature Conservation camping site on the beach that is frequented by anglers trying their luck in the rich fishing grounds off the Namib coast. There is a small store there that sells beer, wine and liquor, plus fishing tackle in addition to a few other basic supplies during the December holidays. It is open 8-1 and 4-7. Petrol is available from 8-1 and 2-6. (You can usually obtain petrol and supplies after hours.) There are long-drop toilets on the beach and wood is available for R2 per bundle. Rates: Camping R10 per site, Showers R1, Water 10 cents/liter.

Shipwreck *Winston*

About 20 km. north of the Mile 108 camping area, there is a small sign that points to the shipwreck *Winston*, a 4 km. drive to the beach. It's a small piece of rusting remains lying in the surf, one of the few wrecks which gave the Skeleton Coast its name that is accessible to tourists.

Road to Brandberg West

Some 10 km. south of the Mile 108 camping area is the D2303 road to the old Brandberg Wes mine. You can explore the mine or the nearby Ugab River (see Kaokoland-Damaraland). The road crosses some incredibly barren dark red-brown landscape punctuated with welwitschia plants.

Skeleton Coast Park

This wilderness area has gained international fame lately from several sources, most notably the February, 1992 *National Geographic* article about the region. It is an isolated and desolate region of barren gravel plains and hills crossed by relatively lush riverbeds. Occasionally, wildlife such as lion will come to the beach from these riverbeds although this is a rare occurrence. Brown hyena and jackal as well as Cape fur seal are a relatively common sight. During good rain years, the rivers can flood from far-off storms and isolate this region. It is a very foggy and often windy stretch of coast offering good fishing and interesting sights for the desert buff. The park gets its name from the skeletons of shipwrecks scattered about the long coastline, remnants of earlier days when ships got lost in the fog and ran aground. Even though some of these wrecks can be seen few are signposted.

The desert ecology here is extremely fragile and has suffered recently from tracks left by off road driving. Think twice before heading off on untracked desert—not only can it bring you a fine, but come back in 50 years or so and your tracks will still be visible! Contrary to what you may think, the wind accentuates rather than covers the tracks with sand. Please stay on the roads to preserve this unique wilderness.

NOTE: To enter the Skeleton Coast Park (anywhere past the Ugab River) you must have a permit from the DNC booking office in Windhoek (Tel. 36975). Additional booking must be made for stays at Torra or Terrace Bay. You must arrive at the Ugab River gate by 3pm and the checkpoint at Springbokwasser by 5pm on the way to Torra or Terrace Bay.

No pets or motorcycles allowed. Entry fee is R8 for adults and R10 per car.

Ugab River Hiking Trail

There is an opportunity to hike from the Skeleton Coast up the Ugab River exploring the fauna and flora of this ecologically fascinating region. There is a hike every 2nd and 4th Tuesday of every month which starts from the gate at the Ugab River crossing about 200km north of Swakopmund. You need reservations well in advance, a medical certificate issued within the past 40 days, and all your own food and equipment. The group size is 6-8 and it cost R80 per person. Reservations are made at the main tourist office in Windhoek- Tel. 36975.

Torra Bay

A primitive campsite open only during December and January, this is similar to other sites farther south. It costs R10 for a campsite which must be booked in Windhoek. (See above). Used primarily by anglers.

Terrace Bay

The furthest north on the Namibian coast where you can stay without being on an expensive fly-in safari, Terrace Bay is open year round and features bungalows with full board, a shop, petrol station and freezer space for the fish you catch! You can travel up to 12 miles north of here, but beyond that a special permit is necessary. The facility is used by anglers and beachcombers and is a windy, foggy desolate area. Perfect for some!

Rates: Single R140, Double R230, full board.

Skeleton Coast Wilderness Area

The only way to visit the northern section of the Skeleton Coast past Terrace Bay is on an expensive fly-in safari with the concessionaire. We have heard that this is a fascinating trip, but at R4600 per person it is a little exclusive. If you are interested, call (061) 224248 or 51269 for more information.

CHAPTER 9

Northern Region

The northern region embraces Etosha National Park with its huge game populations, the plains to the north and the hilly thorn tree savannah to the south and east extending to the Botswana border. It also includes Kaudom Park and the surrounding area where the ancient Kalahari sands form the base of a lush wild area still populated by the San or Bushmen people.

Otjiwarongo

This cattle farming town is a crossroads for both the highway and train line, with road routes going northwest towards Etosha's west gate and northeast towards Etosha's east gate. The main attraction in the area is Waterberg Plateau Park situated some 100 km. by road east of town.

Places to Stay

Hotel Hamburgerhof—Tel. (0651), 2520 Bahnhof St.

One of the Namib Sun hotel chain, the hotel also serves as Otjiwarongo's unofficial tourist information center. They have nice rooms, a restaurant featuring locally produced crocodile cocktails and a beer garden. Alas, no swimming pool.

Rates: Single R121, Double R176 B&B.

Rent-a-Room—Tel. 2517

Since the Hotel Brumme closed, Rent-a-Room has used some of the space for inexpensive accommodations. It's across from the old Hotel Brumme on Bahnhof St. and rooms

NAMIBIA

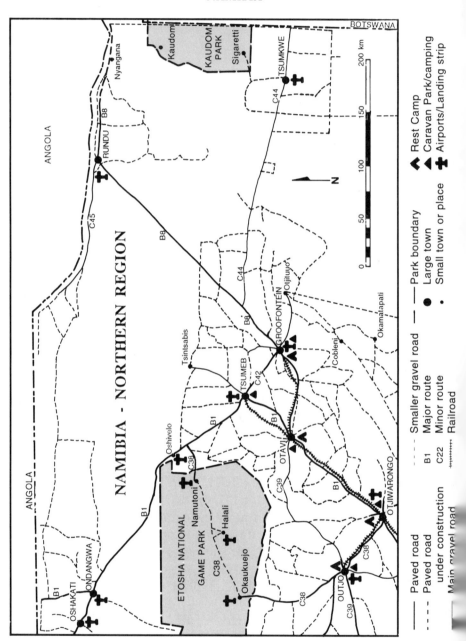

are clean and well appointed with their own baths, coffee machines and fans. Rumor has it that the Brumme may open again soon, though.

Rates: Single R60, Double R95.

Otjibamba Lodge—Tel. 3133 or 3139

Located south of town a couple of km. on the B1 highway, this lovely lodge has a wonderful restaurant with first class food, a small swimming pool and a very friendly staff. They own a large adjoining piece of land which serves as their private game park for guests. Ask for a walking or driving safari through the small park where you can get very close to kudu, springbok, giraffe, wildebeest, several species of birds and other game that are being introduced. This is a very relaxing place just a few hours from Windhoek and can serve as a point from which to see Etosha, Caprivi, Kaokoland, Bushmanland or any of the local sights, such as the crocodile farm in town. The rooms are new and very comfortable, a real bargain.

Rates: Single R125, Double R160 B&B

Municipal Campground

Next to the croc farm (which is well fenced) is a small municipal campground which has a few sites. It was unattended when we arrived but there was some grass on which to pitch a tent, ablution blocks, a washing area and some trees for shade. If no one is there just make camp and presumably someone will come to collect the fees. This was not one of the nicer campgrounds we saw, but it's the cheapest place in town if you're set up to camp.

Rates: Campsites R15 plus R2.50 per person, Day visitors R1.25

Places to Eat

Hotel Hamburgerhof

An interesting menu featuring crocodile dishes including their famous croc cocktail. Crocodile tastes something like a cross between chicken and fish and is worth a try if you like large reptiles.

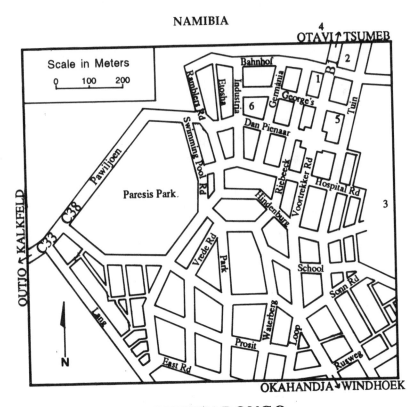

NAMIBIA

OTJIWARONGO

1 Hamburger Hotel   4 Prime Rib Restaraunt

2 Rent-a-Room   5 Bakery

3 Crocodile Farm   6 Alt Otji

Prime Rib Restaurant

Next to Get Lucky Take Aways on the edge of town towards
Otavi, this new diner has a variety of meat dishes and pizzas.

Jacaranda Take Away

At the Mobil station near the middle of town, this is basically a roadside diner with a store and a variety of inexpensive meals. Open 7 days from 8am-10pm.

Bakery

There's a decent bakery on St. Georges St. a block off the

main drag that has light meals, snacks and, of course, baked goods.

Alt Otji

At the corner of St. Georges and Kort Sts., this is the local German club which serves lunch for R10-20 and dinner for R15-30. They have quite an interesting menu with some German specialties. Open 7 days 10-3:30 and 5-11. Live music monthly and bar dice constantly. Tel. 3256.

Things to Do

Crocodile Farm

About 2,000 Nile Crocodile inhabit the croc farm, mostly young ones under 2 meters. The breeders, behemoths up to 4 meters and over 100 years old are kept in a separate fenced pen for viewing with the sign "Enter at your own risk" prominently posted. There they sit statue-like, some with their mouths open to regulate body temperature. The crocs are slaughtered at about 2 years for their skins and the meat is sold locally. There are separate areas for incubating the eggs and raising the young crocs at different stages of their short, reptilian life. They are cold-blooded, mate in the water and have two rows of razor sharp teeth.

Talk to the owner who is more than happy to give information. It's best to get there Saturday just before noon for the once-a-week feeding of waste meat from the local abbatoir, a gruesome sight but well worth the R6 you're charged. Picnics are also possible on the grounds. Open M-F 9-4 and Sat. & Sun. 11-2.

To Get to Otjiwarongo

Take the B1 north out of Windhoek. When you get to Okahandja take the third exit into town before the road curves west. Cross the railroad tracks and turn left at the T intersection. Continue another 160 km. along a very straight highway.

Waterberg Plateau Park

Waterberg Plateau Park is a one of a kind conservation

area; the park lies 200 meters up on a steep island-like plateau which essentially confines wildlife, allowing for introduced and endangered species to be bred successfully. It's the only place in Namibia that you'll find white rhino, for example.

The park was proclaimed a game reserve in 1972 with the aim of boosting the eland population. Now it is used specifically for protection of the country's rare and endangered animals. It is the only remaining home of breeding Cape vultures; in Namibia they face extinction due to poisoning and bush encroachment. There is a "vulture restaurant" where the small colony of about 20 birds is fed animal carcasses.

Due to the wild nature of the park, tourism is extremely limited. You are not allowed to drive your own vehicle around the plateau—the only way to see it is to go on special guided tours arranged by the office or to take the wilderness hike. (See below)

Bernabe de la Bat Rest Camp

Named after one of Namibia's foremost conservationists, it is situated part of the way up the east slope leading to the plateau. You can choose between comfortable bungalows, caravan sites, or camping. There are a few steep trails leading up to the plateau where the view extends east towards the plains that lead to the Botswana border. You are not allowed further than the edge of the plateau, however, unless you're on the wilderness hiking trail.

Rates: 3 bed bungalows R80, 4 bed bungalows R120, Camping R25 per group (Max 8 people, 2 vehicles and 1 caravan) plus R5 per person and R5 a vehicle

To Get There

From Windhoek, take the B1 north towards Otjiwarongo. About 22 km. before you reach Otjiwarongo, you'll see the sign for Waterberg Plateau Park. Turn and follow the C22 for about 40 km. then take a left again following the signs. You'll see the plateau on your left as you make the short drive to the gate.

Waterberg Wilderness Trail

From April-November there is a guided hike through the park every 2nd, 3rd and 4th Thursday. You have to bring all your own gear and the group size is 6-8 which is difficult to arrange unless you happen to be in a group that size. Try posting a notice at the tourist information offices in Windhoek, or if you happen to be there the night before a hike, join an existing group. The hike begins Thursday at 4pm and ends Sunday afternoon. The cost is R80 per person. You must book well in advance for this hike as it is very popular. There is a small group of white rhino on the plateau as well as other imported animals and native game. It is a rare chance to see these creatures on foot in a wilderness area.

Outjo

A stopover for those on the way to Etosha, this small farming community has two fairly nice hotels, 24 hr petrol, and a few well stocked stores.

Places to Stay

Onduri Hotel

Located "downtown" this is a tourist hotel popular with organized tours and is comfortable but not remarkable.

Rates: Single R100-150, Double R160-228 B&B

Etosha Hotel

Located outside central Outjo, this hotel is more African in design and is quite well appointed with a lovely restaurant, which, though a little expensive, has a nice atmosphere—the "house" pets will come and visit you if you're not careful—though the large, friendly Rottweiler is a sight.

Rates: Single R110, Double R212 B&B

Ongava Lodge & Game Reserve—Tel. (06542), Toshari 3413

The Ongava (rhino) Lodge is a brand new luxury lodge on Etosha's doorstep. Built on 30,000 hectares previously used as a cattle farm and bordering the park, Ongava consists of 10 luxurious thatched bungalows and an open air restaurant and bar, all on a small rocky outcrop overlooking the plains below. They feature game drives in Etosha, walking trails on their property, a pool and a first rate menu. Attention to design is evident in the natural rock and thatch construction of many of the buildings. Ongava is a bit on the expensive side, but it's the only full-service accommodations in its class near the west end of the park.

Rest Camp
There is a small rest camp south of town on the road towards Otjiwarongo where you can camp inexpensively.

Getting to Outjo
Take the B1 north out of Windhoek, going into Okahandja on the third exit as the road curves west. Turn left at the T and pass through Otjiwarongo, where you take the C38 to Outjo.

Etosha National Park

This is Namibia's most famous attraction, known for its herds of roaming game that are found throughout the flat expanse. The name Etosha comes from Herero and means *large pan*. Situated 1,000 meters above sea level and covering 22,270 sq. km. (8560 sq. miles) this is one of Africa's largest game parks.

The pan itself, a large, white, often dry lake bed covers about 4590 sq. km. (1764 sq. miles) and is thought to be a former inland lake that dried up, leaving salt deposits on its bed and accounting for its sterile surface. When the pan fills due to heavy rains, the water can be highly saline and undrinkable. The wild game prefer drinking from the perennial springs that line the edge of the pan. The game seen are every bit as spectacular as those in the more famous game reserves in East Africa but the difference here is that you don't feel as if you're part of a crowd. You are also free to drive through the park at your own pace and stop for as long as you like at the waterholes. There is a sense of freedom here to come and go and spend as much time as you like without a fortune in park fees, lodging or guides. You also have the option, how-

ETOSHA NATIONAL PARK

Northern Region

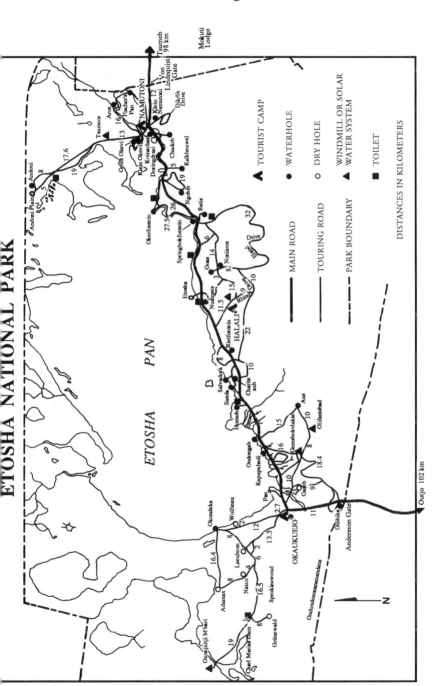

Legend:

- ◣ TOURIST CAMP
- ● WATERHOLE
- ○ DRY HOLE
- ▲ WINDMILL OR SOLAR WATER SYSTEM
- ■ TOILET
- DISTANCES IN KILOMETERS

― MAIN ROAD
― TOURING ROAD
- - - PARK BOUNDARY

ever, of fully inclusive guided tours with excellent accommodations, exquisite food and an opportunity to see one of Africa's great game parks in relaxed comfort. In Etosha, you can camp with your own tent in the rest camps, barbecuing your food, or stay in thatched roof rondavels with all the conveniences of a hotel in town.

As far as wildlife, there is plenty in terms of variety and numbers. The approximate count of larger animals in Etosha is as follows: elephant—1,500; black rhino—300; giraffe—2,000; Burchell zebra—6,000; mountain zebra—700; blue wildebeest—2600; African oryx or gemsbok—4,000; eland—250; kudu—2,500; red hartebeest—600; roan antelope—70; springbok—20,000; black-faced impala—700; ostrich—1,500; lion—300; and an unknown number of leopards and cheetahs, though Namibia has the largest cheetah population of any country worldwide. In addition, there are numerous hyena, jackal, klipspringer, Damara dik-dik, and suricates.

Birdlife is extraordinary with over 340 species recorded in the park, about one-third of these migratory. Bird life is more abundant in the eastern part of the park as it receives more rain. Flamingos, kori bustards (the heaviest flying bird), secretary birds, rollers, weavers and Namibia's national bird, the crimson breasted shrike with its blazing red chest, can all be seen here.

Most of the park west of Okaukuejo is closed except to tour groups, with the exception of the roads around the Sprokieswoud or haunted forest, a stand of moringa trees whose shapes create a landscape that contrasts sharply with the

Springbok, Namibia

acacia and mopane trees seen elsewhere. If you are part of a tour group, the western part of the park consists of mostly mopane woodland along the road, with some hills in the extreme west near the Otjovasandu gate.

Game Viewing

There is an abundance of game at Etosha year round. During the rainy season which starts Oct.- Dec. and lasts until March-April, the animals tend to stay away from the water-holes as water is available elsewhere. As for time of day, mornings and evenings are the best time to view game, but we've seen as much at mid-day as at any other time. Bring a pair of good binoculars and a camera with a telephoto lens (see Getting There).

You must stay in your vehicle except at a few toilets around the park. This is for your own safety as some animals (lions, for instance) are difficult to see in the grass and bushes and they might decide to check you out before you spot them. Look into the trees and bushes for motion or animal colors that make them stand out against the background. Go slowly and you will have a chance to see more.

Ask at the rest camp office about seasonal migrations of animals. Elephants, for example, migrate north during the rainy season and are rarely seen in most parts of the park, while flamingos arrive after the rains near the Fischer's pan area. Dik-dik drive is an excellent place to see the Damara dik-dik, while on the rhino drive you may be hard pressed to see any rhino. Many of the animals have become used to cars and you can approach quite closely without scaring them. They are not used to people approaching on foot, so don't. A good way to locate game is to stop and ask a passing vehicle (if it's going slowly enough) if they've seen something interesting. To really appreciate Etosha, you need to spend at least a couple of days there, as one day may be disappointing while the next offers multitudes of animals.

NOTE: Be sure to arrive back at your rest camp or leave the park by sunset. The gates are closed after this! You risk a fine and/or sleeping in your car if you arrive after this time!

The Cheetahs of Namibia

Namibia has the world's largest population of cheetahs, the fastest land animal on earth. The cheetah, *acinonyx jubatus*, is thought to attain speeds of up to 110 km./hr. (70 mph), but reliable measurements are lacking.

Cheetahs are light, weighing only 50 kg. (110 lbs.) and are built for speed with a lightweight skull and long limbs. They use their meter long tail as a rudder at high speeds to change direction quickly in pursuit of prey. Its claws are non-retractable and its spots solid black, different from the leopard's rosette spot pattern. Females are territorial, while males apparently roam freely between territories. Young average 3 per litter.

The number of cheetah remaining in Namibia is unknown, but many experts calculate about 2-3,000 of the fast cats remain, mostly on farmland outside the parks where they prey on small herbivores such as hares, but consume a quantity of livestock as well, much to the dismay of farmers who often shoot them (legally) as their goats and sheep disappear. The Cheetah Conservation Fund is working with farmers to prevent cheetah predation upon livestock, hopefully elimi-

Tracking radio collared cheetah.

nating the need to relocate or destroy problem animals. One method is placing donkeys with livestock which seems to reduce attacks significantly.

In Etosha, it is thought that there are somewhere between 50-100 cheetahs. These have a significant impact upon the springbok population, especially during lambing season, when young are an abundant and easy prey.

We were fortunate to be part of a research project in Etosha National Park that studied the effect of cheetahs on the plains ungulate population, particularly the effect on springbok, their primary prey. For two months we followed a sibling group of three cats—a sub-adult female and her two brothers 24 hours a day, except for brief trips into Okaukuejo camp for food or showers. The female wore a radio collar to aid in

Cheetah eating a springbok in Etosha.

locating them, particularly at night. This was not going to be a problem, we thought, as cheetahs are primarily diurnal. Our adolescent cats, however, did much of their hunting at night and we spent many late nights and early mornings with little sleep trying to figure what they were doing in the dark without interfering with their hunting. Some mornings we would find them with full bellies, and wonder when and where they ate.

During the day they spent considerable time resting under trees or bushes, often hunting during the cooler hours. Their hunting consisted of slowly stalking prey, sometimes for many hours, trying to hide themselves in the short grass, or running out from the cover of the woodland into a herd. Having a low success rate, they killed approximately every 2 days, sometimes going 4-5 days without a large meal. Cheetahs in the wild almost always eat only what they kill, but in a rarely observed event, we saw them finish off a springbok that had been killed by a caracal and partially eaten by jackals.

Our cats often seemed like large lanky house cats the way they frolicked with each other, pouncing on a hidden sibling or just lying around sleeping—probably their favorite activity. Cheetahs are timid animals, running from predators such as lions and hyenas who chase them from their kills from time to time. Though cheetahs in Etosha are habituated to humans in their cars and you can approach quite close, their numbers may dwindle if they are hunted as pests in other areas of the country. This beautiful, graceful cat that once ranged over Asia as well as Africa could face extinction in the wild.

Where to Stay

Mokuti Lodge—Tel. (0671) 21084

The Mokuti lodge is part of the Namib Sun chain of hotels and is the most luxurious place to stay near Etosha, situated just outside the east gate. It is a bit pricey, but its exquisite thatched roof chalets and incomparable cuisine make it a worthwhile splurge. The rooms are very comfortable and room service is available. Breakfast is included in the price and the dinner menu is unbelievable! Ostrich is certainly worth a try and there are many other game specialties. (Restaurant personnel don't run off into the park to shoot the evening meal for guests; rather they buy from distributors that run well established game farms.) There is a large buffet, complete with game from which they carve slabs of broiled springbok, roasted kudu and eland steaks.

A refreshing pool with bar as well as conference rooms and an excellent bar inside are on the premises. There is a small herd of bontebok roaming the grounds of the lodge that you can photograph at close range. These antelope are not native to Etosha, so this may be your only chance to see these beautiful rich dark brown and white antelopes. Taking the 4 km. trail around the grounds is a good way to see these and other game at close range. Mokuti also will arrange private horseback riding tours and they have a twice daily bus that goes on a three-hour game drive in the morning and evening for an additional cost.

Rates: Single R210, Double R287, 5-Bed Family Chalets R375, B&B

Government Rest Camps
Okaukuejo Rest Camp
Okaukuejo (pronounced *o ka koo'yo*) is situated approximately 130 km. north of Outjo at the west end of the part of Etosha that is open to tourists. This is a government rest camp that offers a variety of accommodations, from so-called luxury bungalows to bring-your-own-tent camping. It has a restaurant, shop, kiosk, filling station and swimming pool. It is the place you'll start if you're traveling west to east through Etosha. Just outside the fence on the west end of the rest camp is a waterhole that is floodlit at night for game viewing. There you can sit in the viewing stand and wait with a hot cup of tea as many of the more elusive and nocturnal creatures appear to drink. The black rhino can often be seen here and

even during the day springbok, kudu, oryx and lion can be spotted.

Halali

Located in the center of Etosha near two small hills is Halali rest camp, named after the bugle call used by the Germans to finish the hunt. There has recently been a waterhole opened on the edge of Halali to attract animals so that tourists staying here can view them. It is floodlit like the one at Okaukuejo and there is a viewing area situated atop a small cliff that serves as a fence. The eerie setting is somewhat artificial but it is a good opportunity to see nocturnal species that inhabit Etosha. It will take a while for the animals to discover this new waterhole. We didn't see much when we were there but given some time it will no doubt become a great place for night viewing like Okaukuejo's famous waterhole.

Halali has the same facilities as the other rest camps plus large 4-person canvas tents with cots.

Namutoni

Located at the eastern end of Etosha, this rest camp was opened in 1958 after its landmark fort was declared a national monument in 1950. Namutoni was originally a spring frequented by cattle and was visited by early explorers. It was used as a control post for the rinderpest and later a post to control smuggling to the north. The first fort was erected in 1903, but was destroyed a year later during battles between German and Owambo soldiers. Two years later it was rebuilt,

Male lion feeds on springbok while lioness, cub and jackals wait their turn.

used as a police post for many years, then rebuilt again in 1956 and opened as a rest camp for tourists two years later. There is a small museum in the fort and a staircase to the top of the fort that overlooks the waterhole.

Rates for All Camps: Admission R8 for adults, R4 for kids, Cars R10; Bungalows R58-104, many have kitchens; Luxury 2-bedroom bungalows R185. Tents available at Halali for R28 (Sleep 4), Camping R25 per site. Day visitors picnic site R25

Where to Eat

All the government rest camps have reasonably priced restaurants with very mediocre cafeteria-style food, or you can go to the Mokuti Lodge for something different. Most people just bring their own food and have a braai in one of the many pits provided—an excellent way to enjoy the African evening.

Getting to Etosha

Depending on whether you want to go through Etosha

Food is never wasted in Etosha: vultures feast on a zebra carcass.

east-west or west-east, you have two ways of getting there from Windhoek.

Going west-east you start at Okaukuejo. You get there by going to Outjo then taking the C38 north out of town about 130 km. You arrive at the gate about 10 km before you get to Okaukuejo itself, but these 10 km. are often full of game. If you're going east-west, then go through Tsumeb, where you arrive by taking the B1 all the way from Windhoek to Tsumeb, a distance of some 420 km. From Tsumeb, continue on the B1 until you hit the C38 about 80 km. northwest, where you turn left and go 35 km. to Namutoni. Here you reach the gate about 6 km. before Namutoni itself. From Okaukuejo to Halali is 70 km., from Halali to Namutoni 75km., and Okaukuejo to Namutoni 134km.

Otavi

About 120 km. northeast of Otjiwarongo on the B1 highway lies Otavi, home of a large Agra grain milling operation. The tourist information office is located in the municipality building next to the caravan park, which is one of the cheapest in Namibia. There's a 24 hour Total station with take-aways, a small hotel, an amethyst mine nearby and a memorial marking the end of German rule in Southwest Africa.

Places to Stay and Eat

Otavi Hotel

It looks like a dive from the front with a seedy looking bar and aging facade, but the Otavi Hotel has decent rooms that the owner embellishes with a complimentary half-bottle of wine and chocolates on the bed, a feature not found in even expensive hotels. The restaurant looked surprisingly elegant with an appetizing menu selection.

Rates: Single R55-75, Double R45-63 per person, B&B.

Caravan Park

Not the most beautiful but one of the least expensive municipal camps in the country with small chalets and campsites with braai pits, shade and a nearby ablution block.

Rates: Campsites R10 plus R1 per person, Chalets R25 plus R1 per person plus GST; showers R1 extra.

Sites to See

Khorab Memorial

Located just outside of town (follow the signs), the memorial is a small stone plaque next to the train tracks. It marks the end of German rule in Southwest Africa in July 1915 when Germany surrendered to South Africa after World War I began.

Grootfontein

Afrikaans for *big spring*, this cattle and maize farming area was once called the Republic of Upingtonia by the Thirstland trekkers who came from South Africa back in 1882. Grootfontein started as a mining town but there is currently little mining activity. The spring from which the town gets its name is not running, perhaps because of the lengthy drought. It's located behind the swimming pool next to the caravan park. Grootfontein is a convenient spot to stop before long drives to either Rundu/Caprivi or Bushmanland/Kaudom. There is 24 hr. petrol as well as a couple of small grocery stores here.

Places to Stay

Meteor Hotel—Tel. (06731) 2078/9, Okavango Rd.

The only decent hotel in town, the Meteor has nicely appointed rooms with phones and TVs. It is located on the main road through town that heads towards Rundu.

Rates: Single R98-122, Double R170-220, Budget 3 beds, R180 B&B

Nord Hotel—Tel. 2049, Kaiser Wilhelm St.

We weren't too impressed with the Nord as it's very basic rooms and restaurant were not completely clean, a rarity for Namibian hotels.

Rates: R55 per person B&B

Municipal Rest Camp—Tel. 3100

One of the nicest small municipal rest camps, this features spotless, new ablution blocks with outlets for 110/220, clothes washing and drying areas, a little stream running through the grounds, lighted braai pits with electricity outlets, and a swimming pool with restaurant next door. The only drawback is proximity to the main road, but traffic is usually light at night. They have some nice bungalows as well.

Rates: Camping R12 plus R3 per person, Bungalows R66 plus R11 for bedding; fully equipped luxury bungalow R138 Single, R165 Double, R193 Triple, R220 Quad

Where to Eat

Swimming pool café

The town pool has a nice bright café that's open 7 days for lunch and dinner. For only R9 you can get a set lunch that includes dessert or an á la carte lunch Sunday for about R20. The pool charges R1.50 (kids R1) and you can rent the Superslide for R30/hour. This is the place for a hot day in Grootfontein.

Le Club

Located on Bernhard St., Le Club has a standard menu of meat and fish for R15-25. They serve 3 meals.

Jacob's Bakery

The place for breakfast in Grootfontein. An excellent selection of fresh baked goods along with bacon, eggs or waffles. Located on the the main road heading towards Rundu.

Things to See

Hoba Meteorite

Very well marked on the Otavi-Grootfontein road is what is believed to be the world's largest meteorite. It fell to earth about 80,000 years ago but wasn't discovered until 1920. Now a national monument, you must pay R2 (kids R1) to see it. It is 82 percent iron, 16 percent nickel and the rest trace elements. The meteorite's roughly cubical shape is rather unique and where the surface has been rubbed away it looks like stainless steel. There is information in Afrikaans, German and English and the trees in the area are identified by number along with a written guide in many languages. You can picnic next to the meteorite and braai pits are provided. Get there either from Tsumeb or Otavi. From Tsumeb, take the D2859 for 20 km. and turn right proceeding for another 1 km. From Otavi, take the B2860 for 20 km. until you see the signs on D2859. All routes are well posted.

Grootfontein Museum

The Grootfontein museum is housed in an old German fort which later became a school hostel, then an army training center and finally a museum. Exhibits deal mainly with the history of the area; it's open Tuesday 4-6, Wednesday 9-11 and Friday 4-6.

Dragon's Breath Lake

Although not on tourist itineraries, something should be mentioned about possibly the world's largest underground lake located on the Haraseb farm 30 km. from Grootfontein on the Tsumeb road. Surface area is 2.8 hectares (7 acres); reaching it is quite an undertaking.

According to a friend who made the descent, you enter the cave through a 1 meter by 3 meter hole and descend with a rope ladder about 4 meters. You then proceed down a 3 meter wide corridor past some boulders where the floor drops off again and you must do a 2-part rope descent of 10 and 15 meters to a tiny ledge, where a 60° slope to the roof of the lake begins. After a roped descent to the roof, it is a 40 meter drop to the water surface! You cross the lake on small rafts or tubes to a beach where tiny straw stalactites are everywhere. Sounds like quite an adventure but to do it you must plan well ahead and probably be part of either a scientific team or possibly an organized spelunking cave exploration trip.

Other Caves

There are many other caves in the area more accessible than Dragon's Breath. Ask at the tourist offices in either Otavi, Grootfontein or Tsumeb if spelunking is your game. The area has a lot to offer!

Road to Rundu

Leaving town past the caravan park, it's 250 km. of very straight tarred road to Rundu on the Okavango River. About halfway between the two towns is the veterinary fence and a 24 hr. petrol and take away. They'll also let you camp closeby if it's late. Further on towards Rundu, there are several road-side stalls selling woodworks and round orange-like fruits of varying sizes. These are *strychnos cucculoides*, known in Afrikaans as klappers or coconuts. Poisonous when unripe, they have a hard shell which broken open yields a delicious, segmented fruit with seeds that tastes like no other we've had. Worth a stop!

Tsumeb

Tsumeb owes its existence to the mine whose smokestacks dominate the sky when you enter town. It's easy to bypass Tsumeb on the way to Etosha but it's worth a stop. It is actually one of the prettiest towns in Namibia with jacaranda, flamboyant and bougainvillea lined streets and a shady park.

The Tsumeb Corporation Limited (TCL) mine produces copper, lead, silver, cadmium and a host of other elements, minerals and crystals and is one of the big three mines in Namibia along with Rössing uranium and CDM diamond mines.

Mining started in 1905 and continues to this day thanks to a huge, rich ore body. Early in the morning you can sometimes hear the dull thud of molten copper slag hitting the water as it cools. There is a small tourist office on Main St. or check with the Minen Hotel for information on current local events. The stores here are better stocked than the ones in Grootfontein, so if you're heading into Caprivi you may want to do some shopping here.

Places to Stay

Minen Hotel—Tel. (0671) 21071/2, Fax 21750, Post St. opposite the park.

Having started in 1907 as no more than a shack, this shady inn has an old colonial atmosphere typified by a large outdoor dining area, which is the perfect place for a drink or dinner on a warm night. There is also an interesting indoor bar where you can drink with the locals and hear stories about the mine and its history. They are frequently busy, so call ahead for reservations.

Rates: Single R80-100, Double R110-140 B&B

Hotel Eckleben— Tel. 21051, Fax 21575

Yet another of the Namib Sun chain, this has little in the way of atmosphere and hopefully will be sold and converted into a Bed & Breakfast. There is a restaurant and beer garden but it caters mostly to business clients.

Rates: Single R110, Double R143

Caravan Park

Run by the municipality, this spacious park-like campground is all grass with a clean ablution block and quite a number of birds that fly amidst the trees, including hoepoes and paradise whydahs. There is electricity, a braai pit and water at the sites, as well as a small sewage water fed lake

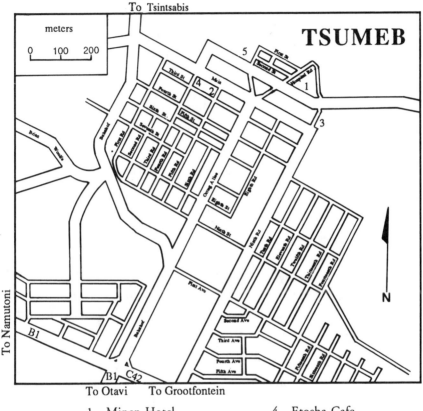

1   Minen Hotel   4   Etosha Cafe
2   Eckleben Hotel   5   Post Office
3   TCR Club

where frogs abound. It is located on the road into town from Otavi.

Rates: R10 plus R5 per person.

Places to Eat

TCR Klub—Tel. 20547

This is a club for mine employees complete with swimming pool, tennis courts, bars and a cafeteria and restaurant which is probably the best in Tsumeb. Officially you must be a member to get in but anyone including the person at the gate can sign you in as a guest, so just ask. The cafeteria has set meals for R8 and is closed Mondays. The Dioptase restaurant is elegant, dark and very reasonably priced with an extensive menu—book ahead and dress up a bit!

Hotel restaurants

Both the Minen and Eckleben have restaurants but for some atmosphere try the outdoor dining at the Minen when it's warm.

Etosha Café

Located on Main St., they're open from 7-5:30 M-F and Sat. 7-1. They offer light meals like burgers and sandwiches inside or in the beer garden. They also sell cakes, homemade jams and curios.

Things to See

Museums, Movies and Markets

The museum has some of the cannons pulled out of Otjikoto Lake as well as a collection of the many minerals found in the vicinity. For a night at the movies, the TCR Klub has shows Fri. & Sat. There is an open air market behind the Model Supermarket selling fresh fruits and vegetables.

Otjikoto and Guinas Lakes

Nearby Otjikoto and Guinas lakes are worth a visit, Otjikoto being a stone's throw off the highway north to Etosha, while Guinas is a 25 km. detour off the B1.

Otjikoto Lake (Meer) is in a sinkhole approximately 10-15 meters below the surrounding terrain depending on the water level. There is a rock stairway leading to the lake surface where the sign says no swimming, but the cool, clear water is just too inviting especially on a hot day. Unfortunately, there is some litter scattered around so please use the trash bins. Water from the lake is pumped for irrigation to the surrounding fields.

The depth of the lake was initially thought to be 55 meters but the lake bottom inclines towards the road into a system of caves and no one has found the bottom yet. During World

War I, German troops dumped cannons into the lake which were eventually hauled out and are currently sitting in the Tsumeb museum. There is a small kiosk selling drinks and snacks as well as wood carvings next to the lake.

Guinas Lake is a dark, deep blue lake situated in another sinkhole off the D3031 road. It is well signposted. There are no facilities here and a system of water pumps are in place for irrigation. The lake surface is not readily accessible but its waters are crystal clear. Camping is allowed but away from the lake where it's not very inviting. Both lakes are popular with divers, but permission must be obtained from the farm owners.

Owamboland

The majority of the population of Namibia live north of Etosha pan in Owamboland. This is where the Namibian independence movement was ignited and where the war for independence was most intense. SWAPO fighters fought South African forces stationed in Owamboland and southern Angola. Many people fled to other African countries to avoid the war and the oppression of the SADF. When South African forces withdrew as part of the peace agreement leading to independence, people started returning to their homes and the area became safe for visitors.

The people of Owamboland currently face a different battle. The drought which has affected all of southern Africa is most critical where the population is dense and land use intense as it is here. The land suffers from overuse as livestock need grass where there is little available and humans need firewood—their main source of fuel for heat and cooking—in an area where much of the once forested land has been decimated. When we visited during the dry season the area appeared to be a white sandy desert with people fetching their water from canals and boreholes drilled into the parched earth, to be used for drinking, washing and irrigation water for largely subsistence crops. After the rainy season, however, this same area was covered with green grassy fields in sharp contrast to months earlier.

When driving through Owamboland keep a watch for donkeys, goats, cattle, bicyclists and people on the road. There are two main towns, Ondangwa and Oshakati. Ondangwa is about 250 km. north of Tsumeb on the tarred B1 highway, and Oshakati about 35 km. farther on.

Ondangwa

This is the first of two major towns in Owamboland. There is one hotel here as well as a pungent open air market where you can buy meat, food, clothes or a local brew called tombo. The road leading into the center of town deadends near the post office, police station and bank.

Places to Stay
Punyu International Hotel—Tel. (06756) 40556
Just 2 km. outside Ondangwa, you'll see signs for this hotel next to the highway. It's a clean place with 28 rooms, some with A/C, TV and phones. It has a bar and restaurant with inexpensive meals—breakfast is only R7 and meals run R7-22. They will allow campers to stay on the small fading lawn. Punyu car hire rents vehicles.

Rates: Single R80, Double R120, Room only; camping R12 plus R5 for shower.

Oshakati

The larger of the two towns, Oshakati has four hotels, 24 hour petrol, a profusion of small bars with strange, colorful names and generally more services than Ondangwa. It's a bustling town, with most of the action taking place on the main highway strip.

Places to Stay
International Guest House—Tel. (06751) 20175
The most luxurious and most expensive place in Owambo-

land comes complete with swimming pool, tennis court and A/C, TV and phone in all rooms. Situated in a residential neighborhood off the main drag, it has a nice restaurant with meals from R15-30. Turn at the tall radio tower and follow the signs to International Guest House.

Rates: Single R95-115, Double R170-195 room only, Breakfast R15; Day rooms available for R35-55.

Continental Hotel—Tel. 20257

This is a clean place on the south side of the main road next to Continental Depot #1 and Phoenix Motors. The restaurant serves three meals and has lunch specials for R12-17. Dinner is about R15-30.

Rates: Single R58-125, Double R75-158.

Club Oshandira—Tel. 20443

This is the place we would stay in Oshakati. It is small with comfortable rooms (all with A/C) and the lawn, gardens and pool make it an attractive little oasis. They also have live music twice weekly and a good inexpensive menu. Right next to the airstrip—you get there by turning left at the radio tower and following the signs.

Rates: Single R89-106, Double R133-150, room only.

Santorini Inn—Tel. 20506 or 20457

This is Oshakati's newest place which is next to the MD electric sign on the north side of the main highway. They have several small A/C rooms and serve light meals and snacks.

Rates: Single R110, Double R180 B&B

Ruacana Falls—See Kaokoland

Bushmanland

Bushmanland and the nearby Kaudom Park have a lot to offer tourists, especially those who want an African wilderness experience. This whole area is isolated from the rest of Namibia and the difficulty in traveling through it is well rewarded by the magical quality of a region little touched by man other than the San (Bushman) people inhabiting it. Remember that you are a long way from civilization (and help) out here, so plan ahead with plenty of water, fuel and food before you head this way. There's only one town, Tsumkwe, which has but a poorly stocked shop and an unreliable gas station.

Tsumkwe

Tsumkwe is not so much a town as a meeting place for people living here or traveling through the area. The store has cold drinks and some food supplies, but don't count on much. The petrol station has petrol and diesel, although they run out occasionally and it may be a day or two before a fresh shipment comes in. There's also a clinic and a modern police station near the shop and a Nature Conservation office located near the large baobab tree several hundred meters past the shop. If you're planning on traveling through Kaudom, the next petrol is at Mukwe on the Caprivi Highway, but your mileage will be severely hampered by the deep sand in Kaudom. Fuel may be obtained at a farm petrol station (watch for the BP sign) between Grootfontein and Tsumkwe but we wouldn't rely on it.

Lodging

If for some reason you're not set up for camping, the only possibility of lodging is a guest house down the road on the same side of the street as the shop. It's a gray building with rondavels around it. Inquire locally.

Camping

You are allowed to camp anywhere in the area, keeping in mind not to pitch your tent near a San community without asking first. The Nyae-Nyae pans and the surrounding area are a truly magical place to visit, provided heavy rains haven't made the going too muddy. There is a small campsite on the west side of the main pan where it's possible to see flamingos, avocets and other water birds when the pans fill with water. Hartebeest, elephant, lion and other game also inhabit the area. To get to the Nyae-Nyae pan, drive to the right of the Nature Conservation office at the end of town (don't take the main road left) and follow the track south for about 18 km. Stick to the main track and don't take tracks

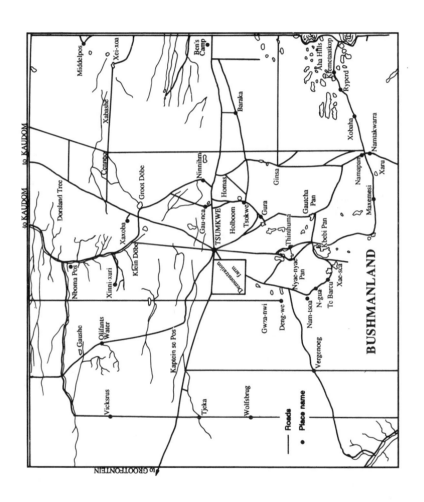

leading off to the left. There are many huge baobab trees (including one that has a massive hole in it) in the area that host a variety of birds. Take your time on the many tracks as it's pretty easy to make your way around with the map provided. Your chances of viewing game are much better in the dry season as are your chances of being able to get around!

The San (Bushmen)

The local population have historically been known as Bushmen, although this has a certain derogatory connotation to it. The problem is that they have no name for themselves as a group. Most scholars refer to them as San, after the Khoi-San language group to which their native tongue belongs. There is a Herero word *Ovakuruvehi*, meaning ancient or original ones, that may aptly describe the San but it is little known or used. Few of the San practice their traditional ways of hunting and gathering and most have been poorly integrated into modern society. Many of the men were inducted into the South African army during the war for independence in Namibia and became accustomed to good food and good pay and plenty of liquor. Now that Namibia is independent, they are trying to survive in a modern world with little employment. Alcoholism and poor health are rampant among the local population. They don't have a tradition of farming or stock raising, so they must be taught the most basic techniques. They are allowed to hunt traditionally with a bow and arrow and Nature Conservation has a policy of involving them in conservation to benefit them as well.

Kaudom Park

Kaudom Park comprises 384,000 hectares (3,840 sq. km.) of dry savannah woodland on old Kalahari sand dunes. Don't expect a desert, however, as the region is lush and the dunes are ancient and have stabilized over the millennia. Do expect very sandy terrain, often very deep, making the going extremely slow. In between the ancient dunes are a system of omurambas, a Herero word meaning vague river courses,

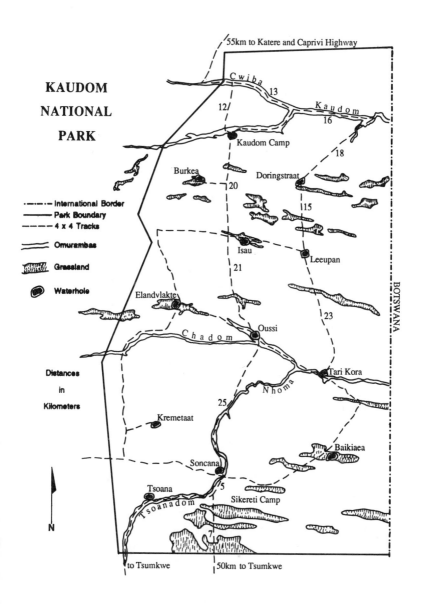

55km to Katere and Caprivi Highway

KAUDOM
NATIONAL
PARK

Cwiba

13

12

Kaudom

16

Kaudom Camp

18

Burkea

Doringstraat

20

15

International Border
Park Boundary
4 x 4 Tracks
Omurambas
Grassland
Waterhole

Isau

Leeupan

21

Elandvlakte

23

Chadom

Oussi

Tari Kora

Distances
in
Kilometers

Nhoma

25

Kremetaat

Baikiaea

Soncana

Tsoana

5

Sikereti Camp

Tsoanadom

N

7

to Tsumkwe

50km to Tsumkwe

BOTSWANA

where game is often spotted. The vegetation is less thick in the omurambas and the waterholes naturally tend to form here, so there are many elephant, giraffe and other game in the dry season.

December through April is the wet season and the game will leave the area as water is abundant elsewhere. Other game such as wildebeest, kudu, roan antelope, tsessebe, reedbuck, eland, lion, leopard, cheetah and wild dog can be seen although not in large numbers. You are allowed to get out of your vehicle wherever you wish but beware of lions which are common in the park. Bird life is abundant with Meyer's and Cape parrots, Bradfield's hornbill, bateleur eagle and white-headed and lappet-faced vultures inhabiting the park. The vegetation is dominated by tall species such as Rhodesian teak, false mopane, camelthorn, kiaat and leadwood.

At this point something should be said about the roads through Kaudom. They are mostly sand which is sometimes very deep, especially in the northern half of the park. **Only four wheel drive vehicles are permitted and there must be at least two vehicles traveling together.** Even four wheel drives get stuck here. If you happen to have only one vehicle, try checking at the caravan park in Grootfontein or Tsumkwe for others traveling through.

We traveled north from Kaudom camp to the Caprivi Highway through deep sand and averaged about 25 km./hour. This was after a rain which compacted the sand a bit. Later we met someone who had taken the same road during the dry season and he said it took him six hours to cover 60 km., getting stuck twice even with a four wheel drive. On these tracks your tires will automatically follow the deep ruts which tend to literally throw you from side to side through the sand. If that isn't enough, the tracks have ridges a meter or two apart, that toss you up and down as well! It's a real roller coaster ride so we'd recommend a light meal beforehand.

Petrol requirements are a much talked about necessity when going through Kaudom. How much you'll need definitely depends on your vehicle, the condition of the tracks and how much exploring you do within the park. We made it from Tsumkwe (where we got petrol) to Mukwe on the Caprivi highway on less than 60 liters but most people recommend taking twice that much. The sand really does eat up petrol and you're a long way from help, so plan ahead.

To Get to Kaudom

As you approach Tsumkwe on the Grootfontein-Tsumkwe road, turn left instead of right into town. Follow the road behind the school where you'll see a Kaudom sign indicating a right turn to the park. Or, keep going past the Kaudom sign for another 300 meters and you'll see a sign for Klein Döbe. Follow this road for 20 km. to a Nature Conservation field station (not open to the public). Continue straight and the road eventually leads to the park after following an omuramba for much of the way. Turning right and continuing on past Klein Döbe will take you back to the main north-south road which also leads to the park.

From Caprivi, there is a small sign at Katere, about 75 km. west of the Total station at Mukwe, where you turn south to Kaudom. It's easy to miss, so keep your eyes open.

No matter which direction you're approaching from, it's best to have a map of the area (available from Nature Conservation or Tourism offices), as well as a topographical map. There are signposts at major intersections of tracks in the park which help in navigating.

NOTE: While in Kaudom Park you must stay at one of two camps provided, Sikereti in the south or Kaudom in the north.

Sikereti Camp

The more southerly of the two camps has basic huts with cots where you must bring your own bedding or sleeping bag. There are also braai pits, water, showers and toilets. It's situated amid trees, and on occasion elephants parade through it.

Kaudom Camp

With a beautiful view overlooking a large omuramba and

a couple of waterholes that animals frequent, this has facilities similar to Sikereti. Both camps must be booked in Windhoek at the main tourist office and cost R25 plus R15 for park and vehicle fees. Neither camp is frequently visited and you may have them all to yourself.

Kavango

The Kavango region is inhabited primarily by the Kavango people, who traditionally have survived by fishing and agriculture along the Okavango River and its surrounding flood plains. Today, some people produce wood carvings which are among the best in Namibia. The main town in this region is Rundu, which sits above the river bordering Angola.

Rundu

On the Okavango River some 250 km. north of Grootfontein is Rundu, gateway to the Caprivi strip and convenient stopover on the way to exploring the Caprivi. It's the starting point for the much awaited Caprivi Highway, which is due to be tarred all the way across the strip sometime in the near future. It is a Wild West sort of town with all sorts of bizarre characters coming through, some of them staying. As someone said of Rundu—"It's not the end of the world, but you can see it from here." Being just over the river from Angola, there is a large Portuguese speaking community here and you'll hear it spoken often around town. There are several places to stay in or outside of town, a 24 hr. petrol, pharmacy, bank, grocery stores, some good places to eat and Namibia's only zoo. It is a center for the fine wood carvings from the Kavango area and the first place you'll be aware of it being a bit more tropical. Rainfall and thus vegetation starts changing here and it often feels like you've entered another country.

Places to Stay
Kavango Guest House—Tel. (067372) 244 or 13, Fax 13
This is a new 5 room guest house close to town with a

beautiful view overlooking the river and surrounding flood plain. The bungalows are well-furnished and have kitchenettes well-stocked with breakfast food so you can make your own morning meal. Hosts arrange boat trips on the river and there is a tennis court. The only drawback is the small grounds and the high barbed-wire fence (presumably for your security) that create a prison-like atmosphere. To get there, follow the road past the post office and when the tar road ends, turn right and you'll see it.

Rates: Single R100, Double R130 B&B (Self-service)

R O K—Tel. 200 or 369 or 5, Fax 200

The Rundu Ontspannings Klub, Afrikaans for Rundu Recreation Club, is just down the street from the Kavango guest house. You don't have to be a member to use the place and they have 9 rooms available for guests, a restaurant/bar, satellite TV with CNN, billiards and snooker tables and room for volleyball and darts. The spacious grounds have a sweeping view of the river and neighboring Angola. Rooms are somewhat plainer than the guest house down the street, but there's more room here.

Rates: Single R90, Double R120 B&B

Sarasungu Lodge—Tel. 161

One of the more colorful characters in Namibia, Volker Preuss has created an interesting world at Sarasungu Lodge, which is named after a tribal chief and means freedom. This is not your run of the mill spot—a large 3–wheel motorcycle out front, a small menagerie of domestic animals, extremely loud frogs when it rains, and a cozy 2-level bar/restaurant serving pizzas and Swiss and German dishes. The signs warning you of "no f—king noise after 10 PM" help to create a bizarre but interesting place. There are thatched bungalows without bath and several camping places, though it's a bit muddy in winter. To get there, turn towards the river at the sign at the edge of town where the old dirt highway begins.

Rates: Camping R25 plus R1.50 per person; Bungalows Single R89, Double R122, Quad R 189 B&B; Breakfast R15 extra for campers.

Kaisosi Safari Lodge—Tel. 265

The nicest of the lodges along the Okavango outside Rundu, Kaisosi has 12 semi-luxurious rooms, a swimming pool, a bar/restaurant with a pool table, and boating when the river is high enough. The á la carte menu runs R15-25 and breakfast is R12.50. To get there, take the old dirt highway east out of Rundu and follow the signs. If you're coming from Caprivi, there are signs on the tarred road. They also allow inexpensive camping.

Rates: Single R100, Double R150, room only; Camping R5 per person.

Penny's River Lodge

Penny's has a handful of primitive bungalows which at R50 per person didn't seem like all that good of a deal. It's a bit farther out than Kaisosi and not as well marked.

Mayana Lodge—Tel. 376

A bit further along the dirt highway and the last of the lodges, this was a former Koevoet base during the war for independence. They have thatched bungalows with reed interior walls and allow camping as well. Two huge bungalows are saved for large groups or big families. Everyone shares a large ablution block as the bungalows have no bathrooms. There's a swimming pool, a peacock that wanders around the grounds and boat trips on the river. The restaurant is decent and inexpensive with meals at R15-20.

Rates: Bungalows R55 per person; Camping R25 per vehicle; Day visitors R5.

The Kavango Motel has burned down under mysterious circumstances and the municipal camping site is no longer operating although rumor has it that it will be turned into a private campsite soon.

Places to Eat

Makalani restaurant

Situated next to the local SWAPO office, this is Rundu's gourmet eating establishment. It is nicely decorated, air conditioned and has a diverse menu that includes Baked Alaska (advance notice required). Many Italian and seafood dishes are on the menu and some fine wines are on the list. Sundays they have a buffet. A beer garden with hot tub is planned. Dinners run R15-40 and they are open 7 days.

R O K

The Wato Inn at the ROK has lunch from 1-2 for R15 and an á la carte restaurant with dinners for R16-26. The menu is typically meat and fish.

Cola Cola Bakery

This is the spot for breakfast, as they have fantastic baked goods and some of the best coffee this side of the Orange river.

Portuguese Restaurant and Take Away

A popular spot with the locals. You can get whole chickens and other precooked meats, cold drinks and some groceries here.

Things to See

Rundu Zoo (Dieretuin)

The only thing remotely qualifying as a zoo in Namibia, this is the place to go if you've missed animals in the game parks because of broken down vehicles or rain or whatever. Oddly enough it is run by the Ministry of Education and is frequented by youth groups who also stay at the youth camp next door. Next to the caged lions, cheetah and caracal are 18 hectares on which game is being introduced. The bird life is incredibly diverse here and is worth the trip for bird watching alone. The manager has lions and cheetah living in his house that are very friendly—at least to him. The house is surrounded by high fences next to the zoo entrance—note the "lion at large" sign.

Entrance is R2 for adults and R1 for kids.

Kavango Woodworks

Near the middle of town you can get locally made wood carvings, T shirts and other gifts although you might do better south of town along the highway where you don't go through the middleman.

The Caprivi Highway

From Rundu it is about 500 km. to Katima Mulilo on the Caprivi highway. The first 50 km. or so from Rundu is paved, then it is dirt and gravel all the way to the Cuando River about 350 km. away. The last 100 km. to Katima Mulilo is a good tarred road. The portion of dirt road closest to Rundu is the worst, and it gets better as you go east. Beware during the rainy season, however, as it can be pretty sloshy traveling.

The entire length is due to be tarred in the next few years. Namibia recently received funding to complete the road and they are supposedly going full steam ahead. This will undoubtedly open up the Caprivi for tourism and commerce from central Africa and will be an important link for goods being shipped overseas from Walvis Bay. There will be many new lodges and roadside businesses opening up in the 90s. It promises to be a boon to the economy.

Eastern Kavango

As you continue along the Caprivi highway, you pass small Kavango villages with their traditional thatch and reed huts. You'll also notice many more people (and livestock) walking next to the road. Usually one family and their animals will inhabit a typical compound which consists of several huts enclosed by a reed fence. As you pass Katere notice the small sign marking the road to Kaudom Park, if you're headed that way. Continuing along the highway, you'll soon come to one of the only chances for petrol in Caprivi, at Mukwe where there is a 24 hour Total station. Fill up here as the next reliable petrol is in Katima 300 km. away. Some 15 km. further on the road splits at Bagani, the left road being the Caprivi highway to Katima and the right going to Popa Rapids, Mahango Park and Botswana and the Okavango delta.

For further information, see the Caprivi chapter.

Guest Farms in the Northern Area

Okonjima—P.O. Box 793, Otjiwarongo, Tel. (0658) 18212

Okonjima (Herero for place of the baboons) is hosted by Val and Rose Hanssen. You should call them for specific directions to the farm. If you turn off the main highway to Otjiwarongo 1-2 km. after the "Otjiwarongo—50 km." sign going north, follow D2515 and just before the settlement of Okonjima take the left onto a dirt road to the farm. From the north, turn off the highway just after the "Okahandja—130 km." sign.

They have 10 double rooms with private baths and a good variety of game. There are pony trails, Bushmen trails and tracking trails, so you should be busy following something! They specialize in night viewing where you can see honey badger, porcupine and aardvark as well as a real good chance of seeing leopard or cheetah. In the heart of the Omboroko mountains, you can swim at the bottom of the waterfall or watch the vultures feed. Over 200 species of birds have been identified here making it a birdwatchers' paradise. They have a rustic camp if you want to forego the comforts of a room and sleep under the stars. Busiest April—October; least busy November- March.

Rates: Single R211, Double R183 full board per person

Waterberg Big Game Hunting Lodge—P.O. Box 973, Otji- warongo,

Tel. (0658) 15313

This is basically an upscale hunting lodge. Swiss managed, it welcomes tourists on a space available basis. To get there, take the B1 north towards Otjiwarongo. About 29 km. south of town turn right to Waterberg Park. Follow signs past Waterberg and to WABI.

The luxurious air conditioned bungalows, swimming pool and excellent meals are part of a package designed to make your stay worry free. Situated on 10,000 hectares (25,000 acres), it has almost every game species available to hunt under a culling program to control the populations of species.

Trophy animals are what you come here for, although game drives and photo safaris are easy to arrange. July-Sept. you must reserve 2-3 months ahead and Feb. & Nov. only 2-3 days.

Rates: R275 per person full board. Hunting rates vary.
Toshari Inn—P.O. Box 164, Outjo, Tel. (06542) 3602 or (06532) 1602

Toshari Inn, hosted by Jake Duvenage, is situated only 26 km. from the Anderson gate (western entrance) of Etosha National Park on the main Outjo-Etosha highway. Drive north from Outjo about 100km. until you see the sign and the buildings next to the road. Conveniently located for those visiting Etosha, the inn has 17 rooms. June-July book ahead 1 month; Nov-Dec 1 week.

Rates: Single R99, Double R128 room only; Meals R9.50 for breakfast; R15 for lunch; R25 for dinner (Children under 12 half price.) Lunch & breakfast packs available.

Other Guest Farms

Bergplaas Safari Lodge—P.O. Box 60, Outjo, Tel. (06542) 1802
La Rochelle—P.O. Box 194, Tsumeb, Tel. (0678) 11002 or 11013
Kupferberg—P.O. Box 255, Otavi, Tel. (06742) 2211

CHAPTER 10

Kaokoland & Damaraland Region

This area is very lightly populated, encompassing the wild and rugged territories where elephant and rhino still roam free. It is largely semi-desert and very mountainous, containing the countries highest point, the Brandberg. People eke out an existence here through stock farming and many, such as the Himba, live in traditional ways. It is a wonderful area for off the beaten track exploration, keeping in mind the delicate nature of the environment, wildlife and peoples here.

Damaraland/Uis

Often overlooked as just a mining town, this small Namib Desert community is in the midst of a transition from an ISCOR company town to a gateway to the many desert wonders close by. These include the Brandberg, Namibia's highest mountain, the Witfrou (white lady) cave paintings and the marvelous Namib Desert, with its harsh dry landscape punctuated with lush dry river valleys that teem with bird and animal life.

Dominated by the Brandberg, Uis is still run by ISCOR, the South African mining giant. But the new rest camp is not run by the company and offers food, drink and accommodations.

Uis store open M-F 8:30-4:30; gas station M-Sat. 7:30-6:30 and Sun. 9-6.

Brandberg Rest Camp—Tel. (062262) 235

The Brandberg Rest Camp was taken over from ISCOR and

NAMIBIA - KAOKOLAND AND DAMARALAND REGION

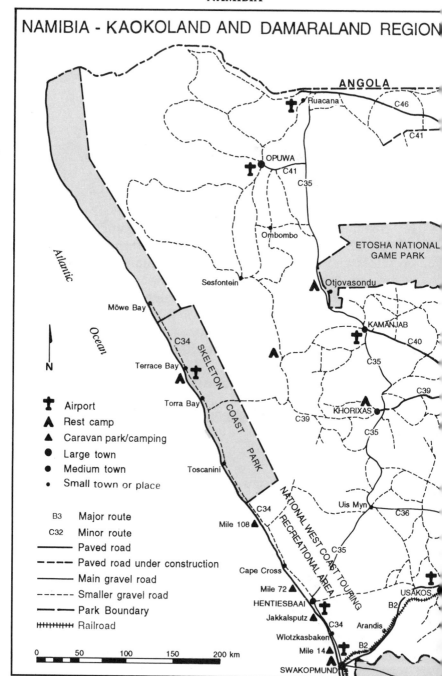

Close encounter with an elephant in Damaraland.

has several 2 bedroom, 4 bed flats which they rent as well as some houses in town. They have an enormous swimming pool that is worth a stop on a hot day. The former mine club has a bar and restaurant and a snooker room.

Rates: Single R45, Double R90, Flat R100

Getting to Uis

From Windhoek, take the B1 highway north to Okahandja; stay on the road as it changes to the B2, then follow it 65 km. to the Wilhelmstal road. This goes to Omaruru, where you take the graded dirt C36 road west 120 km. to Uis. As you approach Uis, you'll see the Brandberg, Namibia's highest point, looming into view.

Brandberg West Mine

An old tin mine shut down in 1982, Brandberg West can be reached by taking the Henties Bay road from Uis and after 14 kilometers turning onto the Brandberg West road. About 85 km. later you reach the gate of the mine after driving around the Brandberg and Table Mountain through a dry welwit-

Playful baboon on the roadside.

schia dotted landscape. As you come close to the mine, notice the fascinating geology in the vertical uplifting of schists that has occurred here.

The mine property has ruins of swimming pools, tennis courts, a clubhouse, living quarters and a small town which looks like any other. At the top of the main road, you'll see old mining equipment on your right and a large quarry on your left with a small lake at the bottom. This emerald colored pond is very cool and refreshing to swim in after the long drive from Uis, but be careful as the pondside is surrounded by sharp rocks.

Ugab River

Near the Brandberg West mine there is an opportunity to visit the Ugab River in all its lushness right in the middle of some of the driest land around. It's hard to imagine vegetation so thick you can't even walk through it out here in the desolation of the Namib, but the subterranean river that makes it possible is right under your feet.

To reach the Ugab take the road you were following past the mine entrance (you'll need a high clearance vehicle but not a 4-wheel drive) and about 1 km. later take the right fork and stay on one of the two rocky tracks to the river. You'll see the pipeline that the old mine used for its water supply along the way. It will help to have a map here as there are many sideroads—just stay on the main one. You will come to a gate after 5 kilometers where you'll see a couple of prefabricated igloo-type houses; someone will let you in. Sign the register and donate whatever you can to local efforts for saving the endangered rhinos in the area and for nature conservation in general. You will need a 4-wheel drive beyond this point. The road continues across the river and up and down the river for a short way. Here you should definitely have a detailed up-to-date topographical map of the area if you are going much farther.

You can camp in the Ugab River bed, but beware of unseen storms in the interior of the country that can cause flooding in the rainy season. Take care to camp away from waterholes as there is plenty of wildlife here. You might hear the baboons screeching closeby, their strange crow like call piercing the early morning. We saw small oryx and zebra herds in the river canyon and some giraffe remains as well. It is one thing to see the thousands of animals from your car in Etosha but quite another to see them on foot from a close distance in this beautiful unspoiled desert wilderness.

The road across the river will take you through the desert to the tiny oasis of Gai-as, a couple of hours away on a rough but discernible road. There is a small spring and a couple of trees in the middle of some incredibly barren terrain. Zebra, springbok and ostrich come for water here and there are some old stone enclosures where you might hide in order to see the animals approach.

Spitzkoppe

This marvelous granite peak situated about 60 kilometers northwest of Usakos is definitely worth a visit. It can be reached from either Uis, Henties Bay or from along the main Swakopmund-Windhoek highway. There are many natural campsites among the large boulders. Although there are no facilities, here is a fantastic opportunity to get away from the often crowded campsites at other popular spots. It is also a good spot for rock climbing and the Spitzkoppe itself is a challenging technical climb for well equipped mountaineers.

Bushman's Paradise

Situated at the eastern end of Gross Spitzkoppe, this beautiful little valley can be imagined as it most likely was: a home for the first inhabitants of Namibia, the Bushmen or San people. Their cave paintings can be viewed on the large overhanging walls around Bushmen's Paradise. Take care not to touch the delicate paintings; they have been here for thousands of years and can easily be wiped out by constant pawing by tourists.

The Rock Arch

Reminiscent of America's southwest, the underlying softer rock has been eroded over the centuries leaving a large arch that adds to the mystical beauty of Spitzkoppe.

Spend a few days here climbing and exploring. You may run into a few Damara miners who scrape the surrounding ground for tourmalines and other semi-precious stones, then sell them to tourists. It is wise to know a little about stones before buying, but you can find a reasonable deal from these locals who eke out a living in the desert.

A journey can also be made to Klein Spitzkoppe but it requires a 4 wheel drive.

Getting to Spitzkoppe

From the Windhoek-Swakopmund highway, take the D1918 about 25 km. west of Usakos and follow it until you see the D3716 turnoff to Spitzkoppe. From Uis, take the D1930 1 km. east of town. Follow it south until you see the sign for

Spitzkoppe and Henties Bay where you turn right and run right into the massif. From Henties Bay, take the D1918 east about 100 km. to the D3716 where you turn left and go the short distance to the mountain.

Okombahe

This small town typifies the small rural communities in Namibia you are unlikely to find unless you follow some of the dirt roads. It lies just 8 km. or so off the main road half way between Uis and Omaruru. There are a couple of stores, a restaurant and a drankwinkel. What is remarkable about Okombahe is that it is much less westernized than other towns and the pace of life here is a lot slower. There is a rug and tapestry making co-operative here that sells their work all over the country.

The Brandberg

This massive mountain totally dominates the desert around it. Those wishing to climb to the peak, Königstein, should try it in the cooler winter months. It is at least a three day trip as the vertical ascent of approximately 2000 meters is steep in places. There are still undiscovered rock paintings here and spending a few extra days to explore could uncover prehistoric art no one has seen to date! Make sure you bring plenty of water as it is often unavailable on the trail, especially during the dry winter months. In the nearby Ugab River and the Namib desert a variety of wildlife can be seen such as rhino, elephant, kudu, oryx, ostrich, springbok and other game.

Brandberg Climb

There are several routes to Namibia's highest point and all should be taken after careful planning, keeping Brandberg's sometimes hostile environment in mind. Detailed maps (1:50,000) of the area can be purchased from the Surveyor-General's office in Windhoek. There may be little or no water available on the mountain no matter what the time of the year, so all water needed must be carried. Plan on at least two liters

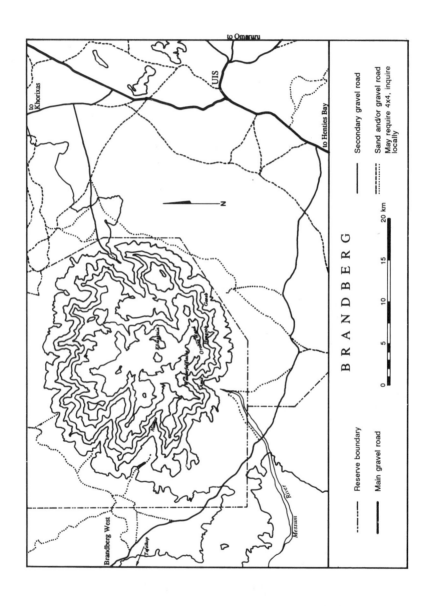

of water per person per day and possibly more during warmer months as during the steep climbing you will lose plenty of it in sweat.

Climbers are rewarded with fantastic views of the Namib desert stretching out to the horizon and cave paintings around the entire Brandberg area. These prehistoric artifacts are part of Namibia's natural heritage and are part of the reason people come here. Unfortunately, some feel that they must have a piece of Namibia's natural history for their own keeping and have chipped away the paintings. Even touching these ancient relics can affect their quality and cause them to eventually be lost to mankind.

The climb we made up to Königstein, Brandberg's highest peak, was through the Ga-aseb ravine on the south side of the massif. The climb starts in the flat desert through sand and quickly becomes a steep poorly marked trail. Ephraim, our guide, had hiked throughout the Brandberg for eight years and he easily found the trail, taking us to cave painting sites along the way. (He accompanied us and our friends from Italy who joined us for the hike.)

Most of the weight of our packs was water as we were there during August near the end of the dry season after five years of drought. We were sure we wouldn't find water anywhere along our hike. We had chosen one of the most direct routes to the top and also one of the steepest. Skirting the riverbed and walking among granite boulders that grew progressively larger, we steadily gained altitude. On a few occasions it became necessary to do a little climbing, using our hands, but the trail Ephraim picked minimized this. As we turned to look back, the desert spread out before us far below, a hazy cream color punctuated with brown granite rock outcroppings.

We stopped for lunch next to a likely looking cave and rock overhang where we spotted some of the ancient red paintings—mostly of prehistoric hunters and the animals they hunted. As the hike grew steeper, we noticed ourselves stopping more frequently for water and near the top of the pass that would lead us to the plateau, we were parched and finished off the better part of a liter. There a small rock overhang yielded yet more paintings and an awesome view of the Namib's flat expanse. The sound of birds interrupted our gaze as a group of a dozen or so rosyfaced lovebirds noisily flew from tree to tree, their bright green and pink hues startlingly incongruous against the dry brown plateau.

A short while later we came to our camp near Wasser-fallfläche on the map. We camped beneath another set of San paintings. Further examination of the small valley we were in revealed many more. Reminiscent of Bushman's Paradise near Spitzkoppe, this area was evidently home to prehistoric peoples who lived high up and came down to hunt on the plains below. After setting camp, we followed the Wasser-fallfläche downstream and to our surprise discovered in the middle of this broad dry streambed a series of round holes carved into the solid granite, some up to several feet deep and a few with icy cold water still remaining. Lying on the warm rocks while we poured water over each other was a totally unexpected reward after our hot thirsty hike up.

Taking a few extra liters from our newly found water source, we boiled some for tea and dinner, saving what we brought up the mountain for the rest of our trip. A small fire and good company with Ephraim and our Italian friends provided the perfect ending to a tough but fulfilling day.

The next morning we started early for the 3-hour climb (with day packs only!) to Königstein. Along the way Ephraim pointed out many paintings. After some climbing along giant boulders and through narrow, flat valleys we saw the peak with its rock pile and stake. A short, relatively easy climb later we stood at the highest point in the country, surveying the surrounding Namib from many different vantage points. The town of Uis with the white mountain of the mine was visible in the distance. We signed the register and had a leisurely lunch.

Across the Tsisab ravine we could make out the Orabes Wand, a broad relatively flat plain high up on the Brandberg where there stood, barely visible, a small airplane that had crashed years ago. Apparently, Jan Botha, the manager of the Uis mine had landed here several times, once to take hikers closer to the summit. In the company of his son, he caught a downdraft when he was taking off from the short runway and crashed. A rescue party reached the injured pair and was able to haul them down, but the plane's wreckage still remains.

On our climb down we took a detour and ended up in an overhanging cave with a series of spectacular rock paintings. More fantastic than the famed Witfrou were the white and orange hues used here in conjunction with the familiar reds. We then headed back to camp spotting several bizarre species of trees and bushes along the way.

After sleeping under the silent starry desert night, we descended the way we came and were surprised to see the fog rolling over the now obscured desert. As we slowly went down the steep slope, the fog lifted and the Namib sun shone through. It became cooler, the result of an inversion layer that became visible as we drove away from the massif. Our three day trip was short and wonderful, with plans for an extended stay during the hotter but hopefully wetter summer. Seeing this mountain with water gushing down the Wasserfallfläche would be a sight worth the hot steep climb to the top of Namibia. For a guide, inquire at the store in Uis or the store at the township location.

Witvrou

The Witvrou or White Lady is a piece of rock art painted by a San artist some thousands of years ago. It is unusual in the fact that it presumably depicts a woman with the bottom half of her body all white. The style resembles similar prehistoric paintings found in the Mediterranean and a possible link to these paintings farther north has been speculated. Now, researchers are not sure if this White Lady is even a lady and most consider it to be a male figure though the name remains. It is part of a group of paintings found on the Brandberg's northeast side, up the Tsisab ravine. There are several other interesting paintings in the immediate area of the Witvrou, which you can find by exploring. The Witvrou is enclosed to prevent vandalism, but there are many less accessible samples of rock art all over the Brandberg that are more impressive.

To get there from Uis, take the road towards Henties Bay; less than a kilometer later the road to Khorixas and Kamanjab turns north. Take this road until you spot the Witvrou turnoff about 15 km. later. Turn here and follow the graded road to the parking area. You must then take a 3 km. trail following arrows (annoying—they're painted on the rock) and after a short scramble you will arrive at the small overhanging cave that hosts the painting.

The more adventurous should try hiking up the Tsisab ravine from the Witvrou. Take plenty of water if there is none visible in the riverbed. Hiking up in the riverbed is extremely difficult due to the large boulders, but coming down you can slide to lower levels that are impossible to climb because of the smoothness of the rock. After a good rainfall, you may come across some pools of water that are too inviting to resist. Be careful as it is very hot here, especially in the summer.

Khorixas

Khorixas (pronounced *kor'ee hahs*) is a small dusty town that is the "capital" of Damaraland and the gateway to north-western Namibia—the rugged northern Damaraland and Kaokoland. Your choice of where to stay in Khorixas is limited to the Khorixas rest camp and the Sunrise Hotel. There is a 24 hr. petrol, a bakery and a hospital here.

Places to Stay and Eat
Khorixas Rest Camp

Khorixas Rest Camp is found just west of town off the main road—just follow the signs. This comfortable spot is very busy, especially March-September and reservations should be made well in advance for bungalows, though camping spaces are easier to get on short notice. Most people visiting this region end up staying here as there is little other suitable accommodation. It is rewarding to find such an oasis in the dry surroundings. There are 40 bungalows and a couple of larger bungalows for groups, a swimming pool, bar/restaurant with an incredible wine list, a collection of local birds in the aviaries scattered about the grounds, and other small pets wandering about.

For campers there is a small campground with ablution blocks and places for cooking and doing laundry. There is a little shop that sells souvenirs, post cards, a variety of food and sundries.

Rates: Single R120 B&B, Double R180 B&B. All rooms have their own toilet. Camping R25 per tent plus R5 per person. Major credit cards accepted. Breakfast R15 for campers. Dinner a la carte-entrees R15-25. Telex and phone available.

Sunrise Hotel—Tel. 382

If you're stuck in Khorixas and the rest camp is full you may want to reluctantly consider the Sunrise. Located across from the post office, this rather seedy looking place has 5 rooms with communal baths for R50 per person.

They will make meals on request. There is also a bar that is a little too close to the rooms and an outdoor "disco" on Wed., Fri. and Sat. This "hotel" looks very much like the budget hotels you find throughout Africa only it is not priced accordingly. The noise on disco nights could eliminate sleep as a possibility.

Khorixas Bakery

You can get fresh bread and cold drinks as well as light meals in the small restaurant here.

Save the Rhino Trust

With Namibia having the world's only surviving free ranging rhinoceros in the Damaraland-Kaokoland area, and poaching becoming a growing problem worldwide, the Save the Rhino Trust was created. Many rhino carcasses had been discovered in the desert here, the victims of unbridled poaching—often by government officials and the South African military. Something had to be done as the number surviving in the area in the late 70s was less than 100.

A grass roots Namibian organization, Save the Rhino Trust is entirely funded by donations. Their objective is to preserve the remaining stock of black (hook-lipped) rhinoceros and increase populations to the carrying capacity of the region, then perhaps create a sanctuary where additional animals can be bred. Local people are employed, providing jobs in a high unemployment area and giving the community a say in conservation, which is in line with the community based conservation philosophy taking hold in Namibia and elsewhere. Teams on foot and with vehicles patrol the area, tracking rhinos and cataloging each individual by photographing and sketching its distinct horn, tail and ears and other characteristics. Over 100 have been cataloged to date and poaching has largely stopped.

Some rhinos have been dehorned to protect them from poachers who sell the horns which eventually make their way to Yemen for dagger handles or the far East for use in traditional medicines. The committed members of the Save the Rhino Trust need donations of cash or radios, clothing and other equipment to continue their effort to save this dwindling species. If you can help, call the Save the Rhino Trust at (061) 222281 or write to Box 22691, Windhoek.

Twyfelfontein

Twyfelfontein, or doubtful spring, is the area where famous rock engravings and cave paintings are located southwest of Khorixas and northwest of Uis. There is a small shaded parking area, picnic tables, a curio shop with locally made arts and crafts, and a new thatched office. The spring flows in a good water year but during the current drought the water level is a few meters beneath the ground. The entry fee is R2 per person which includes a mandatory guide. Guides are necessary as some of the rock engravings have been defaced. With one of Namibia's natural monuments in danger of being lost, it was decided to let the local people have a say in controlling tourism in the area. The guides will show you how to find engravings and paintings as well as some interesting rock formations. There are two walks—the short one taking almost an hour and the longer one of about an hour and a half.

These finely preserved engravings date from a few hundred to several thousand years ago and depict mostly animals. Etched into the sandstone are also geometric shapes and symbols as well as the spoor of some of the animals and human footprints. Why these extraordinary engravings exist is anyone's guess, but some researchers believe that they were drawn during the trances of the San shamans while they communicated with the spirits.

There is another group of engravings located a couple of kilometers away from the main group dubbed "Adam and Eve." Ask Elias if he will take you there as there are no facilities yet.

There are some interesting geological formations in the Twyfelfontein area, notably the "organ pipes" and the Wondergat, or wonderhole. The organ pipes are a formation of dolerite that appears as geometric columns of rock lying in a small stream bed. To get there, take a right 2 km after you leave Twyfelfontein on the road to Verbrandeberg. There is a parking spot just to the left of the road; you must walk a short distance to the stream bed to get a good look.

The Wondergat is a small hole in the middle of the desert about 15 meters deep—it's not too far out of the way so it's worth a look. The turnoff is 4 km. west of the Twyfelfontein turnoff on D2612 or D3254, depending on where you're coming from. You then follow a small dirt road a short distance until it ends. You'll see the hole nearby—but be careful—it's a long drop down!

Another tourist attraction is the Verbrandeberg or "burnt mountain." This has been described as rainbow colored, a beautiful kaleidoscope at sunset or sunrise, but is not all that fascinating. It glows a little at sunset and is interesting geologically, but nothing compared to its giant cousin just south—The Brandberg. It's not far out of the way so you might see more than we did (please tell us if you do.)

Aba-Huab Campsite

A few things have changed near Twyfelfontein recently. The "driving force" behind the development of rustic tourist facilities, Elias Xoagab, has built a campground on the Aba-Huab river a few kilometers from Twyfelfontein. This wonderful campsite has small bashirs (A-frame thatched reed open air beds) running water (conserve it as it is very scarce), a braai pit, a tree or two and a picnic table. The campsite was designed to intrude as little as possible on the natural surroundings. There is a large group braai area and showers, toilets and a bar—sometimes open very late. The cost is R10 per person per night.

To get there from Uis, take the Uis-Khorixas road north until you reach D2612 about halfway between the two towns. Take a left onto D2612 until you come to the sign for Twyfelfontein where you take a left. The way is well signposted.

The Petrified Forest

Situated about 50 km. west of Khorixas, the petrified forest is well marked off the C39 road. There is a shaded place to picnic, toilets and a 20 minute trail among some petrified wood. You can see the growth rings on the larger logs, some of which are over 250 million years old. There is no entry fee at present.

Vingerklip of Damaraland

There are a few vingerklips in Namibia so if you're into strange, solitary rock formations, this is the place for you. To find them, take the tar road east from Khorixas about 40 km. or so, looking for the small sign "Vingerklip." Take this graded dirt road 19 km. until you reach a small house next to the road on the left. You must pay an entrance fee as the site is located on a private farm. The cost is R1 per vehicle plus R1 per adult and 50 cents per child.

The entrepreneurial owner also sells juice, homemade marmalades, jams and biltong for a reasonable price. There is a short drive to the base of the rock and you can walk around and see fairly spectacular scenery in the surrounding area.

Palmwag Rest Camp

Pronounced *pah'lum vahk*, this remote outpost has been run since 1985 by Desert Adventure Safaris which holds the concession rights for the 8000 sq. km. area bordered by the Skeleton Coast Park on the west, the D3706 road on the east, the veterinary fence on the south and the Hoanib river on the north. To get there from Khorixas, take the main road (C39) west about 115 km. You'll come to the Torra Bay turnoff; keep going straight another 40 km. to the veterinary fence where you're stopped to receive regulations for carrying animals back south from northern Namibia. After 6 km. you'll see the small Palmwag Lodge sign on your left.

They are responsible for the game, maintaining the area for tourism and nature conservation in general. The rest camp itself is an oasis on the Uniab river where water springs up year round. Many bird species frequent the area and especially during the dry season, elephants and other wild game come to drink, sometimes crossing (usually harmlessly) right through the campground.

Palmwag gets its name from the Makalani palms that grow there. You can take one of many tours throughout the concession area where lion, elephant, rhino, giraffe, zebra, kudu, gemsbok and springbok are frequently seen, or if you have your own vehicle, with permission and directions you can explore the area.

There is an abundance of wildlife here and no crowds; you can spend hours watching elephants drinking and playing in some of the nearby waterholes. Please get good directions before setting out and stay on the roads and tracks (a good topographical map would help), as people have gotten lost here. It's not particularly fun or cheap for the staff to arrange to rescue lost travelers—so plan ahead.

The nearby Aub canyon and Van Zyl's *gat* are accessible with 4-wheel drive vehicles. Animals frequent these areas due to the year round water.

For deluxe accommodations, Palmwag has 9 rooms, 7 of them in thatched huts. There are also 5 excellent campsites with water, table, sun shelter, light and braai pit with communal toilet and showers. There are 2 small swimming pools which are soothing especially in the summer months. There is a cozy and well stocked bar and a restaurant which serves 3 meals. They are busiest during May-September when you should book a few months ahead, though there is usually some camping space available. There is an airstrip close for those wishing to fly in.

Rates: Campsites R20 one time charge plus R10 per person; Bungalows R140-160 per person includes breakfast and dinner; Breakfast R12.50, Lunch R8-10, Dinner R35-40. Petrol Mon.-Sat. 8-12:30 and 3-6, Sun. 8-12:30, R2 after hours service (only petrol for a long ways in any direction).

There is a very small store for some provisions. M-F 8-12:30 and 3-6, Sat. & Sun. 8-12:30.

Etendeka Mountain Camp— Tel. (061) 225178 or 226174, Fax (061) 33332

Etendeka is a permanent tented camp in the Grootberge range east of Palmwag. The area hosts many of the same game as Palmwag including black rhino and elephant and here you have the opportunity to camp and hike around an isolated area of the country with all equipment provided by your hosts. You need only carry drinking water and camera as you hike to a trail camp. Meals are taken care of by the staff and as water is sometimes scarce, bucket showers are provided—a real wilderness experience!

Khowarib Restcamp

This primitive, yet lovely, rest camp is one of the few community based rest camps created recently by the local people of Damaraland. By creating a way for the local Damara people to survive off tourism, they will have an incentive to protect wild game which is sometimes in conflict with their way of life. It is also a way for the Damara and others to have more of a say in their own destiny rather than just working for traditional tourist sites.

A small stream runs through the middle of the rest camp, separating the traditional mud hut accommodations on top of the cliffs above the river from the bashir grass A-frame beds situated on the sandy banks. Here you have a chance to live in a primitive style like so many of the Damara and Himba people in northwestern Namibia. There are not many facilities here, but you will find a nice toilet hidden among the river bush and bucket showers. There is a small gift shop selling handmade curios but no cool drinks yet as the money for propane refrigeration is not available. There is good water on tap but please conserve. You can also take a ride in a traditional donkey cart up the canyon for R15 per half hour—max. 3 people. Traditional dancing and singing are available on request for a donation. Hiking guides will show you around the area for R15 per half day or R25 a full day.

Rates: Huts R25/night; camps on river R20-30 for up to 4 people, R50 for 8 person camp, tent space R10; showers R2 per bucket; wood R5 (exact change helps).

Ongongo Waterfall

This lovely waterfall spills into a clear pool that is welcome relief after the long, hot, dusty drive you take to get to this area. It is popular with both locals and tourists but if you come at the right time you'll have it all to yourself. The water is usually cooler in the morning and late afternoon as it is fed by a small, shallow stream.

This is another spot that the local community has developed in a limited way. Camping is possible although there's not much in the way of facilities. Being one of the few ways that the people have of surviving here, they now charge a few rand per person to use the pool and R10 to camp overnight. They keep the place clean and prevent goats and other livestock from fouling the waters. Some of the local youth will have you sign the guest book and pay the entry fee.

To get there from Warmquelle, turn right at the sign for Warmquelle school and follow the signs. After 2.7 km. you come to a gate and another 2 km. you cross a small river and follow a pipeline constructed to bring the town water. After another 1.3 km. you'll come to the gate where you can park or take a 4-wheel drive road down another 100 meters or so to get a little closer to the waterfall. It's only 50 meters from here to the pool.

Warmquelle

A small Damara goat farming community about 25 km. southeast of Sesfontein, here is a store with the barest of provisions. There is a school and a pipeline from the Ongongo waterfall to bring water to the town.

Sesfontein

Situated as far north as you should go without a 4-wheel drive, this is the gateway to the wild rugged region of Kaokoland, where there is not a lot in the way of services. If you want to explore beyond this point, bring up to date maps, water and plenty of petrol as you won't find any north of here unless you're going to Opuwo. There are a few shops in town, though some are off the main road and you may need directions to find them. We arrived here on a hot Sunday and drove around a maze of small roads looking for stores (all but one were closed) and we were out of luck for a cold drink. After we settled for a warm Fanta we met lots of friendly people in front of the store who were as curious about us as we were about them.

There is no petrol here, so make sure you fill up at Palmwag and be sure Opuwo has petrol before you head up that way. Talk with travelers for information about the area as this is often helpful in the case of washed out roads.

Kamanjab

This small town has a 24 hr. Shell station and a store where you can stock up on goods for a trip into the veld (Hours M-F 8-1 and 1:30-6) Tel. (0020) 2 or 45. The store will also change foreign cash for you at decent rates. The owner is working on a rest camp but as of early 1993 there is no lodging in town. If you're fortunate enough to be flying in, phone ahead and he'll get you fuel.

There is a drankwinkel for ice and cold drinks and a small bakery. The Total station has a garage for repairs and there is a clinic for medical emergencies.

Rock Engravings

Kamanjab's only real tourist attraction is a quantity of rock engravings just outside town at Peet Alberts Koppie. About 4 km. north on the road to Outjo you'll see a small dirt road on the left. Follow it for 2 km. until it deadends at a gate. Park here and climb around the upper portions of the koppie where there are thousands of crude engravings, not as defined as those of Twyfelfontein but certainly more numerous. Judging from the content, there were lots of giraffe at the time they were etched.

Huab Lodge—Tel. (06542), Otjikondo 4931

Though not scheduled to open until late 1993 or early 1994, this place promises to be unusual. About halfway between Khorixas and Kamanjab on the C35 road turn west and travel 33 km. on a good road through no fewer than 10 gates (although many are planned to come down) to get there.

Two couples, Jan and Suzi Van de Reep and Udo Weck and Dorothea Daiber, have purchased and are renovating an old rest camp and adjoining farm on the Huab River. They are in the process of trying to get other farms to join in and create a sort of reserve for the elephants that live along the Huab and in the surrounding desert.

The elephants and farmers along the river have been at odds in the past when the elephants destroyed gardens and fences in their search for food and farmers sometimes killed them or had them removed by Nature Conservation officials. Their idea is to create a buffer zone and fence-free habitat for the remaining animals to minimize human-animal conflict. By allowing tourism and by getting the community involved in protecting the game so they benefit as well, they hope the elephants will flourish.

We camped in the river one night next to the lodge site and were awakened by two large elephants standing just two meters from our small tent! They soon left and went up river to eat but it was an unforgettable experience.

The Huab Lodge is planned to be an upmarket lodge of 10 thatched bungalows with baths and a swimming pool. Fences will be torn down and solar power will be used instead of generators. A nearby hot springs may be developed as well.

Hobatere Lodge—Tel. (0020) 2022

Situated in the northernmost finger of Damaraland that juts between Etosha and Kaokoland, this is a wonderful place to stay if you want a chance to spot big game close up. Elephants are frequently seen cruising through the camp or drinking out of the swimming pool, and the roar of lions can be heard at night. Our first afternoon here was spent watching elephants come through the camping area munching their way down to the waterhole a few hundred meters from the lodge. All sorts of game frequent the waterhole but to see even more, go on one of the day or night game drives.

Hobatere sits in a 320 sq. km. concession area bordering Etosha National Park with the lodge itself 16 km. off the Kamanjab-Opuwo road. They are planning some unusual accommodations at Hobatere such as a tree-house suite, where you should be able to see lions from a safe vantage point.

Guided hiking for R60 per hour—6 people maximum—is

possible during your stay. There is a primitive bush camp a few kilometers from the lodge where guests can stay for R50/night. This is definitely a place to check out. Camping is also possible at Hobatere though the campsite is closer to the road. For more information about Hobatere, see the Guest Farm section in this chapter.

Kaokoland

Kaokoland gets its name from Herero for the left arm, meaning the left bank of the Kunene. It's a forbidding territory that is home to one of the tribes least affected by civilization, the Himba. It's a rugged but fascinating place to explore though care must be taken to safeguard the fragile environment.

Opuwo (Opuwa)

Opuwo is the only real town in Kaokoland where you can get such essentials as petrol, food and ice, but is strikingly different from other towns in Namibia, mostly due to the presence of the Himba who make their home in the surrounding hills. The name Opuwo, meaning finished or enough, dates to when the old South African administration wanted to build a town at Kaoko Otavi to the west. The local Himba chiefs said that the town could only be built at the site which is now Opuwo. After some discussion, the chiefs decided that the matter was finished (opuwo in the Ovahimba language) and that was that.

Being a real frontier town it's the place most people in Kaokoland stock up before heading off into the rough, rocky tracks of the territory.

To get to Opuwo, take the TransNamib bus from Outjo that goes once a week or try hitching a ride, though traffic is often sparse, at best. Getting further will require your own vehicle or hitchhiking. If you're driving, take the C35 200 km. north of Kamanjab, where you turn left at the sign and proceed for 50 km.

Where to Stay

Your choice of lodging in Opuwo is limited to the ENOK-FNDC guest house which charges R25 per person. It is fairly well equipped, so you just need to bring your food. There are 18 beds in 8 rooms and you must contact Mr. Grobbelaar at the Groothandel Wholesale to get a bed here. If you're calling, try him at work (0020) 17, or at home (0020) 36. His fax number is (0020) 85. Many people, however just drive out of town for a few kilometers and camp.

Stocking Up

The BP petrol station is open from 7-6 although they sometimes run out of fuel and you must wait for a day or two. They have a limited supply of spare parts as well. The nearest fuel is Kamanjab (245 km.) or Ruacana (130 km.) There is a bakery open from 7-6 M-F and 8-12 Sat.and Sun. for fresh breads and some sweets. The Groothandel Wholesale mentioned earlier is the biggest market in town—they have a decent selection of food, frozen meat, hardware, auto supplies, camping stoves, frequently ice, sometimes vegetables and old newspapers. Hours are 8-1 and 2-5 M-F and the last two Saturdays of the month from 8-12. If he is not open, there's another smaller market on the main road that's open Saturdays from 2-7. There's a drankwinkel next to the Groothandel for beer, liquor and cold drinks. A post office and hospital are also part of Opuwo. There is a Nature Conservation office on the main street where you can get additional information about Kaokoland if you wish—however, staff are frequently out in the field and the office is not always manned.

The Himba

The Ovahimba people who call Kaokoland home share a common ancestry and language with the Herero people. They maintain their traditional dress with the men usually wearing a necklace of beads or shells dyed dark brown, a belt draped with fabric, and a small metal arrow tucked into their cloth-

*Married Himba woman
in Kaokoland.*

bound hair for itches. The women are adorned with copper
or lead belts, anklets, bracelets, and necklaces, goat skin
headdress, skirts made of animal hide and a beautiful white
sea shell around their neck. The women also dye their body
orange-brown with an ochre-animal fat mixture and coat
their hair with it as well. Hair styles and dress vary with age
and marital status, with some of the younger boys having
amazing hairdos.

There are approximately 5000 Himba inhabiting the area,
though census figures are difficult to obtain due to the re-
moteness of the region and the fact that they also cross the
border with Angola freely and inhabit southern Angola to a
certain extent. They are a fascinating and friendly people, not
accustomed to dealing with the outside world except in

Himba youth.

chance meetings with tourists in the region and an occasional trip to Opuwo. They are herders of cattle and goats and live off them almost exclusively at times. For the most part they speak only Ovahimba, but some have learned a bit of Afrikaans, Portuguese or English. In general, expect to use universal sign language to communicate. Here are a few words in Ovahimba for those interested:

Hello, good day	*moro*
Thanks	*dankie*
How's it going?	kapiri nawa
Goodbye	karup oo nawa
Water	omia
Living area	onganda

Good, OK   nawa
Thank you   okawipa

Cultural Dos and Don'ts

It is considered proper for the Himba to come and join your campfire as it shows respect and curiosity. It is also OK to join their fire, however, when entering a village it is best to ask a resident or the headman for permission to walk around. Don't go poking into people's houses, even abandoned looking ones, as they are semi-nomadic and leave their mud, cattle dung and branch houses and some belongings when they are moving with their herds. Don't enter the area between their house entrance and the fire ring and cattle corral as this is considered bad manners.

They are as curious as you probably are, so ask questions and interact freely—they are quite friendly. Most will ask you for something, particularly tobacco, pain medicine, matches, food or money. Many have probably been given things by tourists or aid workers in the area and since they don't have these things available and it is often several days walk into Opuwo, they see your bakkie packed with things and assume that you have scarce goods. It is not impolite to refuse but to have the Himba depending on handouts is not encouraged. What is now being promoted is to trade them food or tobacco for something of value like wood carvings or something else they are willing to trade. If you want to photograph them, ask first and possibly give them something in trade for this as it will be appreciated.

You may find some Himba on the track asking for a ride. It may take several days to walk from their home village to Opuwo, traveling with most of their belongings wrapped up in a cloth or skin, getting food from people along the way. Both men and women smoke pipes, often lighting them with a flint or burning embers enclosed in a small tube made from bone or antler.

Kaokoland Interior

There has been for some time a proposal for a Kaokoland

Reserve to be established as there are currently no laws to control tourism and off-road driving in the area. The reserve area would include extending the Skeleton Coast Park eastwards to include a chunk of Kaokoland. Currently, there are no permits required for the area but this will change when the reserve is approved by the Namibian legislature. Some sort of permit for tourists will be required to enter the area, so check with the tourist office before coming to the interior.

Once you get away from Opuwo, there are many interesting tracks to explore, nearly all of which require a 4-wheel drive vehicle with high clearance. It is recommended that you travel in a party of two 4-wheel drive vehicles because help may be a long ways away. Some of these tracks are incredibly rocky and rough; don't expect to average more than 25-30 km. per hour on a good road here. One section of road we took would definitely have been faster by foot— we averaged less than 5 km. per hour! Some pieces of track must be repaired before going on and others are impassable after good rains. A good recent topographical map of the area, a compass and asking directions from people you encounter are essential to make your way around without getting lost. Spare tires, lots of fuel in jerry cans or a spare tank or both, plenty of water and food, and patience are necessary for traveling through the area. Remember that the only fuel available is in Opuwo, Palmwag or Ruacana, so plan accordingly. Gas consumption will certainly be greater on the slow tracks of Kaokoland— figure about 50-100 percent more than normal depending on your vehicle and the track. You might want to bring some extra food such as mielie meal, sugar, aspirin or non-prescription pain pills, matches or tobacco to trade with the Himba. If you happen to break down, you may wait for a few days before help comes depending on where you are. Ask the Himba for help as they will probably help you with what they can.

Game in Kaokoland has taken quite a beating due to uncontrolled hunting and elephants that used to roam the area have all but disappeared. Lately, however, poaching has been largely controlled with the co-operation of the Himba and populations have rebounded, with game such as springbok and zebra being re-introduced. Don't expect to see herds of game as much has been hunted over recent years and the vegetation is often thick. Fishing in the Kunene can bring in bream, barbel and pike, though hunting in Kaokoland is strictly prohibited.

Stay on the main track and don't create tracks where there are none as the environment is fragile and often takes years or even decades to repair itself. Also, many tracks increase the chance that others will get lost as the main track is sometimes just barely discernible. A recent article in a popular South African travel magazine touting Kaokoland as the ultimate test for a new 4-wheel drive resulted 4-wheelers creating tracks and roads in many sensitive areas. Treat the area and people with respect and your time there will be extremely rewarding. The following are a few of the places in Kaokoland which can be visited.

Epupa Falls

Epupa gets its name from Herero meaning flow or wash. Situated on Namibia's northern border with Angola, Epupa Falls is an incredible cascade of the clear Kunene surrounded by palms and baobabs, abundant with bird species as well as a few crocodiles and possibly a few hippos. Some of the bird species include rosyfaced lovebirds, blue waxbills, Rüppels parrots, scarlet sunbirds, golden weavers and bee-eaters. Be sure to take a dip in the cool water above the falls, checking first for crocs or hippos, both of which tend to avoid the rapids. When swimming anywhere along the Kunene, remember there are many hungry crocodile waiting for an easy meal and they are extremely difficult to spot. There are only a handful of hippo left in the Kunene in Namibia, but it's best to look out for them as well! Rocky pools surrounded by rapids are the best bet for swimming, while reeds or nice sandy beaches are to be avoided.

The campsites along the river's edge are kept clean by the

resident Himba and they ask for a donation as part of a plan to involve the local population in tourism and reap them some benefit. Use the toilets provided and take out all trash with you. The service of keeping the site clean is well worth it, so give what you can while this wonderful place lasts as it is due to fall victim to a hydroelectric dam which will inundate the falls itself and the surrounding region. Due to future dam construction a semi-decent road has been built to the falls from Onkangwati; you can make it with a 2-wheel drive in the dry season although one with high clearance is preferred.

Getting There

To get there you must take the D3700 towards Epembe and Okangwati, also shown on the map as Otjijanjasemo. Drive slowly as the dips in the road are quite steep and can be filled with water after rains. When the road splits, take the left fork to Okangwati as the right goes to Epembe. About 110 km. from Opuwo, you come to Okangwati, where there is a small store which often has cool drinks and some food. Turn right past the store and go through a part of town with ramshackle housing. You will end up on a good road heading north-northwest. The road gets a little rougher from here on as you cover the 75 km. to Epupa Falls. The Kunene comes as quite a surprise after crossing through the often dry rocky terrain.

From Epupa, you can travel east along the Kunene with a 4-wheel drive for about 150 km. to Ruacana or about 100 km. to Swartbooisdrif and get back to Opuwo from either location. The road is extremely rough and the trip will take all day. There are many Himba living along the river with their goat and cattle. At Swartbooisdrif the road splits and you take the south road back to Opuwo. After 5 km. you pass a small sodalite mine, a dark blue mineral found only here and in Siberia. You can collect small pieces of sodalite along the road past the mine. Take care as you approach the Opuwo road as it's easy to get lost among the tangle of back roads here.

If you continue on from Swartbooisdrif along the river you come to the Okauahone Lodge, a shady primitive place where you can camp for R15 with an extra R15 for your vehicle, or try a 3 bed hut for R30 or 4 beds for R45. They have cool, though not cold, drinks and a small swimming pool. You can boat or fish along the river here at the lodge. If you want to camp along the river anywhere, do so away from people's homes and kraals or ask permission to camp within their settlement area.

West of Opuwo

If you are heading west of Opuwo up to the Marienfluss or the Kunene river west of Epupa Falls, there are several tracks to take, the easiest being the track heading southwest through Kaoko Otavi and Orupembe that passes many Himba settlements along the way. Another more difficult route is northwest through Okangwati, Otjihende and down Van Zyl's pass into the Marienfluss. The road is good up to Okangwati, but afterwards deteriorates into a rocky track where you might average 10-15 km./hour or less in some places.

Spend a couple of days getting to the Kunene—any faster and your bones will surely be jarred to the point where you will agonize at the thought of returning. Ask for the way to the next place name on the map as tracks are small and barely discernible in some points. Keep in mind that these place names are just that—there is often no habitation visible from the track. Otjihende, for example, is just a small stream crossing and you may or may not see people there. Just after Otjihende the track goes steeply downward as you descend Van Zyl's pass. **DO NOT attempt Van Zyl's pass in a west to east direction—it is a steep, slippery and rocky climb and you'll probably get stuck miles from help.** Locals who have lived in Kaokoland for years say they will not go this way; it is bad enough going down in first gear using the brakes and trying to see the track over the front of the bakkie as you lurch over one boulder at a time!

The surrounding terrain starts getting noticeably drier as you cross the pass and enter the eastern fringes of the Namib Desert. It's about a 70 km. drive on a good flat sandy road through the Marienfluss. It feels great to be able to drive at normal speeds again! Keep in mind that this area is very sensitive to off-road driving so stay on the main track!

The Marienfluss is a grassy broad expanse with panoramic views of the Hartmann's range on the west and the Otjihipa range on the east. The area looks like it could support herds of game, but the lack of water won't allow it, although near the Kunene you will probably come across ostrich, springbok, oryx and possibly zebra.

As you are driving up the Marienfluss, you'll notice thousands of circular areas amid the grass where nothing grows. What causes these so-called fairy circles is the subject of many theories. They could be caused by termites that come in a good rain year and start building circular mounds, only to have them blown away by the winds. Another theory has it that when euphorbia plants die they leave a toxic substance that inhibits growth of other grasses; yet another postulates that the circles are hard pans that won't allow water to penetrate, thus preventing growth. In any case it's a strange sight in this beautiful area.

Arriving at the Kunene, you'll see a sign for Syncro Camp where you can follow the track to the right and find a small shaded camp with primitive but well built reed huts as well as a cooking and washing area and toilet. It is used by tour groups but anyone is welcome to stay in the hut or camp for R10 per person. There are no beds in the huts.

About 3 km. north beyond the sign is a track to the right where there is a nice camping spot under some trees. Another 3 km. north takes you to a place where the track divides into 3 parts—the right one goes to a secluded campsite, the middle to a beach where swimming is a welcome relief (keeping in mind the crocs) and the left track to a viewpoint above the river. The level of the river can fluctuate greatly in any given day so don't camp next to the river! There is a good quantity of bird life here including bee-eaters, black crake, herons, cormorants and many raptor species. This is a truly out of the way place and you might find yourself alone with the few

Himba residents who may trade wood carvings for food. Again, please take all your trash with you as this place hasn't been spoiled yet and should continue to remain this way.

Leaving the Kunene, you travel back down the Marienfluss about 40 km. from the Syncro Camp sign where the road forks. You'll want the right fork here as the left takes you back to the dreaded Van Zyl's Pass which should not be attempted going towards Opuwo. Another 30 km. after taking the right fork you'll come to Rooidrum (Red Drum) where, sure enough, there is a red oil drum which marks another split in the track—the right fork leading to a sandy track up the Hartmann's Valley to the Kunene and the left fork heading towards Orupembe another 50 km. beyond on a semi-rough track. Hartmann's valley is a beautiful drive ending in sand dunes that descend to the Kunene, a seldom visited spot! Check in Opuwo before coming this way. At Orupembe, you can take the track back to Opuwo or continue on to Purros and Sesfontein, reaching Palmwag for fuel and perhaps a cold beer!

Ruacana Falls (Valle)

Although politically part of Owamboland, Ruacana Falls is geographically part of the rocky, mountainous Kaokoland region and is included here. If you come from Owamboland you'll be surprised as you first see this area after hours of flat terrain. It's a beautiful, relatively unused area with the Kunene flowing down from Angola and the distant mountains of Kaokoland visible. The Kunene's water is used for the power station and is also diverted through pipes and canals into Owamboland up to about 100 km. past Oshakati. The falls were not flowing when we were there as the water level in the Kunene was not sufficient to run the hydroelectric station and keep the falls running.

The hydroelectric station at Ruacana Falls is run by SWAWEK, the Namibian state electrical company and can in the best of times supply Namibia's entire electrical needs and even sell surplus. The water comes from the Calueque Dam in Angola and is fed into the turbines through pressure tunnels. It currently produces about 50-60 megawatts which supplies only 30 percent of Namibia's electricity but has a capability of 250 megawatts. The turbines are shut down daily to allow water pressure to build up; when the flow reaches 220 cubic meters/second, the falls can be turned on. March-April are reputedly the best time to see the 100 meter high falls.

To get there follow the sign to the falls (valle). You'll come to a small sign on a tree where you turn right. There is a border station here where you go straight through the gate to the falls or right into Angola, where you see a crumbling border station with a tattered flag.

There is a camping spot on the Kunene which you can get to by following the tar road past the waterfall turn-off and turning right when the tar ends. Unfortunately, this sight has been thoroughly trashed and bottles and cans are lying everywhere. It seemed like an ideal site for a community rest camp if it were cleaned up! If you follow the road straight past where the tar road ends, it's about a 2 hour drive to the Okauahone Lodge on the Kunene and a rough, long road to Epupa Falls.

Ruacana Town (Dorp)

The fortified town of Ruacana is 5 km. from the main road on a smaller road that provides the sole entry or exit to the town. It's mostly inhabited by SWAWEK people but used to be a military base, evidenced by the earth berm and barbed wire surrounding the entire town and bomb shelters in many backyards. There is a fenced section of land outside the town that still has land mines! A small market and BP station has petrol during the day. It's possible to stay in the SWAWEK guest house but it must be booked in Windhoek at the SWAWEK office.

Guest Farms in the Kaokoland-Damaraland Area

Hobatere Lodge—P.O. Box 110, Kamanjab, Tel. (0020) 2022
Hugging Etosha National Parks' western border, Hobatere

Lodge guest farm is hosted by the Brains. A prime game viewing area for all species, it offers 11 accommodations all with twin beds, their own toilets and showers. There is a bar and restaurant with a set menu and a swimming pool. Game drives are their specialty—both day and night—and you may see elephant, lion, cheetah, leopard, giraffe, aardvark, aardwolf and many other species. During the dry months, elephants often come around the lodge itself along with other animals. Game drives are R70 per hour—maximum 5 passengers during the day—and R80 per hour at night. They are busiest June-Sept. when you should book 3 months in advance but 1 year in August! During Dec.-Feb. 1 week in advance is usually enough.

To get there out of Outjo, take the C40 west to Kamanjab and then the C35 towards Ruacana for 65 km. where you turn left and after another 15 km. arrive.

Rates: Single R180 B&B, R220 Full board; Double R155 per person B&B, R195 per person full board.

Bambatsi Holiday Ranch—P.O. Box 120, Outjo, Tel. (06542) 1104

Situated on a hill with a great view of a mopane forest, Bambatsi is 65 km. east of Khorixas or 75 km. west of Outjo on the Outjo-Khorixas road; turn north at the small sign. They have 8 bungalows with private bathrooms and offer walking and driving trips on a 10,000 hectare cattle ranch where game is also seen. Local trips may be arranged to Vingerklip, Twyfelfontein and other attractions. Open March—October, they have electricity only 4 hours in the evening. Aug.-Oct reserve 3 months ahead; May & June 1-2 weeks.

Rates: R130 per person B&B, R175 per person full board.

Otjitambi—P.O. Box 2607, Outjo, Tel. (06542) 4602

The Otjitambi farm, hosted by J. Schlettwein, is located on the southeastern border of the Kaokoveld and comprises 11,650 hectares. To get there from Outjo take the Kamanjab road to D3246 and turn left. Hiking trails, bird and game viewing from blinds next to waterholes, a swimming pool and hot thermal baths will keep you busy. Five double and three single rooms come with private bathrooms. They specialize in sightseeing flights by airplane (R500 per hour) or microlight! (R140 per hour).

Apr.-Aug. reserve 1 month ahead, Oct.-March 1 week.

Rates: R180 per person full board; discount for kids under 15.

CHAPTER 11

Caprivi Region

The far northeastern strip of land known as the Caprivi is vastly different from the rest of the country in terms of its appearance and the people found here. Jutting into central southern Africa, it is more lush and green with the feeling of an entirely different country.

Caprivi

Upon crossing the Okavango and the checkpoint at the Bagani bridge, you enter western Caprivi and the West Caprivi Game Park. A park in name only, it has not been developed and currently there is no accessibility for tourists except for a settlement of some ex-SWAPO fighters and San-Bushmen at Omega and the small triangle outside the eastern park boundary next to the Cuando River, which is administered by Nature Conservation as part of a core conservation area.

The Caprivi has an interesting and unusual history. It is a long narrow strip of land bordered by Botswana on the south and Angola and Zambia on the north with the far eastern tip just touching Zimbabwe's far west. Varying in width from 30 km. to 100 km. and approximately 500 km. long, it is named after General Count Georg Leo von Caprivi di Caprara di Montecuccoli, who was chancellor of Germany after Bismarck.

It was supposedly given to Germany by Great Britain in exchange for Zanzibar. Germany hoped it would lead to a trade route through central Africa from the then German-administered Southwest Africa. When World War I began, the

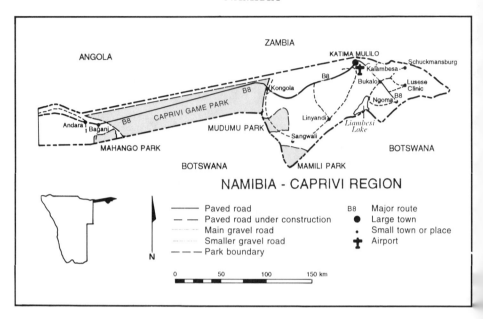

NAMIBIA - CAPRIVI REGION

story goes, the British commander was having tea with his German counterpart across the river in what is now Zambia. A servant brought in a sealed message saying Britain was at war with Germany which the commander handed to the German while simultaneously declaring him a prisoner of war. Britain subsequently took the territory in what is now Namibia without a shot being fired, this being the first Allied occupation of enemy territory of the war.

After the war the Caprivi was administered by British ruled Bechuanaland (now Botswana) until being handed over to South African ruled South West Africa in 1929. Upon independence it remained part of Namibia.

The main tribes in the Caprivi are the Bafwe who inhabit the Cuando river area and eastward toward Katima Mulilo, and the Basubia who live in easternmost Caprivi. They have a great degree of autonomy in managing their affairs with chiefs, tribal courts and elders laying out the law in some cases. The common language which the locals use is Silozi, while English is a common second language and Afrikaans is rarely heard. The people herd cattle and goats and grow mahango (millet), sorghum and maize.

Community Based Conservation

One of the challenges facing modern day Caprivi is how people whose livelihood depends upon stock animals and crops can co-exist with wild game, whose presence often conflicts with agriculture. Elephants can rampage through a field of maize leaving a wake of destruction and lions can kill off livestock, causing devastating economic losses. The traditional solution is to remove the offending predator or shoot it. If game numbers continue to dwindle due to this conflict as well as poaching, Namibia stands to lose one of its potentially valuable resources and irreparable damage may occur to the ecosystem.

One possible solution now being explored is so-called community based conservation, an idea supported and run with the co-operation of the Department of Nature Conservation, non-governmental organizations like Integrated Rural Development and Endangered Wildlife Trust, the local community and some local businesses like Lianshulu Lodge. The philosophy is for communities to benefit from conservation through money made from increased tourism, professional hunting (which can generate large trophy fees) instead of culling, nature conservation jobs and revenue from arts and crafts and community based campsites. The current challenge is changing legislation so communities get this money directly rather than have the money go into general coffers. To date a few jobs have been provided. Seeing wildlife as a benefit rather than a pest is necessary to make the scheme work. Community based conservation is being applied in many localities in northern Namibia.

Popa Rapids Rest Camp

Though technically in eastern Kavango, this part of Namibia is geographically within the Caprivi strip. Known as

Popa Falls on all tourist information brochures and maps, this is actually a small set of rapids on the Okavango where it crosses the Caprivi strip and heads into Botswana to form the famed Okavango delta. Meaning "here" in the Kavango language, Popa is where you'll find one the nicest rest camps in all of Namibia. It is famous for abundant and diverse bird life that thrives in the riverine forest. We spotted black-collared barbet, paradise flycatcher, Heuglin's robin, several species of bee-eaters, pied kingfisher and many sun birds. It also happens to be just down the road from Mahango Park, with its large elephant population.

You can have a roomy 4 bed bungalow in the forest near the river or camp in one of several closely spaced campsites with water and braai pit. The ablution blocks are spotless and there is a building for cooking complete with gas stove and fridge with lantern lighting at night. The office has a surprisingly well-stocked store where frozen meat, eggs, milk, cool drinks, bread and other groceries are sold. A small tributary of the Kavango river runs through the camp area and creates a shallow swimming pool and rapids in which to take a refreshing dip. There are trails to the main river and rapids which are frequented by bird watchers. Be on the lookout for snakes, crocs and hippos! (It is not advisable to swim in the river as crocs and hippo are often present.) If you like to fish, get a license at the office for R2. Collecting firewood is prohibited but they sell it at the office.

Rates: Bungalows R70 for up to 4 people; camping R20 per night plus R5 per vehicle or person one time charge.

Suclabo Lodge— Tel. (067372) 6222

A few kilometers down the road from Popa Rapids is the Suclabo Lodge named after owners Susie, Claudia and Boris. Five small basic bungalows with communal ablutions are situated around a grassy area which can be used as a campground. The restaurant sits high above the Okavango's banks where you can watch hippos playing in the water. River access is down a short trail where you can rent canoes for

R20/hour or take a cruise on a motor boat up to the rapids for R25 per person/hour. Dinners R30.

Rates: R95 per person B&B; camping R17 per person per night.

Ngepi

Still further down the road towards Mahango is Ngepi Camp. Ngepi means "How is it?" in Kavango. In answer to the question, we found it a pleasant place to camp with a bit more room than Popa Rapids but not as organized. But for solitude along the lazily flowing river, it will do. You can fish, have a drink at the bar, or take a boat or canoe trip. At present only camping is possible.

Rates: Camping R12 per person. Boat trip R20 per hour plus R2 liter petrol.

Mahango Park

Mahango is a 25,000 hectare (62,500 acre) game reserve and National Park nestled between the Okavango river and Botswana. It is known for 350 species of birds and a large elephant population in addition to lechwe, reedbuck, sable and roan antelope, bushbuck, warthog, zebra, hippo, crocodile, wildebeest and lion. We were there at the beginning of the rainy season around Christmas and saw all of the above game except lion in addition to a plethora of bird species. A highlight was following a herd of elephant swimming and frolicking in the river.

A wonderful feature of Mahango is the ability to wander about the park on foot (taking care to move slowly) as elephant are likely to be encountered. The park seems to have too many elephant, a fact acknowledged by several people familiar with the area. Elephants tend to destroy their habitat when overcrowded and there are uprooted trees and smashed bushes. It's still a fantastic place to visit, especially along the river and flood plain which supports much of the wildlife.

The road to Botswana runs right through the park and is suitable for 2-wheel drive vehicles. There is one picnic spot

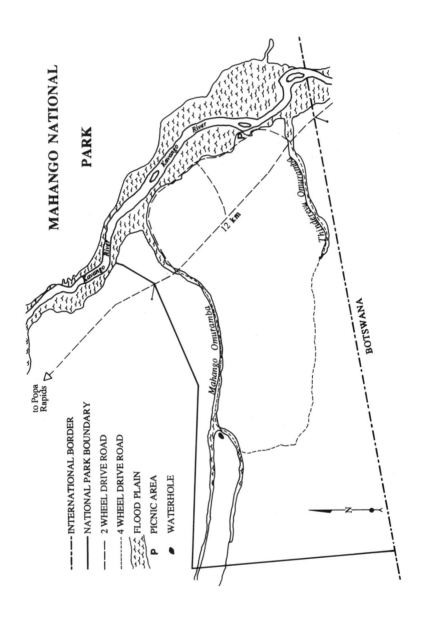

MAHANGO NATIONAL PARK

to Popa Rapids

Kavango River

Kavango River

12 km

Mahango Omuramba

Thinderevu Omuramba

BOTSWANA

N

INTERNATIONAL BORDER
NATIONAL PARK BOUNDARY
2 WHEEL DRIVE ROAD
4 WHEEL DRIVE ROAD
FLOOD PLAIN
P   PICNIC AREA
●   WATERHOLE

next to the river along a side road that is great for exploring or watching the hippos closeby or the game wandering about the flood plain. There is also a less frequently visited sandy 4-wheel drive loop that runs for approximately 30 km. past omurambas and waterholes surrounded by thick teak woodland. There is no overnighting allowed in Mahango and the gate hours are 7-6. It's only 15 km. down the road from Popa Rapids and the entry fee is R15 per vehicle, which you need not pay if you're traveling through to Botswana.

To Botswana

If you're planning a trip down to Botswana from here, there are a couple of places to stay not too far over the border and we've heard the road is now paved to Maun except for the first 70 km. or so past Shakawe Fishing Camp. The only problem you may have is petrol, as there is none between Mukwe and Maun, a distance of about 430 km. Check locally before proceeding. The border post at Mohembo is open from 6-7 and you must have your tires and soles of your feet sprayed with disinfectant to control foot and mouth disease. You must also pay 5 pula (R7.50) for third party insurance, good for one year, upon entering Botswana. Reporting to the police in Shakawe is no longer necessary.

Lodging in Botswana

The first thing you'll notice about Botswana are the prices, which are much higher than Namibia's.

Drotsky's Cabins

Located about 20 km. south of the border past the small town of Shakawe, Drotsky's has a new restaurant and bar, 6 comfortable chalets and a camping area. They accept most foreign currencies. During Aug.-Nov. bee-eaters, including the reddish-pink carmine bee-eater, form nesting colonies in the banks of the river.

Rates: Chalets R165 per person; camping R18 per person. Meals run from R37 for breakfast to R67 for dinner.

Shakawe Fishing Camp

Another 3.5 km. past the Drotsky's turnoff is the Shakawe Fishing Camp, which was not nearly as nice as Drotsky's. The grounds had a noticeable lack of grass but it seemed like a good spot to fish and drink beer. They'll rent you fishing gear if you don't have your own.

Rates: Chalets R150 single, R225 double; Camping R22 per person.

The West Caprivi Triangle

This small roughly triangular shaped piece of land wedged between West Caprivi Game Park and the Cuando River is currently administered by Nature Conservation. An entry permit can be obtained at the offices in Windhoek, Katima Mulilo or the local Susuwe office just off the Caprivi Highway. Elephants can be seen in abundance here, especially during the dry season (May-August). Herds of up to 1,500 have been reported recently and have actually been a problem for some tourists. (Imagine yourself on a road in the middle of such a herd!) They can be quite aggressive so inquire at the office about the current behavior of the pachyderms. It is also not advisable to drive at night, especially on the faster Caprivi highway (The Golden Highway) where elephants are hard to see.

Other game include buffalo, hippo, lion, roan, giraffe, sable, kudu, impala, lechwe, wild dog and the hard to spot sitatunga. Wattled cranes, saddlebilled stork, narina trogon and ground hornbills are some of the more interesting birds spotted here. A system of undeveloped 2 and 4-wheel drive tracks make this remote region accessible. There are currently two secluded, primitive campsites which have no facilities and are ideal for those wishing to be alone in this beautiful area. The northern site at Chisu is difficult to find and sometimes has a problem with tsetse flies, which sting and leave a large welt but are otherwise harmless. The site overlooks the Cuando and the surrounding flood plain and is close to the border with Angola—which you should be careful not to cross.

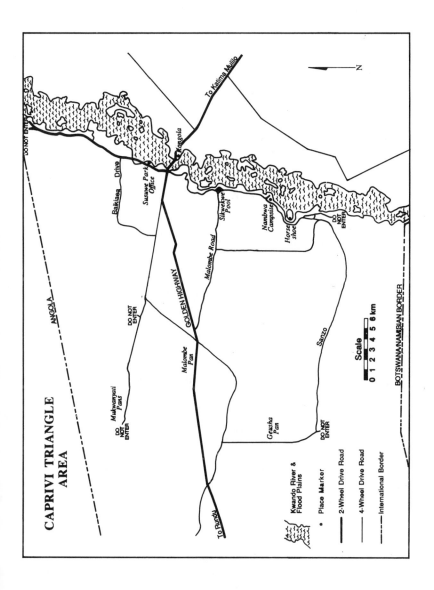

The southern Nambwe campsite is across a causeway over the flood plain. It is on a small "island" next to the reed and papyrus lined river. On the way you pass a former South African military base which was used during the war for independence. The mosquitoes can be bad during April-June; the best time to visit is probably July-December. Campsites are currently free of charge if you have a permit. To get a permit, turn left off the Caprivi Highway at the Nature Conservation sign just before you come to the Cuando River crossing at Kongola. Drive 3 km. taking the left fork in the road until you see the Susuwe office signposted. Here you can get information, permits for the Triangle, Mudumu or Mamili National Parks and buy an interesting selection of locally made curios. If no one is there, just wait awhile.

East Caprivi

Upon crossing the Cuando River, whose source is in the highlands of Angola, you enter East Caprivi at Kongola. You go through a checkpoint here and have the option of continuing on tarred road to Katima Mulilo or detouring south into a seldom visited part of Namibia which includes Mudumu and Mamili National Parks and the Linyanti Swamps. The terrain in east Caprivi is very much different from the rest of Namibia with flood plain accounting for about half of the region and Rhodesian teak, mopane and silver terminalia woodland the other half. The only real town where supplies are available is Katima Mulilo, but several smaller settlements have drinks and a few basic supplies. There are several camps along the Cuando—also known as the Mashi—some of which will fade away and some of which will flourish as tourism grows in the area.

Touch Africa Safaris—Tel. & Fax (067352) 453

Touch Africa has two camps along the Cuando, the first being Sitwa which is signposted about 10 km. from the Caprivi highway south of Kongola. About 53 km. from the Caprivi highway south on the Linyanti road is the turn off for Touch Africa's other camp, Mvubu. Follow the sign and it's another 4 km. to the camp itself. It's located in Mudumu National Park and has good game during the dry season (April-November).

At present there's a few thatched huts at Sitwa but the plans are for developing a lodge with an all-inclusive package at about R350 per person per day. They have very basic A-frame huts which are available when there are no tour groups, but they offer camping as well. Guided mokoro or motorboat safaris are available for a reasonable price. These camps may be developed soon and prices will rise accordingly.

Rates: Huts R25 or R37 with bedding per person; camping R15 per person.

Lianshulu Lodge—Tel. (061) 225178, Fax 33332

The only full service private lodge situated in a national park, Lianshulu is definitely one of a kind. A former hunting camp, it has been transformed into a natural paradise that does more than just provide food and lodging to weary travelers. It is an active force in the area of conservation and their philosophy is to promote tourism while running a progressive company. They have started the Lianshulu Lodge Community Conservation Fund used for helping the community develop small enterprises which benefit from tourism and conservation. They also work closely with Nature Conservation and Integrated Rural Development to ameliorate damage to crops and livestock by problem animals.

Nearly all game species numbers are down and some have disappeared from the Caprivi entirely due to uncontrolled hunting and conflict with human settlements. Namibia's policy is in line with restoring game numbers (and tourism) while providing much needed employment through conservation. Currently, a traditional village called Lizauli is planned 12 km. north of the lodge as part of community based tourism; ask about it at the lodge.

The turnoff for Lianshulu Lodge is 40 km. south of the Cuando River crossing at Kongola down the Linyanti road, which is good graded gravel. Turn at the sign and it's a short

4 km. drive to the lodge itself. Consisting of 8 luxurious A-frame thatched huts and run by committed conservationists Grant Burton and Marie Holstenson, the lodge is built in harmony with natural surroundings. It's in Mudumu National Park but there are no signs or development in the park so it sits on the Cuando by itself with birds and game closeby. Hippos have been known to wander across the grounds at night and bird life is prolific. You may see the broad-billed roller, open billed stork or any of a number of bee-eaters along the slowly flowing water. The birds wake you up in the morning and the xylophone-like bell frogs put you to sleep at night. The lodge is lantern lit at night, adding a romantic touch. You can take a drive on Mudumu's few roads or a sunset boat trip along the Cuando. The personal attention you receive here is unmatched.

Rates: R175 per person full board or R275 per person activities included.

Mudumu National Park

Named after a Bafwe chief and declared a national park in 1990, Mudumu is totally undeveloped—there is currently not even a sign saying you are entering a park! Some roads exist, but nothing to guide you. Check with the Nature Conservation office in Windhoek or Katima Mulilo or with Lianshulu Lodge for more information as things may develop in the future with increased tourism.

Mudumu National Park is just over 1,000 sq. km. in size and borders the Cuando on the west where small numbers of lechwe and sitatunga occur. A great place to explore if you keep in mind its undeveloped and fragile nature.

Other Lodging or Camping

About 20 km. down from the Caprivi Highway on the Linyanti road is the turnoff for what is presently a former police camp with plans to make it the Mashi Lodge. They will offer camping in addition to 8 bungalows.

About 18 km. from the highway, the Siloli camp was a campground with ablutions but was in disrepair when we

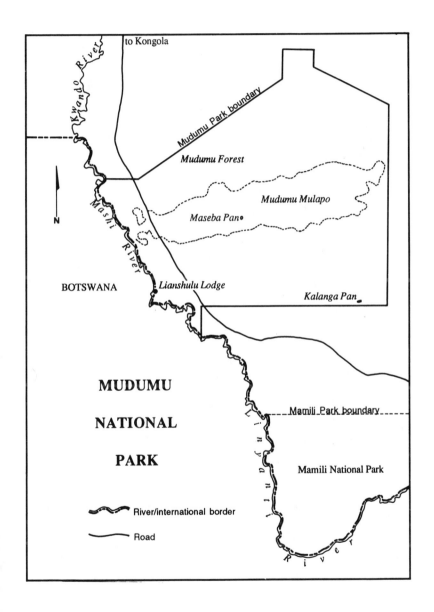

to Kongola

Kwando River

Mudumu Park boundary

Mudumu Forest

Mudumu Mulapo

Maseba Pan

N

Mashi River

BOTSWANA

Lianshulu Lodge

Kalanga Pan

MUDUMU

NATIONAL

PARK

Mamili Park boundary

Linyanti River

Mamili National Park

〜〜〜 River/international border

——— Road

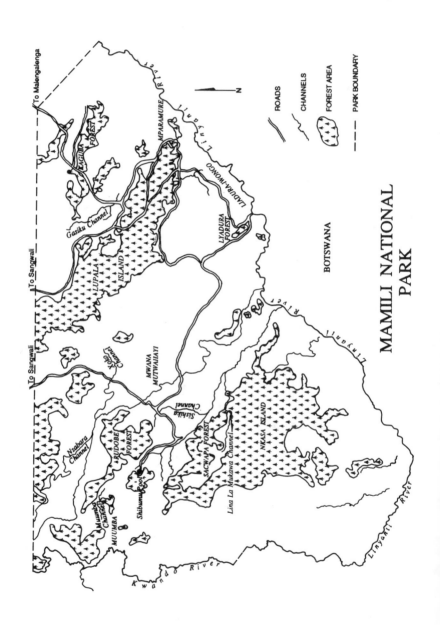

MAMILI NATIONAL PARK

ROADS

CHANNELS

FOREST AREA

PARK BOUNDARY

N

To Malengalenga

To Sangwali

To Sangwali

ZAGUBA FOREST

Gasiku Channel

MPARAMURE RIVER

Linyanti

LIADURA-IWONGO

LIADURA FOREST

LUPALA ISLAND

BOTSWANA

Linyanti River

MWANA MUTWAIIAYI

Xobo Channel

Nzabara Channel

RUDOBE FOREST

Shibumu Pool

Sishilo Channel

SACWAPA FOREST

NKASA ISLAND

Lina La Mukawa Channel

Muumba Channel

MUUMBA

Kwando River

Linyanti River

296

were there. The owner had plans for development into an inexpensive campground.

Mamili National Park

Named after a Bafwe chief, Mamili was declared a national park along with Mudumu in 1990 and is the largest conserved wetland in the country at 320 sq. km. It is centered on the Linyanti Swamp with the Cuando-Linyanti River forming its western and eastern boundaries. (This river becomes the Chobe River before its confluence with the Zambezi at Namibia's eastern tip.) The area can be flooded or dry for lengthy periods depending on the rains. The flood plains and islands are pristine and inhabited by a variety of game such as lechwe, hippo, elephant, buffalo, reedbuck, baboon, lion and cheetah. There are a few basic undeveloped campsites scattered throughout the park and a system of tracks that are generally good in the drier months. Two large islands, Lupala and Nkasa, dominate the flood plain and provide safe ground during floods.

You can enter Mamili via Sangwali or Malengalenga from the main road. It's best to ask locally as roads disappear with floods and new ones are created. Another option is taking a small dugout canoe or mokoro as this may be the only way to enter during the flood. Either way it promises to be an adventure if you have the time to check it out.

We entered at Sangwali and drove through town, then past a washed out old road into the park, where there are no signs whatsoever. Following the tracks and being aware of kilometers traveled and turns made seems to be the best way to avoid getting lost. After about 30 km. we arrived at a tiny island and camped for two days surrounded by lechwe grazing in the grassy flood plain and hippos who made their presence known by their groaning laugh. We were alone except for a Botswana Defense Force patrol boat that happened by as we were leaving.

Note: If you have a small boat, be wary of hippos and crocs and do not wander into backwaters which could be Botswana territory. One man we talked with in Katima Mulilo found himself inadvertently in Botswana waters and was taken by boat then helicopter to a BDF base, questioned, then flown back two days later and released! There is currently a minor dispute over a piece of land on the Chobe River further east and both Namibian and Botswana forces have been involved in minor hassles, so make sure you know which side of the border you're on.

The D3511 road which loops south passing Lianshulu Lodge and Mamili National Park is a good 2-wheel drive gravel road, though it can get mucky during summer rains. Check locally before proceeding.

Petrol is available at the settlement of Linyanti (122 km. from Kongola and 80 km. from Katima) along the D3511 road, from 6am-7pm every day.

Liambezi Lake

You may see a large lake on the map of Caprivi called Liambezi Lake. If you get there perhaps you'll see the lake, perhaps not. The lake comes and goes depending on the weather and has some interesting history. It used to be 10,000 hectares in size and a ton of fish a day were caught by the local populace, providing much needed protein. In 1985 it dried up, leaving the hippos wallowing in the mud where they eventually got stuck and were shot for food. The last 50 or so were escorted day and night by Nature Conservation rangers to safer waters such as the Zambezi, 50 km. away.

Another interesting phenomenon occurred in 1987-89 when the dry lake bed started burning. The rich organic material on the lake bottom heated up like a compost heap and smoldered for several months, burning to ash. Eventually the fire was confined to holes in the lake bed into which a few cattle fell and were lost. If you happen to see smoke rising off the dry lake, walking across is not recommended!

Another interesting phenomenon occurs when the level of the Zambezi floods high enough to fill Lake Liambezi through the Bukalo channel and reverse the flow of the Chobe River.

Katima Mulilo

Katima could be described as Namibia's wild east as smugglers, poachers and vagabonds have inhabited the area for decades. For tourists, it's a convenient place to stop while exploring the eastern Caprivi or continuing on to Botswana or Victoria Falls in Zimbabwe 220 km. away. The name comes from the Silozi language, and means to quench the fire. There are two explanations: one has it that the rapids near Katima would douse the burning embers that were carried on long mokoro journeys and used to start fires each night; the other has it that travelers wading across the crotch deep water would have any burning passions cooled off by the time they reached the opposite shore.

There used to be quite a bit of game coming through the area but poaching and human encroachment have made this a much less frequent occurrence. You do, however, see hippos popping their eyes out of the Zambezi River and abundant bird life—the call of trumpeter hornbills floats like the cry of a baby out over the still waters.

There is a bank, a couple of supermarkets with a good but not great selection, bakery, butcher, 24 hour Shell station, a Namib Air office, a clothing store and an open air market where some vegetables, fruits and clothes are sold. To get to the town center take the paved roads 1/2 kilometer either side of the Total station.

Places to Stay

Guineafowl Lodge—Tel. (067352) 418

A former military guest house, the Guineafowl has some stark prefab rooms and camping by mango trees on the river. They offer river and flying tours to almost anywhere—just ask. The restaurant features an inexpensive but not extensive menu of pizzas, burgers, steaks and chicken for R15-20. It's a backpacker friendly place and is located right in town—just follow the signs through a residential neighborhood—less than a km. If camping, watch your things, as belongings have been reported stolen at night.

Rates: Single R65-95, Double R95-125, Triple R155, Quad R180 B&B; Camping R10 per person.

Zambezi Lodge—Tel. 203

Certainly the nicest (and most expensive) place in town, the Zambezi Lodge has 27 clean, comfortable rooms with A/C, a gym, swimming pool, sauna, conference room, a bar floating on the Zambezi, and an adjacent golf course which is free for guests. The restaurant is for residents unless you call ahead and reserve, and expect to spend R40—50 per person for dinner. They offer rental cars and boat trips are possible when the river level is high enough. The Zambezi Queen, a riverboat that plies the river during high water will take you on a luxurious all-inclusive river tour with your own stateroom, but expect to pay about US$600 per day double occupancy.

On the lower end of the budget, they allow camping on the grounds along the river separate from the lodge. There are decent ablutions, braai pits and shade but beware of thieves at night! Keep a lookout for the beautiful Knysna louries that fly through the trees on the grounds. Follow the signs just east of town to get there.

Rates: Single R160, Double R184, Quad R253 room only; Camping R10 per person plus R5 per vehicle. Breakfast R12.50

Hippo Lodge—Tel. 685

Settled on the banks of a backwater of the Zambezi 6 km. east of town, the Hippo provides a shady, tropical ambience that is a switch from its former role as an army camp for South African forces. The island across the water can be reached by canoe (free to guests renting chalets) and explored on foot— you may even camp there—but again look out for crocs and hippos. There is an excellent restaurant where you can have delicious steaks on a veranda perched above the river for R15-30. Camping is allowed and though the ablution blocks were not in very good shape it seems safer from theft than the other two lodges. We awoke one morning to investigate noise in the vicinity of our vehicle and found one of the staff cleaning it!

Rates: Single R100, Double R140 B&B; Camping R10 per person.

Things to Do

Caprivi Art Center

The Caprivi Art Center is located near downtown and is easy to find. They sell locally made wood carvings, baskets, pottery, paintings and jewelry very reasonably in addition to having dances and workshops. Don't expect to bargain much. Open M-Sat. 8-5.

Swimming in the Zambezi

There's a good swimming hole which is relatively safe from crocs and hippos about 5 km. northwest of town on the Zambian border. It has a nice set of rapids and if the water level isn't too high it's a refreshing dip. Take the dirt road past the Total station until you see the border post. About 30 meters or so before the first border sign turn right and follow the left fork.

To Botswana, Zambia and Victoria Falls

To cross into Zambia from Caprivi take the dirt road past the Total station and swimming hole to the border post. After customs formalities, get on the ferry, which runs whenever it's full and costs R50 for a vehicle. If you're going to Livingstone/Victoria Falls, the road through Zambia may be in bad shape and police roadblocks are fairly common, though mostly just a formality.

To Botswana, continue on the unpaved Caprivi Highway to the border post at Ngoma. This is a decent road in dry conditions, but can get quite muddy during the rainy season. After you complete your exit papers drive across the Chobe River to Botswana where you drive through the foot and mouth disease treatment and complete customs formalities. You must pay the five pula third party insurance here. You then come to the Chobe National Park entrance which does not require the expensive entrance fees if you are in transit.

Wear your seatbelt to avoid being shaken down for a 40 pula fine for not having them on. The border is open here from 7-5:45 but it's best to get there midday to avoid the possibility of early closing.

To Victoria Falls it's about 220 km. and about 4 hours from Katima including border formalities. You must first cross the aforementioned border into Botswana, then after driving through Chobe Park, cross the Zimbabwe border near Kazungula. You'll need third party insurance (which they'll sell you right there for a nominal fee if you don't have proof that you are covered by another policy) and a police clearance stating that you do in fact own your car. From here it's a good tar road through to Vic Falls about 75 km. distant.

For more information on border crossing formalities, see Border Crossings in the Getting Around chapter.

Sources

"Acacias of SWA/Namibia: Tree of the Year 1989," Herta Kolberg.
Afrikaans-English Dictionary. Hippocrene Books:1992.
"Aloes of South West Africa," W.J. Jankowitz. *Nature Conservation: 1975*
Automobile Association of Namibia, Windhoek
"Conserve Our Plants," Amy Schoeman. *Nature Conservation:* 1983.
Department of Nature Conservation of Namibia
A Dictionary of Southern African Place Names, D.E. Raper.
Earth Link Survival Guide to the Outdoors, James Clarke. Earth Link Publications: 1987.
Etosha, Daryl and Sharna Balfour. Struik Publishers.
Field Guide to the Mammals of Southern Africa, Chris & Tilde Stuart. Struik Publishers: 1991.
A Field Guide to the Trees of Southern Africa, Eve Palmer. Collins Publishers: 1977.
Guide to Namibia & Botswana, McIntyre & Atkins, Bradt Publishing
A History of Resistance in Namibia, Peter H. Katjavivi. UNESCO: 1988.
Manson's Tropical Diseases 19th edition, P.E.C. Manson-Bahr and D.R. Bell. Bailliere-Tindall.
Ministry of Wildlife, Conservation & Tourism
"The Namib: Natural History of an Ancient Desert," Mary Seely. *Shell Guide:* 1987
Namibia 1990—An Africa Institute Country Survey, edited by Erich Leistner and Peter Esterhuysen.
Namibia: Africa's Harsh Paradise, Anthony Bannister and Peter Johnson. Struik Publishers.
Namib Flora, Patricia Craven. Hamsberg Publishers: 1986.
Namibia Weather Bureau, Windhoek.

Newman's Birds of Southern Africa, Kenneth Newman. Southern Book Publishers: 1991.

Peoples of SWA Namibia, J.S. Malan. HAUM Publishers: 1980.

Stay Alive in the Desert, K.E.M. Melville. Publisher Roger Lascelles: 1987

Teach Yourself Afrikaans, Helena van Schalkwyk. Southern Book Publishers.

"Trees and Shrubs of the Etosha National Park," Cornelia Berry. Nature Conservation.

Trees of Southern Africa, Keith Coates. Struik Publishers, Palmgrave: 1977.

Visitor's Guide to Namibia, Willie & Sandra Olivier, Southern Book Publishers

Waterberg Flora: Footpaths in and Around the Camp, Patricia Craven. Hamsberg Publishers: 1989.

Appendix
Additional Maps

NAMIBIA

NAMIBIA - OLD REGIONS

NAMIBIA- NEW REGIONS

Index

Index

Index

HIPPOCRENE
AFRICAN LANGUAGE LIBRARY

For travelers to Africa, for African-Americans exploring their roots, and for everyone interested in learning more about Africa and her languages, we offer the new African Language Library.

ENGLISH-SOMALI/
SOMALI-ENGLISH DICTIONARY

Somali, the national language of Somalia, is spoken by 6 million in this easternmost African country, as well as 1 1/2 million in Ethiopia, and 300,000 in Kenya. Features 11,000 up-to-date entries with clear pronunciation.

276 pages • 5 1/2 x 9 • $29.50 cloth • 0-7818-0269-5

SWAHILI PHRASEBOOK
T. Gilmore and S. Kwasa

Presented simply, with a minimum of grammar, this is a straightforward guide to basic communication in many African countries from Botswana in the south to centrally situated Zaire to Kenya and Ethiopia in the east.

184 pages • 4 x 5 3/8 • $8.95 paper • 0-87052-970-6

TWI-ENGLISH/
ENGLISH-TWI CONCISE DICTIONARY
Paul Kotey

Twi is the major language of Ghana and it is spoken by 6 million people. Brand new and easy-to-use, this is **the only Twi-English/ English-Twi dictionary available in the U.S.** Each of its 8,000 entries is accompanied by common-sense phonetics to facilitate correct pronunciation of this important African language.

425 pages • 3 5/8 x 5 3/8 • $11.95 paper • 0-7818-0264-4

A NEW CONCISE XHOSA-ENGLISH DICTIONARY
J. McLaren
One of the Bantu languages, Xhosa is spoken by about 4 million people, primarily in the Transkei territory of South Africa, which borders Lesotho and faces the Indian Ocean.

A standard among students of Xhosa since 1914, this edition of *A New Concise Xhosa-English Dictionary* contains approximately 6,000 modern entries and an extensive section on pronunciation, emphasizing the distinct Xhosa tone and accent, as well as an outline of grammatical rules. Also featured is a helpful appendix of place names.

194 pages • 4 3/4 x 7 1/8 • $14.95 paper • 0-7818-0251-2

YORUBA-ENGLISH/
ENGLISH-YORUBA CONCISE DICTIONARY
Olabiyi Yai
One of the major languages of Nigeria, Yoruba is spoken by 15 million people, principally in the southwestern region of the country.

The only Yoruba-English/English-Yoruba dictionary to be offered in the U.S., this concise reference provides a thorough grounding in vocabulary for students of Yoruba. It also serves as an indispensable guide for Yoruba-speakers learning or improving their English. The dictionary features a clear, easy-to-use guide to pronunciation, emphasizing the rise and fall of the voice, essential to speaking this beautiful tongue.

375 pages • 3 5/8 x 5 3/8 • $11.95 paper • 0-7818-0263-6

ZULU-ENGLISH/ENGLISH-ZULU DICTIONARY
G.R. Dent and C.L.S. Nyembezi
Zulu is one of the major Bantu languages of South Africa, originating in the easternmost part of the country. Over 4 million people speak Zulu.

With 30,000 updated and modern entries, most with multiple definitions, this dictionary is one of the most comprehensive Zulu-English dictionaries available anywhere. In addition, its lightweight and compact design makes it perfect for the student or traveler who needs a portable *and* thorough dictionary. Invaluable for everyone from the beginning student of Zulu to the scholar.

519 pages • 7 1/4 x 4 3/4 • $29.50 paper • 0-7818-0255-5

TRAVEL GUIDES TO AFRICA...

The Michael Haag Guide to West Africa
Kim Naylor
"Writer, photographer and anthropologist Naylor's carefully researched and thoroughly informative guide will become the traveler's bible to the region." —*The Traveler*
index, b/w photos, maps
224 pages • $14.95pb • 0-87052-728-2

Guide to East Africa: Kenya, Tanzania & the Seychelles
Nina Casimati
A most detailed guide to the increasingly popular east Africa. Includes tips on safaris, scuba diving, and game fishing.
194 pages • $14.95pb • 0-87053-883-1

Thorton Cox Guide to Kenya and Northern Tanzania
Thorton Cox
"An invaluable book for tourists and Kenya residents alike."
—*Sunday Nation*
index, b/w photos, maps • 280 pages • $14.95pb • 0-87052-609-X

CARTOGRAPHIA HANDY MAPS:
The Countries of Africa

These maps cover the entire country with major roads, outlines of major cities, and other national concerns.

Algeria Map	Angola Map	Ethiopia Map
(301) • $8.95	(522) • $8.95	(302) • $8.95
Libya Map	Mozambique Map	Tunisia Map
(302) • $8.95	(540) • $8.95	(631) • $8.95

LITERATURE ABOUT AFRICA

DESERT AND WILDERNESS
Henryk Sienkiewicz
Newly edited and revised by Miroslaw Lipinski

Sienkiewicz's late 19th century novel, beloved by Polish youths, is brought to fresh life in a newly edited and modernized translation. Set in Africa, this story follows the adventures of Stas (pronounced "Stosh") and Nell as they encounter wild beasts, warring tribes, and the fanatic hordes of the Mahdi, the Islamic leader who planned to conquer the world.

At once a coming of age tale and a vigorous adventure saga, *In Desert and Wilderness* rivals such classics as *Robinson Crusoe* and *Treasure island.*

278 pages • 5 1/2 x 8 1/2 • 0-7818-0235-0 • $19.95

WEATHER IN AFRICA: Three Novellas
Martha Gellhorn

"This is a surprisingly good book." —*New York Times*

The look and feel of Africa, the scents and colors are so true that one might be there, and the weather is perfect. Europeans live in this magnificent scenery but their inner weather, very different from the sunshine around them, is turbulent and unpredictable.

263 pages • • 5 1/2 x 8 1/2 • 0-90787-101-1 • $14.95pb

MOROCCO THAT WAS
Walter Harris

"Many interesting sidelights on the customs and characters of the Moors... intimate knowledge of the courts, its language and customs... describes a thorough understanding of the Moorish character."
—*The New York Times*

338 pages • 5 1/2 x 8 1/2 • index • 0-90787-140-2 • $14.95pb

A YEAR IN MARRAKESH
Peter Mayne

"A notable book, for the author is exceptional both in his literary talent and his outlook.... Mr. Mayne is that rare thing, a natural writer... no less exceptional is his humor."
—*Times Literary Supplement*

"He has contrived the air of an English November to the spicy odors of North Africa; he has turned, for an hour, smog to shimmering sunlight. He has woven a texture of extraordinary charm." —*Daily Telegraph*

250 pages • 5 1/2 x 8 1/2 • 0-90787-130-5 • $14.95pb

(Prices subject to change.)

TO PURCHASE HIPPOCRENE BOOKS contact your local bookstore, or write to: HIPPOCRENE BOOKS, 171 Madison Avenue, New York, NY 10016. Please enclose check or money order, adding $4.00 shipping (UPS) for the first book and .50 for each additional book.

HIPPOCRENE INSIDER'S GUIDES

Hippocrene Insider's Guides provide you with tips on traveling to not-too-familiar lands. You'll be guided to the most interesting sights, learn about culture and be assured of an eventful stay when you visit with the Insider's Guide.

INSIDER'S GUIDE TO THE DOMINICAN REPUBLIC
Jack Tucker and Ursula Eberhard
212 pages • b/w photos, maps • 0-7818-0075-7 • $14.95

INSIDER'S GUIDE TO HUNGARY
Nicholas Parsons
366 pages • b/w photos, 20 maps • 0-87052-976-5 • $16.95

INSIDER'S GUIDE TO JAVA AND BALI
Jerry LeBlanc
222 pages • b/w photos, maps • 0-7818-0037-4 • $14.95

INSIDER'S GUIDE TO NEPAL
Prakash Raj
136 pages • illustrated, maps • 0-87052-026-1 • $9.95

INSIDER'S GUIDE TO PARIS
Elaine Klein
224 pages • illustrated, maps • 0-87052-876-9 • $14.95

INSIDER'S GUIDE TO
THE WORLD'S MOST EXCITING CRUISES
Shirley Linde and Lea Lane
230 pages • illustrated, maps • 0-7818-0258-X

INSIDER'S GUIDE TO POLAND, 2nd revised edition
Alexander Jordan
233 pages • 0-87052-880-7 • $9.95

INSIDER'S GUIDE TO ROME
Frances D'Emilio
376 pages • b/w photos, map • 0-7818-0036-6 • $14.95

COMPANION GUIDES FROM HIPPOCRENE

COMPANION GUIDE TO BRITAIN, *by Henry Weisser*
Highlights are cited and explained clearly, describing what is best to see in London and the provinces: castles cathedrals, stately homes, villages, and towns. This essential practical guide lists history, geography, politics, culture, economics, climate and language use.
_____250 pages • 0-7818-0147-8 • $14.95

COMPANION GUIDE TO AUSTRALIA, *by Graeme and Tamsin Newman*
With helpful tips on preparing for your trip, this cheerful guide outlines the distinctive characters and main attractions of cities, describes picturesque countryside, and links the things tourists like to do with the history and character of the Australian people.
_____294 pages • b/w photos and 4 maps • 0-87052-034-2 • $16.95

COMPANION GUIDE TO MEXICO, *by Michael Burke*
Along with the usual tips on sites, this guide outlines contemporary realities of Mexican society, religion and politics.
_____320 pages • b/w photos • 0-7818-0039-0 • $14.95

COMPANION GUIDE TO POLAND (Revised), *by Jill Stephenson and Alfred Bloch*
"This quaint and refreshing guide is an appealing amalgam of practical information, historical curiosities, and romantic forays into Polish culture."—*Library Journal*
_____179 pages • b/w photos, maps • 0-7818-0077-3 • $14.95

COMPANION GUIDE TO PORTUGAL, *by T.J. Kubiak*
Learn about the land, the people, their heritage and much more with this guide to the unexpected bounty of Portugal.
_____260 pages • maps • 0-87052-739-8 • $14.95

COMPANION GUIDE TO ROMANIA, *by Lydle Brinkle*
Written by a specialist in Eastern European geography, this modern guide offers comprehensive historical, topographical, and cultural overviews.
_____220 pages • 0-87052-634-0 • $14.95

COMPANION GUIDE TO SAUDI ARABIA, *by Gene Lindsey*
Gene Lindsey, an American who has spent much of the last decade in Saudi Arabia, traces the history of the region, religion, development, harsh environment, foreign policy, laws, language, education, technology, and underlying it all, its mindset.
_____368 pages • maps • 0-7818-0023-4 • $11.95